UNIVERSITY LIBRARY PRACTICES
IN DEVELOPING COUNTRIES

UNIVERSITY LIBRARY PRACTICES IN DEVELOPING COUNTRIES

Dr Nazir Ahmad

Assistant Professor,
Faculty of Arts,
King Abdulaziz University,
Jeddah

KPI

London, Boston, Melbourne and Henley

First published in 1984 by KPI Limited

Routledge & Kegan Paul plc
14 Leicester Square, London WC2H 7PH, England

Routledge & Kegan Paul
9 Park Street, Boston, Mass. 02108, USA

Routledge & Kegan Paul
464 St Kilda Road, Melbourne,
Victoria 3004, Australia and

Routledge & Kegan Paul plc
Broadway House, Newtown Road,
Henley-on-Thames, Oxon RG9 1EN, England

Set in Times Roman
by Hope Services, Abingdon, Oxon
and printed in Great Britain
by St Edmundsbury Press, Bury St Edmunds, Suffolk

Library of Congress Cataloging in Publication Data

Ahmad, Nazir.

University library practices in developing countries.
Includes bibliographical references and index.
1. Libraries, University and college – Developing
countries.   2. Libraries, University and college – Arab
countries.   3. Libraries, University and college – Islamic
countries.   I. Title.
Z675.U5A42   1984   027.7'09172'4   84-4366

British Library CIP data also available

ISBN 0-7103-0058-1

Dedicated to the memory of my mother

Contents

Contents

Illustrations

Tables

Foreword

Scarcity of library science literature on Arab Islamic countries is no doubt prevalent and this remarkable attempt made by Dr Nazir Ahmad to survey and evaluate the university library practices of eight rapidly progressing states is of tremendous significance.

The necessity to acquire, process, preserve, retrieve and utilize knowledge efficiently, economically and conveniently makes it imperative to devise procedures to facilitate and optimize service to the university community. The task of management in an atmosphere of inadequate staff, finances and space becomes more challenging and even complex, due to the computerization of certain aspects in some of the Arab university libraries.

The author has tackled the subject with diligence, profundity and judiciousness. He has recorded contemporary practices, methods and applications, thereby presenting a titillating contrast between the functioning of prosperous and economically starved university libraries. Considerable emphasis is placed on collection development policies and the planning of library buildings in tropical climates. The author analyses the drawbacks and commends provocative designs of some university libraries in Saudi Arabia, Jordan, Kuwait, Qatar, Sudan, Malaysia, Pakistan and Nigeria.

Although Dr Nazir does not claim to have made an exhaustive study, and considers this a humble contribution, I personally believe the investigation is the most extensive yet conducted in the field and it is indeed a substantial contribution which provides the reader with a reliable review of current developments. The author has unquestionably succeeded in writing this book plainly, clearly and energetically, aiming to reach a wide audience in both the advanced and less developed countries.

Dr Hisham A. Abbas
Dean,
Library Affairs,
King Abdulaziz University,
Jeddah,
Saudi Arabia.

Preface

This book presents a penetrating analysis of contemporary procedures, practices, applications and operations of university libraries in eight Arab Islamic countries. The author synthesizes various areas of investigation – library functions, structures and organization, managerial systems, selection and collections development policies – to comprehend analytically university library building plans and design and the need for coordination of resources to maximize utility.

Considerable emphasis is placed on acquisition methods, selection tools for both Arabic and Western materials which are crucial for the enrichment of libraries for posterity. The author demonstrates how to be an effective manager and discusses communication networks which constitute one of the inevitable and essential components in the efficient running of libraries. The book delineates the service concept, which is closely linked to a reference and information-oriented approach to readers, and focuses on the key issues of library planning in Arab Islamic countries by appraising a selection of building projects carried out in some of the countries surveyed.

The information for this book was gathered by field observations in some countries and material collected from statistical summaries, library publications and reports, as well as through questionnaire data, interview data and personal correspondence with university libraries. An interesting contrast is documented between the ambitious development plans of prosperous university libraries and those which are economically disadvantaged and struggling for survival with meagre allocations. Since internal cooperation on an organized scale within the country is vital for the sharing of the fruits of international coordination, a critical evaluation of both the Malaysian and Nigerian cooperative ventures is presented and the enhanced interest for introducing cooperative schemes in Saudi Arabia, Jordan, Kuwait and Qatar is recorded.

It will be a relief for my critics and stimulation for others to read that the study is not an exhaustive one, but is a humble contribution to the literature of Arab Islamic librarianship. It will help motivate library scholars to use it as a stepping-stone for further investigation and research.

However, this profusely illustrated book, comprising plates, diagrams and statistical tables depicting the diversity of university library practices and building design will appeal to both students and librarians alike in developing and developed countries.

Introduction

The acquisition of knowledge serves to increase awareness of God the Creator and belief in Him and the concept of life and death. Islam is the religion of God and the Qur'an is the Holy Book revealed by God to the Prophet Muhammad (may blessings and the peace of Allah be upon him). As the last religion, the last Prophet and the last Holy Book embrace all the previous teachings of prophets and divine books, Islam is accorded the status of the distinct and supreme religion of all mankind. The Holy Qur'an encourages the pursuit of knowledge: 'Allah will exalt those who believe among you and those who are vouchsafed knowledge.' (Holy Qur'an-Al-Mujadila-11) 'But be ye faithful servants of the lord, seeing that ye are wont to teach the Book and seeing that ye are wont to exercise yourselves therein.' (Holy Qur'an-Al-i-Imran-79)

The Prophet Muhammad (peace be upon him) once narrated: 'Ilm is the flame lighted by Allah in the heart of whomsoever He chooses.' 'When a man sets out to seek Ilm his footsteps are rewarded with benefactions.'

The fourth caliph of Islam, Ali bin Abi Talib, once said to a companion 'O Kumail, Ilm is better than wealth. Ilm protects you whilst you have to protect wealth. Wealth diminishes through spending but Ilm increases with use.'

The first verse of the Holy Qur'an to be revealed to the Prophet was 'read in the name of the lord who created you' (Al-Alkq-1). The significance of Ilm (knowledge) is evident from the fact that it is mentioned 770 times in the Holy Qur'an.

The common characteristic of Arab Islamic countries is the teachings of the Qur'an and the Prophet Muhammad (peace be upon him) and these form the basis for the conduct of social and political life in this world and preparation for eternal life. The education of Muslims begins in early childhood at home, and is followed by formal Quranic education in mosques. To expand the horizons of the human mind, knowledge of sciences, mathematics and nature is imparted through schools, colleges and universities, so that members of the society become skilled, trained and capable of illuminating others and contributing to the industrial, social, moral, cultural and technological development of these nations.

Since this book deals with eight Arab Islamic countries, it is vital to cast a cursory glance at the higher education structure, university objectives in particular, to form the basis for the discussion of university library systems in subsequent chapters. Some might argue that Nigeria is not a totally Islamic country, or that a fair proportion of non-Muslims is settled in Malaysia. I do not entirely disagree with the critics, but the fundamental reason for the inclusion of Nigeria is that its population includes a substantial number of Muslims and her six big universities are striving to specialize in the collective acquisition of Arab Islamic materials. Moreover, Nigeria, being labelled as a developing country, has much to offer in the field of university library development to other countries around the world.

Nigeria is one of the largest countries in Africa and remained under British rule from 1914 to 1960. It comprises nineteen states, and nearly 394 different languages are spoken, but the three major ones are Hausa, Ibo and Yoruba; English is the country's lingua franca. Until 1967, there were only five universities, the oldest being the University of Ibadan, established in 1948. During 1968–78 eight more universities sprang up in Benin, Calabar, Jos, Kano, Sokoto, Ilorin, Port Harcourt and Maiduguri. The five oldest universities were set up in Ibadan (1948), Nsukka (1960), Ife (1961), Lagos (1962) and Zaria (1962). With regard to the objectives of universities, the Unesco conference on the development of higher education in Africa, held at Tananarive (now Antananrivo) in Madagascar from 3–12 September 1962, made certain recommendations. The outcome of the conference was the emergence of the following objectives:

1 to teach and advance knowledge

2 to maintain adherence and loyalty to world academic standards

3 to ensure the unification of Africa

4 to encourage education and the appreciation of African culture and heritage and to dispel misconceptions about Africa

5 to evolve over the years truly African institutions of higher learning dedicated to Africa and its people, yet providing a bond of kinship to the larger human society (Unesco conference report, Paris, 1963)

To accomplish these objectives the Nigerian National Universities Commission, set up in 1962, has given considerable support to promote the cause of universities.

Malaysia, previously called Malaya, secured independence from British rule in August 1957 and was expanded in 1963 to incorporate Singapore, Sabah and Sarawak. But in August 1965 the Federation of Malaya was bisected to give independence to Singapore and the country was renamed as Malaysia. There are three major groups of people in the country, the Chinese, the Hindus and the Malaysian Muslims, the latter by far the largest group in the country. The economy of the country is dependent upon the export of rubber, agricultural products, palm oil, coconuts, timber, tea and various other items. The country has been continuously promoting sustained economic growth and has launched, through successive five-year development plans, an imaginative programme for the improvement of higher education. For instance, the first Malaysian plan for 1966 to 1970 was directed to create an environment in which the various ethnic groups in the country could live in harmony and dignity. The second Malaysian plan for 1971 to 1975 concentrated on education and training programmes and the consolidation of the system of education to achieve national development objectives. The third Malaysian plan for 1976 to 1980 visualized the need for the development of higher education and outlined the government's expectations that the universities should play a vital role in the social and economic advancement of the country.

In Malaysia, there are five universities altogether; the first one, the University of Malaysia, was established in 1957 and the remaining four were set up from 1969 onwards. They are the Universiti Sains Malaysia (1969), the National University (1970), the Technological University (1971) and the University of Agriculture (1970). No further university has been founded, but these few universities are making an invaluable contribution by producing skilled and professionally trained manpower and by promoting research and creating understanding amongst diverse races, sects and religious groups. Islam is the dominant faith of the majority of people and the educational system is structured according to the Qur'an and Sunnah. All the universities have fabulous mosques and even the university libraries are built with a provision for mosques on the premises, so as to facilitate praying at fixed times during the day. All Malaysians can speak, read and write Arabic, since it is the language of the Qur'an and is taught in schools throughout the country.

Pakistan is one of the largest Islamic countries in the world, where only 2 to 3 per cent are non-Muslims. It was also under British rule and came into existence when India was partitioned in 1947. Several languages are spoken. Although English is common and widely spoken among the educated community, Urdu is the national language. Recently, Arabic became a compulsory language at elementary and secondary school level. The country is struggling with a poor economy and the pace of higher educational development is surprisingly slow. It has, however, produced many distinguished scholars, who are serving in different countries of the Middle East and the Western world. At present there are twenty universities located in four provinces of the country. The first one was the University of the Punjab, founded during British rule in 1882. Instead of concentrating on improving the quality of education and injecting adequate finances into the older universities, new universities are continuously being founded. These universities, the Islamic University, Islamabad, the University of Engineering and Technology, Peshawar and the University of Agriculture, Peshawar, were established in 1981.

Sudan is the largest country in Africa, where around 115 languages are spoken, but Arabic is the major one, and is widely understood. It was also under British rule. It is one of the poor Arabic-speaking countries of Africa and, like Pakistan, lacks the financial resources to fulfil the objectives for which four universities have been founded.

In contrast, the state of Qatar is an Arabic-speaking, rich Arab country where higher education was initiated with the foundation of the University of Qatar in 1973, and since that time several faculties embracing scientific and technological disciplines have been opened in accordance with the ambitious government projects for meeting manpower needs in developing the society.

Jordan is another Arab country, but not as rich as many neighbouring countries. It was also a British colony, but was made independent in 1946. There are only two universities; the University of Jordan was established in 1962 and Yarmouk in 1976. Both are well established and are bent on turning out well-trained manpower capable of managerial positions, as well as technical positions in the country.

Qatar is another prosperous and oil-rich Arab country. Its population is just over 220,000. The peninsula of Qatar projects northwards into the Arabian Gulf from mainland Arabia for some 160 km. Arabic is the language of all Qatari people, though the moderately educated tend to speak English fairly well. Not only is education free, but students are also provided with free transportation, books and other educational materials and equipment. At present there is just one university in Qatar which was set up in 1973, but every year new faculties are being established so as to produce manpower capable of assisting the government in meeting its ambitious development plans.

Oil revenue has provided a tremendous boost to the implementation of the Kuwaiti government's educational, social and technological projects. The University of Kuwait emerged in 1966 and, with adequate financial backing, has set up numerous faculties and initiated a wide range of disciplines to meet the objectives of higher education.

The situation is similar, and rather improved, in the Kingdom of Saudi Arabia, where the discovery of oil has added new dimensions of wealth to the lives of the Saudi people. Education is absolutely free at all levels and there are promising rewards for those who prove their excellence. The first university was that of King Saud at Riyadh, founded in 1957, followed by King Abdulaziz University, Jeddah, in 1967. Now there are seven universities altogether in the kingdom and the standard of education is relatively high. The objectives of the university were diligently described by the late King Faisal Ibn Abdul Aziz:

it is not important to build colleges and celebrate their openings, but it is important to do our best to obtain the most benefits from the colleges in order to fulfill the hopes and aspirations of our nation, and to find from among our sons those who aspire to a bright and flourishing future to serve their religion, nation, and country.

Within this framework, the universities in Saudi Arabia seek to contribute to the promotion of scientific, technological, social and moral advancement, the furthering of the industrialization process, to prepare students for imaginative and creative participation in the development of Saudi society, and to encourage students in their search for excellence in every sphere of human activity within the Islamic ideology.

It is unwise to judge every Saudi student on the basis of his understanding and knowledge of the English language. Arabic is the language of instruction, study and learning and it is the only medium of communication between all the Arab countries. A vast amount of literature is being produced by Arab scholars and published in the Arab world for imparting knowledge to students. It needs to be adequately procured, processed, preserved and disseminated. Whether there is an abundance of funds or a scarcity of resources in the universities, national development has to continue. Universities must contribute to it through research and trained manpower, and the libraries must act as a tower of light and reservoir of knowledge.

Chapter 1

Library systems and organization

To explicate the system and organization of university libraries in eight Arab Islamic countries necessitates the evaluation of the purposes, goals, objectives and functions of a number of university libraries in these countries. Political and economic considerations, coupled with the recognition accorded to each university in the national context, have great impact on the pace of development of libraries. Universities in many Western countries are partly or completely financed by taxpayers' money, whereas in most Islamic Arab countries the funding situation is entirely different. It is an undeniable phenomenon that university libraries in Pakistan and Sudan are suffering from neglect, and to some extent are institutions of little significance. In contrast, government policies in Saudi Arabia, Qatar, Kuwait, Jordan and Malaysia have augmented the role of the universities in national development. The expansion of all the universities and the establishment of new ones, especially in the past decade, has resulted in enhanced financial support and backing from the respective governments.

Nigeria in no way lags behind her counterparts and the universities continue to grow with an increasing rapidity. The universities have, by and large, assumed the role of institutes of great importance and are playing their part in producing competent products, which in turn assist in nation-building. Consequently, intensified government support for universities has also given the libraries a new image and a new challenge.

In some countries, like Nigeria and Pakistan, a national commission or committee liaises between the government and the universities in identifying needs and making recommendations. For instance, the national universities commission in Nigeria has set up offices in the USA and Europe for settling the overseas accounts of university libraries.[1] It has also established a formula of an allocation of 5 per cent of the total educational budget to university libraries.[2] Also, all grants to Nigerian university libraries are made through the National Universities Commission. In Pakistan, there is a University Grants Commission which coordinates the activities of the library standing committees and study groups, and holds workshops and sponsors projects related to libraries. These commissions are in fact similar to the British University Grants Committee which acts as a 'buffer between the Government and the Universities, interpreting the one to the other, and enabling public funds to flow into the universities without direct Government intervention'.[3]

One of the remarkable achievements of the British committee has been the Parry Report, published in 1967.[4] Apart from considering the most effective and economical arrangements for meeting the needs of university libraries, it recommended that the libraries should be included on any sub-committees set up by the library committee.[5]

It is appropriate to cast a cursory glance at the role and functions of university library committees, which play an indiscriminately important part in shaping policies and formulating systems which are most suited to meet the aims of universities. In different Arab Islamic countries, some university library committees are so powerful that they have reduced the role of the chief librarian to a mere custodian. In other instances, committees simply exist on paper, which is delightful for library directors who consider themselves 'Dr Know-all'. In Saudi Arabia, for example, four university libraries out of seven have a library committee. The dean of library affairs acts as chairman of the library committee, which includes the director of the library and a number of faculty members chosen by the university president or rector. There is no student representation on the committee.[6] The composition of the library committee of King Saud University is as follows:

1 Dean of library affairs (chairman)
2 Vice-Dean of library affairs
3 University librarian/director
4 Five professors from various faculties appointed for two years by the university council

5 Two members from the university or outside the campus, in consultation with the deanship of library affairs and with the agreement of the university council. They are appointed for two years and their appointment may be renewed once.[7]

Regular monthly meetings of the library committee are held to discuss various matters. The recommendations of the committee may be rejected by the president of the university within fifteen days, but upon the insistence of the library committee they may be referred to the University Council which may reject them outright, accept them or suggest modifications. The library committee takes active interest in library development, helps to formulate policies and plans for meeting needs with regard to serials, books and equipment.

The composition and functions of library committees in other countries are not so dissimilar. One of the biggest university libraries in Nigeria is that of Ahmadu Bello University. Its library committee consists of the vice-chancellor as chairman, the deputy vice-chancellor as ex-officio member, and the university librarian, who acts as secretary. Its terms of reference include (a) making regulations governing the use of the library, (b) allocating at its discretion, money for the purchase of books, journals, manuscripts, etc., (c) submitting as many financial estimates and reports on the work of the library as may be required, (d) examining the relation between departmental libraries and the main library.

In addition, it considers various other aspects, e.g. hours of opening, library building maintenance, renovation or improvements and the conditions of service of the library staff.[8]

Almost all universities in Pakistan have library committees, each consisting of twelve to fifteen members, most of whom are appointed by the Academic Council for a two to three-year period. The functions of these committees are:

1 To frame rules regarding the use of library materials and the hours of opening
2 To advise in the preparation of the library budget
3 To allocate funds to various departmental libraries
4 To lay down procedures for selection and purchase of books, journals and other reading materials

5 To take decisions on requests for the transfer of books and
  journals to departmental libraries
6 To formulate the general policy of library development.[9]

The committees also have the power to write off losses and
reduce or remit the delay fine.[10] Also, the committee may take
disciplinary action against the library staff. 'The efficiency of a
university is measured by its central organ – its library – and the
strength of the library is gauged by its committee.'[11] There are
certain committees who can exercise their power, if necessary, to
defer annual increments or even reduce the pay of any member of
the library staff upon finding him neglecting his duties. The
committees normally act in an authoritative and administrative
capacity, thereby exerting undue pressure or interfering in the
internal library affairs. The library committee should be carefully
composed, representing all faculties and both undergraduate and
postgraduate students. The presence of influential members on the
committee will inevitably help the library in the accomplishment of
its aims and objectives.

Functions and objectives

If the two major functions of a university are teaching and
research,[12] the essential function of a university library is to
support the teaching and research programmes of the university by
acquiring print and non-print materials, processing them and
making them available for use. Moreover, there is increasing
recognition in Western countries of the educational function of the
university library; special provision is made for library instructions
to users with the sole purpose of creating 'a broad and positive
form of education designed for the recognized potential users of
the library and which makes use of the materials and services
peculiar to the library'.[13] The University of Petroleum and
Minerals library in Saudi Arabia has formed an information
services unit, previously a research division, to provide formal and
informal instructions to users in the use of the library's facilities
and collections.[14] In the United Kingdom, a paper on university
libraries, prepared in 1964 by the Association of University
Teachers, states precisely that the 'prime function of a university

library is to provide facilities for study and research'. Many university libraries in Islamic countries have failed to recognize the educational function as a vital component, as is evident from their deficient staffing provision which prevents their providing even a very basic readers' service. King Saud University library, Riyadh, is set to meet the following objectives:

1 To provide the academic community with comfortable facilities with which to utilize the information and documentational services of the libraries
2 To facilitate scholarly research
3 To make known the results of scholarly research by keeping up-to-date collections
4 To cooperate with libraries in the kingdom and abroad.

The objectives of Yarmouk University library, Jordan, are quite similar to those stated above. Its first objective is to offer a source of information and services in accordance with academic disciplines in the university and to continue to service the needs of research and higher studies. It should coordinate with other libraries in Jordan to ensure the existence of a comprehensive information service at the national level and to promote library development in the country. One of its objectives is rather different from the concept of a university library's duty to members of its own institution, as its aims are to offer information services to the area in which Yarmouk University is located and to the people, as well as educational establishments in the region.[15]

The objectives of the University of Jos library in Nigeria are to provide a variety of resources, book and non-book alike, and ancillary services which support and extend the university's programmes of instruction and research. To achieve these objectives the university library is destined to (a) ensure a high degree of relevance of its collection to the needs of the university community, (b) ensure that maximum use is made of the resources and facilities it provides, (c) give qualitative reference and information services to its clients and (d) join its staff with their teaching colleagues in making the use of its resources an integral part of the educational process.[16] Likewise, university libraries in Malaysia share most of the objectives so far discussed and are destined to meet them by the provision of excellent accommodation for readers, efficient advisory services and the comprehensive acquisition of materials which are essential to the pursuit of higher education and research. The University of Qatar and the University of Kuwait have set very high goals which are being accomplished due to tremendously high budgets allocated to the libraries.

Library systems

University library systems, whether centralized or decentralized, vary in size and formation, depending on the number of faculties, colleges or departments in each university. In Malaysia, for instance, at the University of Malaya, the policy has been to discourage departmental libraries and strengthen the services and activities of one central library which extends its services to ten of the eleven faculties, the faculty of medicine being located at some distance from the university campus.[17] Although different faculties do possess a small proportion of reading materials, the technical services are completely centralized. The university was founded in 1962 and its faculties include arts and social sciences, dentistry, economics and administration, education, engineering, law, medicine, science, shariyah (Islamic law), usuluddin (legal basis of religion) and an institute of advanced studies. The National University of Malaysia (Universiti Kebangsaan Malaysia), comprising seven faculties, has a central library at the main campus in Bangi and coordinates the collections and services of other libraries of the university. Apart from the Tunseri Lanang library at the main campus, there is the science library. The former is a temporary arrangement and as soon as the faculty of science building in Bangi is completed, the present science library will be merged in the collections at Bangi. Unlike the University of Malaya, both the medical library and the library at Sabah campus are entirely decentralized.[18] Similarly, at the Universiti Sains Malaysia, there is a central library and two faculty libraries with decentralized technical services. Other universities in Malaysia, namely the Technological University of Malaysia and the University of Agriculture, have no faculty libraries and both the library systems are fully centralized.

While some university libraries in Nigeria are centralized, the

12

others follow the usual pattern of decentralization, as is the case with Ahmadu Bello University, where a number of libraries located at some distance from the campus have their own library budgets.[19] At present, they have a decentralized library system with four faculty libraries, in which technical services are completely decentralized. The University of Jos with eight faculties and the University of Calabar with six do not have any faculty libraries and central libraries are responsible for servicing the needs of individual faculties. At the University of Benin, in addition to the central library, two of the nine faculties and colleges have independent faculty libraries, but technical services are based at the main campus library. Three out of four faculties of the Rivers State University of Science and Technology possess their own libraries, but the technical services are fully centralized.

The University of the Punjab in Pakistan, founded in 1882, is the largest of the twenty universities in the country. The institutional structure and physical layout of the university led to a decentralized and uncoordinated pattern of library services. There are thirty-four teaching departments which have their own departmental libraries, totally independent of the main university library. One of these libraries is the Institute of Education and Research library which contains a rich collection of materials. The second largest university is the University of Karachi, which has a completely centralized library system. It was established in 1952 and subsequently a large number of departmental libraries sprang up. When the library moved to its newly-constructed building comprising six floors, all departmental libraries merged into the central library. Obviously, the strong personality of the university librarian, a powerful library committee devoted to the cause of developing the university library and geographical proximity contributed to the formation of one central library. The library of the University of Engineering and Technology, Lahore, has fourteen teaching departments, of which four departments have their own libraries, but the technical services, e.g. acquisition, processing, cataloguing, etc., are centralized. Similar to the University of Karachi is the University of Agriculture library, conceived from the beginning as a central organ. The Quaid-e-Azam University, Islamabad, was set up in 1965 to accommodate only postgraduate and research students. Most of its institutes have established libraries and the library services are not centralized, although the main university library is playing its full part in meeting the educational and research needs of the university community. The Allama Iqbal Open University has neither a centralized nor a decentralized library system. It has established study centres conveniently located in different parts of the country.[20] The instruction is imparted through radio, television and correspondence, and printed notes, as well as home experimental kits, are despatched to students prior to the lectures which are broadcast on the radio and television. The university maintains a small library at its main campus in Islamabad and has not so far introduced a postal loan service for distant borrowers. Bahauddin Zakariya University, Multan, set up in 1975, to some extent follows the pattern of the University of the Punjab in that it has, besides the university library, twelve departmental libraries which are administered by library assistants who are responsible for ordering, receiving and processing reading materials for their departments. Norugi Edlgi Dinshaw (NED) University of Engineering and Technology, Karachi, founded in 1977, has no faculty library and is operating a unified library system. In contrast, the University of Baluchistan, Quetta, established in 1970, has developed nineteen departmental libraries but still pursues a policy of centralized technical services and takes care of all the libraries in the system. Total decentralization of library services is an uneconomic proposition as it hinders the strengthening of central library resources. Azad Jammu and Kashmir University, founded in 1979, and formed by the amalgamation of a number of colleges, does not have a central library and the colleges have independent libraries with no real cooperation between them.

In Sudan, the University of Khartoum library system consists of one main library and six branch or faculty libraries having partial control over their affairs, with complete decentralization of technical services. It is considered to be the 'most important academic library in the Sudan'.[21] On the other hand, the University of Al-Gezira has a central library and three faculty libraries, but acquisition, technical processing and servicing material for use are carried out on a centralized basis. The Omdurman Islamic University has just one faculty library besides the main library where part of the technical operations are centralized.

Economically disadvantaged countries cannot gain from partial or complete decentralization of their university library services, manpower resources and reading materials. However, the geographical location of departments or faculties is sometimes the cogent and compelling reason for having libraries on the faculty premises.

The State of Qatar has just one university, the University of Qatar. Although the university initiated its activities in 1973 with the faculty of education, a library in the real sense did not exist until 1977.[22] There were no catalogues, no circulation system and no accessions procedure. At the present time, while the new library building is being erected, the library materials are scattered among a number of locations within the campus. Collections for men's usage are stored at present in the three faculties of humanities, science and education. Likewise, two women's libraries are in existence. Also, there are fair-sized reading rooms in both the men's and women's dormitories. The Director of Libraries, A. M. Tilbani, has no plan to decentralize the library services of the university. A huge modern central library is to be developed as the materials are moved to the newly constructed building.

Unlike many universities in Arab countries, the University of Kuwait, set up in 1966, has a decentralized library system.[23] Mr Sulaiman Kalendar, British-trained Chief Librarian of the university, has helped in the setting up of nine faculty libraries, whilst his own central library has consistently developed a collection of 383,991 volumes and 34,102 items of non-print materials. One of the libraries contains a unique and comprehensive collection on the Gulf area and the library provides an outstanding and efficient service to patrons conducting research in this field.

In Jordan, both the University of Jordan and Yarmouk University have only centralized library systems, operations and services, although Yarmouk University has established five reading rooms in some of the faculties which are under total control of the central library. Similarly, the University of Jordan, conceived from the beginning to have a central library complex, has not permitted the decentralization of technical services, resources and finances, but, in an attempt to improve access to reading materials for the teaching staff and students, it has maintained ten reading rooms in faculties such as agriculture, economics and commerce, education, medicine sciences and sharia (Muslim law). The most relevant materials and periodicals form part of the reading room collections.

The library systems of Saudi Arabian universities are centralized. Dr Abbas Tashkandy draws the picture vividly. Each university has, he says,

> a central library and a number of smaller library units at several locations on the campus. The central library is responsible for almost all the activities of the system, controlling the acquisition and processing and the distribution of the staff.[24]

The oldest and the largest is the King Saud University, Riyadh, which has a network of fifteen faculty, college, departmental or institution libraries. The faculties include arts, sciences, pharmacy, engineering, medicine, dentistry, nursing, allied medicine, and the graduate school, as well as the Arabic Language Institute.[25] In addition to the massive central library with centralized technical and related activities, a number of faculty libraries are scattered around the city, owing to the physical location. Also, there is a central library for female students. The faculty of science and pharmacy is adjacent to the dental library complex and their collections are housed in the central library. Acquisition, budgeting, cataloguing and classification are fully centralized and normally, for any item purchased on behalf of any faculty library, an additional copy is acquired to be kept in the central library. The same policy is adopted by the King Abdulaziz University which comprises nine faculties and institutions, including a women's campus which commenced its operations in 1967, the year this university was founded.[26] Some of the faculties, e.g. the faculty of marine science, are located over forty kilometres away from the university, which makes it essential to have reading facilities for all those students and teaching staff who cannot have easy access to the central library facilities. Faculty libraries, especially those of engineering, arts and humanities, economics and administration, science, earth sciences and the English language centre, are situated fairly close to the central library, all within very short walking distance. In spite of that, it has been the policy of the university to permit the development of faculty libraries independently, except that materials are purchased and processed by the technical services department of the central library.

The University of Petroleum and Minerals library, Dhahran, is one of the kingdom's excellent libraries. Library services are completely centralized, but there are about sixteen research institutions with reading rooms within the campus. One of them, previously termed the 'compound library', is called the recreation centre library. In the early days of this university there was

> an unofficial effort by the ladies of the North compound to fill a need which they felt – the need for recreational libraries for the families. These libraries have had no financial assistance from the university. The material large paperbacks, were donated by the families themselves.[27]

At present the library possesses 7,500 volumes and receives one hundred popular magazines. Also, there is a small collection of cassettes, records and sheet music. In addition to the libraries in the research institute, data processing centre, English language centre, College of Environmental Design and College of Industrial Management, reading rooms have been set up in the departments of chemical engineering, civil engineering, electrical engineering, mechanical engineering, petroleum engineering, computer science engineering, chemistry, earth sciences, Islamic and Arabic studies, mathematical sciences and physics.

The King Faisal University libraries system is set up along the lines of other university libraries in the Kingdom of Saudi Arabia. The university has two campuses located at a considerable distance from each other, which has made it necessary to have libraries at both campuses. The system consists of the following libraries:[28] the central library, Dammam, which also houses the collections of the college of architecture and planning located in the same building; the College of medicine and medical sciences, two libraries for male and female students;[29] and the central library, Al-Hasa, which in fact houses collections of the college of veterinary medicine and animal resources, the college of agricultural sciences and food and the college of education.

In addition, the dormitory libraries in Al-Hasa and Dammam and the department of home economics library at Al-Hasa will be started shortly. The technical services, including acquisition, classification, etc., are carried out centrally at the Dammam campus.[30] However, the cataloguing is done by a commercial firm in the United States and multiple copies of a periodic print-out of a computer-produced catalogue are sent to all the university libraries in the system.

So far the discussion has focused upon the prevailing pattern of university library systems and faculty or departmental libraries or reading rooms with full or partial control over their activities and affairs. Naturally, there are a number of factors which strongly support the process of decentralization, as it permits convenient access to the reading materials. In developing countries especially, students are not library-minded, and are less likely to approach the library if it is not in the proximity of their teaching departments. Many central libraries do not provide European or American-style reference and advisory services. The library staff lack the concept of 'reaching out' and do not consider their first and foremost duty to the readers, other responsibilities being secondary. Where departmental libraries exist and are manned by competent staff, there exists a better chance of more personalized service to users. In West Germany, as quoted by James Thompson, the

> pattern of strong specialist libraries attached to the departments as the focus of reading has, therefore, much to recommend it to the user, particularly in view of the highly specialized rather than synthetic nature of much research and study.[31]

Panal Buck of Harvard University suggested a 'co-ordinated decentralization' in which materials on a particular subject, as well as less-used works, could be stored separately. But in Islamic countries inefficient communication channels in some universities may be a major hurdle in accomplishing coordination among the departmental libraries. In the University of the Punjab and Quaid-i-Azam University in Pakistan, departmental libraries in certain cases are operating effective services which are far superior in quality to the main campus libraries. No doubt the teachers find it handy to frequently consult the libraries attached to their respective departments and also they can persuade students to carry out projects and to work on their assignment in the libraries under partial supervision. The famous Parry Report, which was produced by the Committee on Libraries of the University Grants Committee and published by Her Majesty's Stationery Office in 1967, put forward some guidelines in regard to the formation and running of departmental libraries.

(a) All libraries in the university should be under the juris-
diction of the library committee or similar library authority
which will be responsible for their organization and the
regulations for their operation

(b) A union catalogue of the holdings of all the libraries in a
university is essential and, where it does not exist, should be
compiled as soon as possible

(c) No library outside the central library should contain items
which are unique in the university, unless it is large enough
to justify the appointment of library staff adequate to offer
services of the standard of the central library, including
extended hours of opening

(d) No library should be set up outside the central library unless
there are sufficient funds to support both the initial
purchase of its stock and its continued maintenance.

Several points emerge from the guidelines of the Parry Report
cited above. A union catalogue is maintained by all the university
libraries in Saudi Arabia, Jordan, Qatar, and many libraries in
Nigeria, Sudan and Pakistan. University libraries in rich Islamic
countries can certainly afford to have branch libraries, although
decentralization is undesirable. In Pakistan, some universities,
e.g. the University of the Punjab and Quaid-e-Azam University,
maintain departmental libraries with total decentralization, whereas Karachi University outrightly rejected the idea of any departmental libraries which consume finances and duplicate effort and
materials. It is more logical to group together all the departments
and form a faculty of arts and humanities library. This idea has
gained popularity where most universities have established faculty
libraries, centrally controlled by the deanship of library affairs. In
Saudi Arabia, for example, Imam Muhammad Bin Saud Islamic
University has eleven faculty libraries and each faculty consists of
a number of departments.[32] An ideal system has been developed
by the University of Petroleum and Minerals library, Dhahran,
Saudi Arabia; no departments have independent libraries, but
reading rooms have been set up in sixteen departments which are
organized and operated through the central library system. The
new King Saud University complex, the largest in the Arab Islamic
world, will soon accommodate in one building all library units
scattered at the moment.

It is an undeniable phenomenon that duplication of collections occurs in a decentralized set-up and this eats up a substantial slice of the financial loaf. Provision of a consistently high-standard readers' and reference service to students and staff cannot be maintained in a fragmentary library system. Perhaps one could consider the institution of a self-renewal policy, whereby dead wood of little use and less frequently used materials might be deposited in reading rooms attached to each department for consultation and research. Needless to say, the upkeep of these collections would not consume a painful proportion of central library allocations.

Library organization

An overview of the functional organization of main libraries and the physical management of collections within these university libraries in various countries would reflect different service patterns and effectual or ineffectual organizational styles. Numerous components of every system contribute towards the formation of departments within the central library. In Saudi Arabia, at the King Faisal University, Dammam campus, the library operations are grouped under three sections: readers' services, acquisitions, and classification and cataloguing. Great importance is attached to the reference department, although the quality of the reference service needs to be improved for the benefit of readers. The University of Petroleum and Minerals library is organized into five functional divisions. As is evident from Figure 1.1 the processing division takes care of the acquisition procedure, invoice settlements and cataloguing activities, while the selection of reading materials is left with the collection use division, and the non-print material selection is the responsibility of the educational aids division. Moreover, user assistance or an advisory service to readers is offered by both the educational aids division and information services division. The latter division provides a superb reference service and aids research students in techniques of investigation. The physical layout of the library indicates diligent planning by Dr Saleh Ashoor, Dean of Library Affairs. The materials are arranged thus:[33]

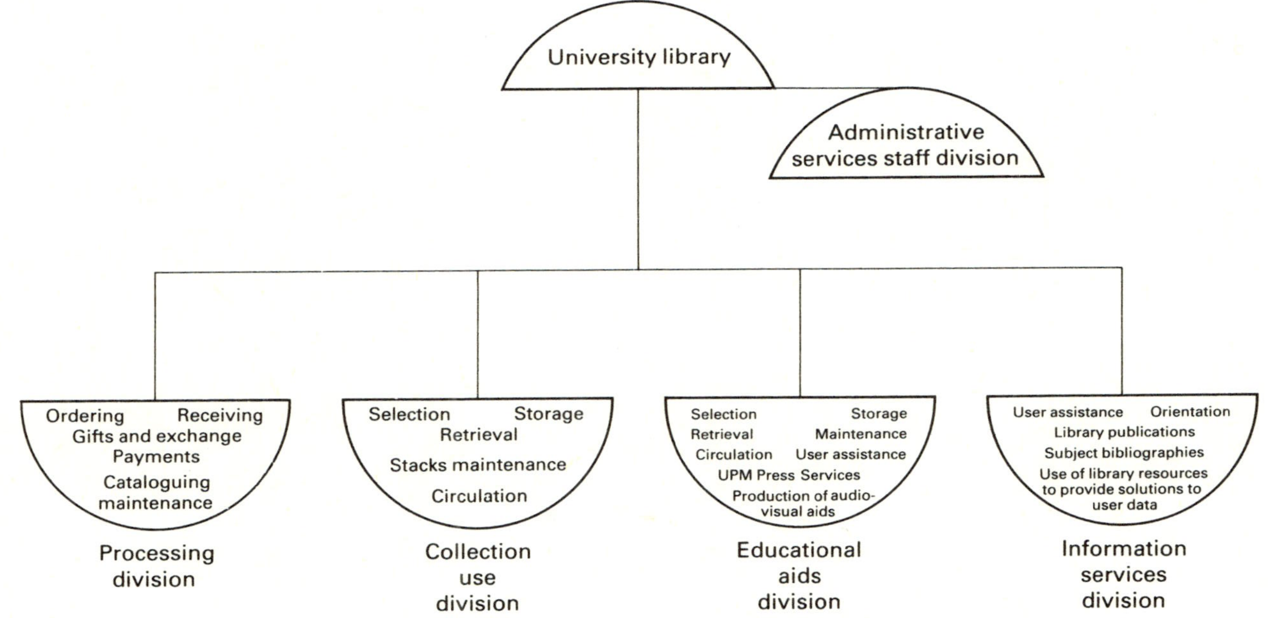

Figure 1.1 *Functional organization, University of Petroleum and Minerals library, Dhahran, Saudi Arabia*

Basement level	16mm films, photo laboratory and auditorium
Plateau level	Reference, research, online retrieval circulation; public catalogues: authors and titles, subjects; current periodicals and newspapers; Near Eastern collection; theses & dissertations; media centre, educational aids
Level 2	Dean of Library Affairs; administrative services, processing services
Level 3	Humanities and social sciences – books and periodicals (A–P), maps, microforms and reader/printers; research reports: National Technical Information Service (NTIS), Educational resources Information Centre (ERIC).
Level 4	Pure and applied sciences – books and periodicals (Q–Z)

Ideally, periodical holdings, both current and back issues, would have been stored as well as displayed on one particular level rather than split into three floors. Presumably, space considerations may have hindered the process of material organization. The second expansion of the library building, due to start in 1985, will obviously help in overcoming structural organizational problems and facilitate the use of collections.

The King Saud University library in Riyadh functions under ten departments: acquisitions, research photography, exchange and exhibitions, periodicals, cataloguing and classification, special collections, manuscripts, government publications, audio-visual resources, and research publishing.[34] King Abdulaziz University library, Jeddah, is organized as in Table 1.1.[35]

Table 1.1 *King Abdulaziz University library, functional organization*

Library services dept	*Special collection dept*	*Technical services dept*
Reference	Manuscripts	Acquisition
Circulation	Government documents	Cataloguing
Photography	Audio-visual materials	Serials
	Microfilms	

An apparent shift in emphasis is shown by a change in the organizational pattern of these university libraries in Saudi Arabia. One common aspect which emerges from their departmental segregation is the increasing importance accorded to the establishment of audio-visual resource units.

The central library of Kuwait University has three major departments: acquisitions, cataloguing and reference. Under each are grouped all the activities for the efficient performance of attendant responsibilities. On the other hand, the University of Qatar library functions under the following divisions: circulation, readers', advisory, cataloguing and classification, bibliographical services and training. The training division is involved in preparing and teaching user education courses for four hours weekly for two consecutive terms to undergraduate students.

The library operations of the University of Jordan are split up into five departments: acquisition, cataloguing and classification, reference and special collections, periodicals and circulation. But Yarmouk University library in Jordan is organized in several units, all functioning under two major divisions: public services and technical services. The process of sectional and divisional arrangement is illustrated diagrammatically (see Figure 1.2). Each unit represents specific areas of user services and technical operations. One of the areas of the public services division is the rooms control department, unheard of in other university libraries. It is primarily concerned with the supervision and running of reading rooms in the university library.

The organizational structure of university libraries in Nigeria differs greatly, depending on the librarian's capability and the circumstances which sometimes dictate either functional or subject organization. The University of Calabar library pursues the former method, whereby all operations are separated into three divisions. As Figure 1.3 shows, all the library activities are logically arranged under three divisions, namely resource development, technical services and readers' services. The readers' services division is solely responsible for providing advisory, reference and consultancy services to users. It deals with users, enquiries for specific information and undertakes to search for such information. Expert library staff help readers to find desired items and any piece of information systematically and efficiently. Library staff in both the lending and reference departments coordinate their

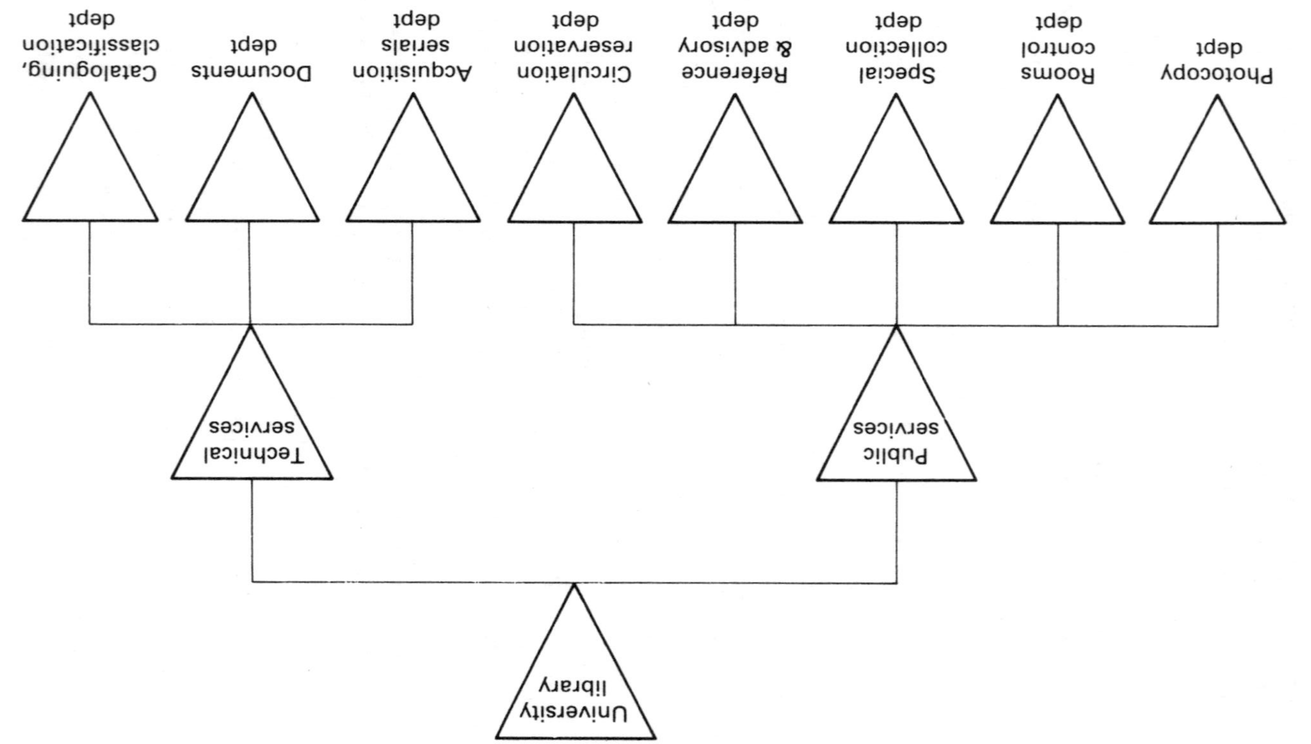

Figure 1.2 *Functional organization, Yarmouk University library, Jordan*

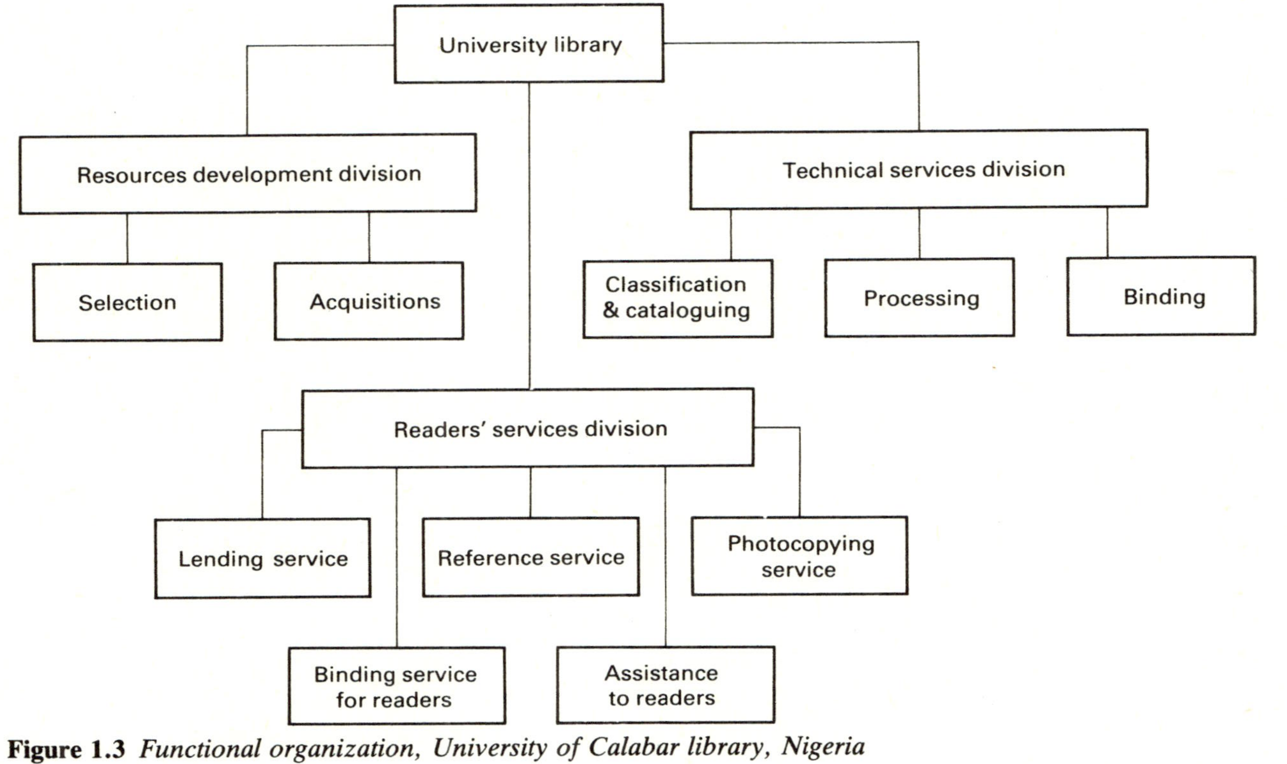

Figure 1.3 *Functional organization, University of Calabar library, Nigeria*

efforts to give readers the best services which are lacking in many university libraries in other countries. Some universities regard acquisitions and selection as segments of the technical services division, but the University of Calabar library has established an independent resource development division. In contrast, the University of Jos library, Nigeria, follows a pattern of subject approach to library operations, as it is seen as a more effective way of discharging responsibilities and providing efficient services. There are two major divisions: subject libraries and support services. The former consists of seven service points related to the number of faculties in the university. The latter includes orders, material processing, binding and reprography and other areas concerning technical processing. The subject organization in the university libraries is considered by the majority of users as the most convenient arrangement which permits unobstructed access to periodicals, books and other materials on a particular subject in one place. The advantages of the continental system of subject specialist librarians is summed up by Professor J. D. Pearson. With the advent of centralized cataloguing, he says,

> whether by means of LC cards or MARC tapes, this time-consuming function will cease to absorb the minds of our senior staff, releasing them to work with readers, enabling them to become expert in the bibliography and librarianship of a subject or group of subjects or an area. The expertise should be put to the disposal of students and staff and all users of the library.[36]

In the University of Jos library the Chief Librarian, B. U. Nwafor, strongly supports the concept of subject specialization and, therefore, subject libraries are systematically organized so as

> to concentrate at one point and for the convenience of the reader, the range of library materials of interest to him irrespective of their formation. For example, in this social services library, all the reference and lending books as well as current and retrospective journals in that subject are brought together with reading tables in close proximity.[37]

The subject organizational procedure is also in operation at the University of Karachi library, where the combined readers' services and administration division controls the circulation and reading rooms located on various floors offering informational,

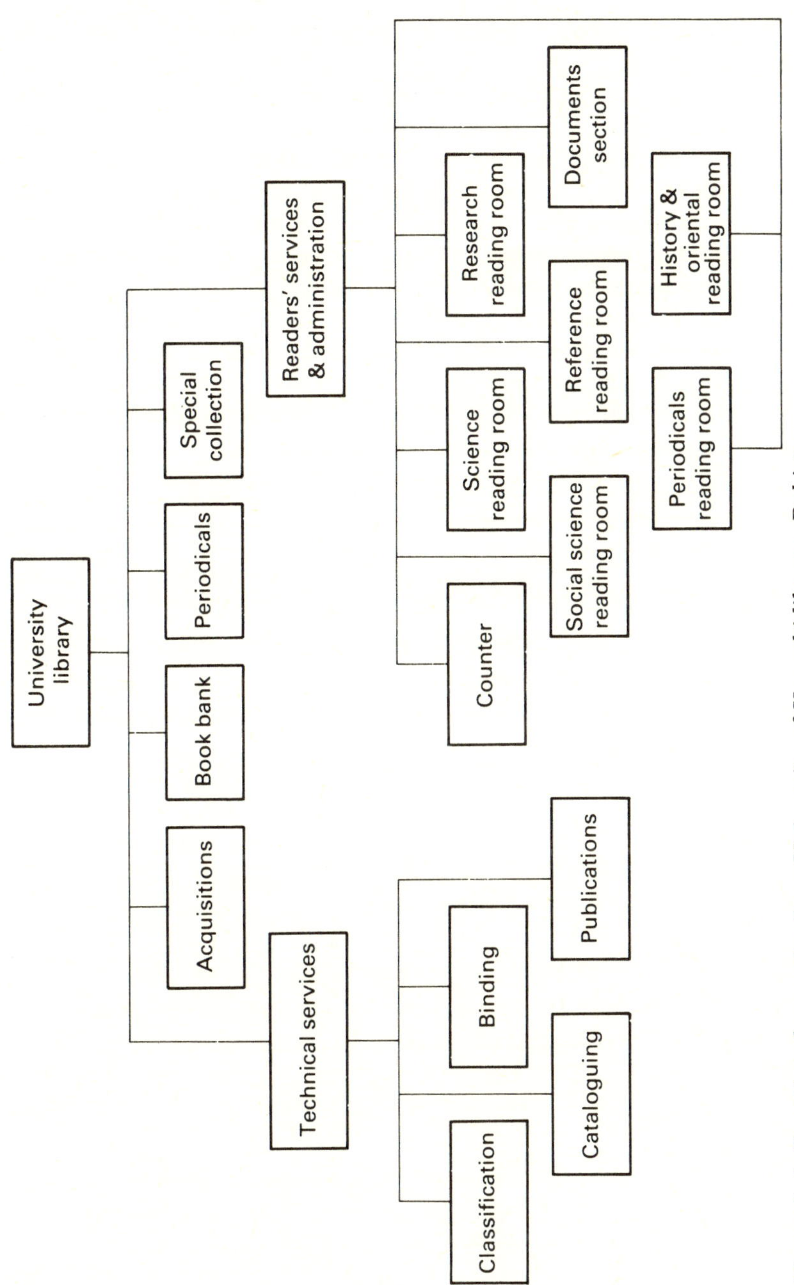

Figure 1.4 *Functional organization, University of Karachi library, Pakistan*

reference and advisory services to users in different subject fields. As Figure 1.4 shows, library activities are grouped under six divisions, i.e. technical services, acquisitions, book bank, periodicals, special collections and readers' services. Here, acquisition and periodicals are not part of the technical services division. Although the arrangement is functional, the readers' services and administration division reflects subject organization, which is not a common pattern shared by other university libraries in Pakistan and many other Islamic countries. Budgetary limitations, the lack of accommodation for materials and services, the scarcity of staff in qualitative and quantitative terms, the traditional policy of the university library, and the non-service-oriented attitude of the chief librarian are some of the fundamental reasons which may dictate the organizational structure of the library.

Chapter 2

The management of university libraries

The first objective of a hospital is the care of the patient, whereas the fundamental objective of the university library is to serve the readers. This needs the 'intellectual and professional services of men and women who have been trained for precisely such purposes'.[1] Technological innovations and the proliferation and utility of multi-media systems have significant implications for library management. In Arab Islamic countries most university libraries have concentrated their attention on the functioning and performance of technical service units and have somewhat neglected the public service area, which is unquestionably the heart of the library. The library manager is primarily concerned with the accomplishment of two major functions:

(a) He has to acquire and organize books, periodicals and other materials and see that they are made easily available to students

(b) He must maintain an administrative organization in which a sufficient number of appropriately qualified workers may serve the clientele effectively and at the same time attain maximum profesisonal development and satisfaction.[2]

Several points emerge from these two functions, but on the whole the matter revolves around the characteristics of the university librarian, who should be versatile, very intelligent, intellectual, knowledgeable, and an excellent coordinator, in order to be able to pursue the goals mentioned above and attain a high degree of success. As early as 1878, at the London Conference of Librarians, it was mentioned that 'to properly fill the office of a librarian requires the best qualities of a scholar, a gentleman, and a man of business'.[3] He should have an over-whelming desire to enhance his knowledge for the benefit of readers rather than for personal satisfaction. He should not only be professionally trained, but he must also have a broad and active interest in scholarship and scholarly attainments that will gain for him the respect and esteem of his colleagues and students. He must make the library a thoroughly pleasant place for users and the staff of the library must be indispensable. Since 'the more rapidly changing and novel the environment, the more information the individual needs to process in order to make effective rational decisions',[4] it places greater responsibility upon the management to develop the library along those lines which will best fulfil the varied needs and interests of faculty and students. This calls for a library manager with extraordinary qualities: perception, insight, flexibility, adaptability, politeness and a positive attitude towards subordinate staff and readers. Thus, the 'selection of a highly qualified librarian is of central importance'.[5]

According to Elizabeth Stone, the university librarian is chiefly responsible for planning, organizing, staffing, directing, coordinating, reporting and budgeting. But Waddington sums up the librarian's major functions under five headings: planning, decision making, delegating, staffing and reporting.[6] He has grouped organizing, coordinating and budgeting under the planning heading, whereas directing is part of the decision-making function. Hasan Ali Al-Zayer, as stated in his article, 'The image of change in library administration in Saudi Arabia', believes that the librarian's role is no different from that of physician, engineer or professor, and he is involved in library planning: 'The planning includes setting the goals and objectives, developing the library policy, and determining the financial classification for each department in the library.'[7]

There appears to be undue emphasis on the planning component, but 'you cannot plan without a policy'.[8] Policy should be devised to facilitate the service to readers, not as an end in itself. The most important single element of any policy is the provision and management of library personnel, whose performance, actions and commitments obviously shape and influence procedures and policies. If the university librarian is to achieve predetermined objectives, he must make intelligent use of human effort. Since the author is concerned with the managerial styles of university libraries in eight Arab Islamic countries, it is pertinent to discuss and analytically describe the staffing levels and structure prevalent in these countries.

Staffing structures

The quality and strength of the library staff as a matter of principle is dependent upon the size of the student population and faculty, the breadth and range of curriculum, the existing stock and annual acquisition rate, the nature of the library building, its location and internal organizational pattern, opening hours and the type of reference, circulation and informational services rendered. In addition, the personality of the library manager plays a part when it comes to forcefully pleading his case, based on sound and solid arguments for adequate professional and support staff. In spite of his ability to present his case reasonably and exert charismatic influence in seeking approval for his projects, such reports score little success in poor countries, where universities are encountering stringent economic reductions in their annual expenditure.

In some countries, the size of the professional library staff is directly related to the size of the student population. In 1943, the American Library Association considered very large institutions 'as being too complex and too highly individualized to permit the application of a standardized pattern'.[9] Naturally, a wide variety of tasks in libraries do not require professional training and can be comfortably performed by the support staff, who relieve the trained personnel to deploy their energies in carrying out jobs of high significance involving professional knowledge, experience and skill. Also, it is feasible, economical and relatively easy to recruit non-professional staff, as compared with the professionally qualified, who are likely to expect higher salaries etc. It is, therefore, appropriate to maintain an internationally recognized standard concerning the professional and non-professional staff ratio. McNeal recommends a ratio of two non-professional staff to one librarian. Likewise, Peter Durey, in his work, *Staff management in university and college libraries*,[10] quoted the *Guide to Canadian University Library Standards*, produced in 1965, in which it is recommended that 31 per cent of the total library staff should be professionally trained. The Association of College and Research Libraries Joint Committee on

University Library Standards 1969 proposed a figure of 35 per cent.[11]

An analytical examination of the statistics relating to professional and non-professional staff in Table 2.1 indicates wide variations in the professional staff ratio in different university libraries in different countries. Either the percentage of professional to non-professional staff is much higher than the standard 30 per cent or far lower. Overall staff shortages prevail in almost all the university libraries in Nigeria, Pakistan and Arab countries. In October 1981 Qatar University library suffered from an acute shortage of professional staff. There were only ten librarians for the women's section and twelve librarians for the men's section and many of them did not hold professional degrees in library science.[12] During the last couple of years, the ratio of professional to non-professional staff has been reversed, due to the fact that the university library sought the consultancy services of an Egyptian-born Australian national as their Unesco expert. Similarly, the University of Kuwait library hired Dr Ahmad Badr as an advisor. He helped in the organization and administration of library services, before moving in September 1982 to King Abdulaziz University as Professor of Library Science. He acted as Director of the Kuwait University library for a number of years and was replaced by Suleiman Kalendar, a Kuwaiti national who had completed his professional postgraduate library education in England. In Qatar, Kuwait and Saudi Arabia, the vast majority of staff are not natives and they are hired from several countries around the world. In Saudi Arabia, 'even disregarding the lack of native professionals, the overall number of professionals is inadequate for the volume of library collections and the increasing size of university enrolments'.[13]

In Malaysia, all university libraries are relatively well staffed; most of the personnel are trained either in Great Britain or the USA. Another equally important aspect is the balanced percentage of professional and non-professional staff; the figure ranges from 16 to 20 per cent. Of all the Arab Islamic countries, the Malaysian university libraries are at the top of the list in recruiting and retaining the high proportion of non-professional staff which is so essential for the efficient conduct of library services and operations. The same is true of the Nigerian library scene, where the emphasis on the appointment of support staff corresponds to a great extent with that in Malaysian university libraries.

Table 2.1 *Professional and non-professional staff, 1983*

University library	Percentage of Professionals	No. of Professionals	No. of Non-professionals
University of Qatar	68.5	37	17
University of Kuwait	14.6	23	134
University of Jordan	28	23	59
Yarmouk University, Jordan	30	12	28
University of Petroleum and Minerals, Saudi Arabia	64.1	34	19
King Abdulaziz University, Saudi Arabia	45	18	22
King Faisal University, Saudi Arabia	54.5	6	5
University of Khartoum, Sudan	28.5	8	20
Omdurman Islamic University, Sudan	25.8	8	23
University of Al-Gezira, Sudan	1.5	2	17
National University of Malaysia	16.6	36	180
University of Agriculture, Malaysia	20.5	29	112
Technological University of Malaysia	17.6	25	110
Universiti Sains, Malaysia	17.6	25	117
University of Engineering and Technology, Lahore, Pakistan	2.4	9	35
University of Baluchistan, Pakistan	37.5	9	15
NED University of Engineering and Technology, Karachi, Pakistan	32	8	17
Islamia University, Bahawalpur, Pakistan	44.4	8	10
University of Agriculture, Faisalabad	22.5	7	24
Islamic University, Islamabad, Pakistan	26.6	4	11
University of Benin, Nigeria	21.7	30	80
University of Jos, Nigeria	16.4	14	71
University of Calabar, Nigeria	15.1	13	73
Rivers State University of Science and Technology, Nigeria	11.8	9	67

Staffing structure and hierarchies in university libraries have great implications for managerial styles and the successful functioning of administrative, public and technical service units. In both Nigeria and Pakistan, the libraries are usually led by the university librarians, and further down are the deputy librarian and heads of department; where the structure is subject-oriented, subject specialist librarians are appointed below the rank of deputy librarian. Some university libraries, including Ilorin in Nigeria and Yarmouk in Jordan, tend to favour a hierarchy, where two deputy librarians, one each for technical services and public services, work under the authority of the university librarian, who is responsible for policy formulation, planning and coordination.

In Malaysia, the chief librarian is at the top of the ladder and normally one senior librarian and a number of qualified personnel are in charge of serials, acquisition, cataloguing and other departments in the university library system. In Kuwait, Qatar and to some extent in Saudi Arabia, the university librarian is designated director of libraries, followed by the heads of departments who each control a set of functioning units.

The administrative structure of university libraries in Saudi Arabia is entirely different from that of most other countries. There are deans and, in some cases, deputy deans of library affairs. They are solely responsible for the 'planning, administration, and operation of university libraries'.[14] Next in command are the directors of libraries, who are 'responsible for the direct administration and supervision of the university library and report directly to the Dean of Library Affairs'.[15] The concept of deputy librarians or deputy director of libraries does not prevail in this part of the world. In some of the universities, such as King Faisal University and the University of Petroleum and Minerals, the post of director of libraries does not exist at the present time, although both these universities were headed in the past by directors of libraries. The staffing structure of the University of Petroleum and Minerals library is distinct and does not relate in any way to other university libraries in Arab Islamic countries:

Dean of library affairs
Director general, educational aids
Manager, collection use services
Manager, information services
Systems analyst

Head of monographic acquisitions
Head of circulation
Head of serials
Head of cataloguing
Head of Arabic section
Head of reference
Audio-visual librarian

At the University of Petroleum and Minerals all the heads of departments report to the managers of their respective divisions and there are no deputy librarians or a library director, as is the practice of several other university libraries in that country.

In Arab Islamic countries, a few university libraries do not appear to differentiate between professional librarians and support staff. In this world there will always be the 'hewers of wood and drawers of water'. Librarians should not despise those who perform such tasks, nor the tasks themselves, but it is a false economy to continually use librarians for carting boxes of books, for tidying up the library or for typing book orders, when other untrained and less qualified people can be hired to do that work at less expense.

Management techniques and styles

A library manager should design a system without idiosyncratic elements and which would involve the efficient deployment of the effort, skills, abilities and enthusiasm of individual staff members without the visible waste of those energies which might otherwise be dissipated in tasks of lesser significance. Personnel management is that part of management which is concerned with people at work and with their relationships within the library. It aims to achieve 'both efficiency and justice, neither of which can be pursued successfully without the other'.[16] It welds the individuals into an effective organization for the attainment of projected goals and objectives. According to Pigors and Myers, 'personnel administration is the management of people. It is accomplished primarily through direct supervision and the development of official policies'.[17] In fact, the manager need not manage people, he should simply provide expert advice to the sub-heads so as to make effective and economical use of manpower resources. But where the library manager is given unrestricted executive powers, the problem of dividing or sharing those powers remains and it has to be solved logically.

Amongst the various styles of management there are (a) line organization, (b) line and staff organization, (c) functional organization and (d) committee organization. In the (a) type, the library manager simply gives orders to subordinate staff to carry out his instructions. The (b) type involves team work, in which a team of consultants within the library helps the manager in identifying and solving problems and even in making decisions. He does not make any decision without consulting his senior staff. Functional organization is a mixture of both the (a) and (b) types. In this case, the library manager delegates authority to the heads of department in the library and gives them responsibility to study the problems and come up with solutions. Finally, there is the library committee which, in the words of Corbett, 'is a means of testing opinion and gaining support and helps the librarian clarify his own thoughts'.[18] If it undermines the authority of the manager, it would be unduly obstructing the administration of the library and the implementation of predetermined policies and the pursuit of institutional goals. The committees should not exercise close supervision nor deal with minute administrative affairs, but should act in an advisory capacity and coordinate the work of the library.

Participative management

In Western countries, library committees make recommendations for the solution of library problems and such committees provide some background for staff participation. In the past, library managers were accustomed to seeking informal advice from their staff. In the USA, the Association of Research Libraries set up a Management Review and Analysis Programme, which was based on team-building, group decision-making and general library staff participation. Maurice Marchant believes participative management requires and generates a high degree of mutual trust and confidence between superiors and subordinates.[19] Equally significant is the comment made by K. D. Metcalf that 'staff participation in the management of a large library benefits the head librarian by keeping him in touch with his staff and by helping to make his decisions and policies effective.'[20] Even if the library manager is versatile, intelligent and imaginative and firmly believes in his superior judgment in tackling extremely complex and delicate situations, he would still be totally unwise to ignore and disregard the library staff's contribution in advancing solutions to problems which may have never occurred to him. According to David Weber, Director of Stanford University libraries, 'subordinates are likely to give greater weight to practical matters, assistance with procedures, and departmental personnel issues. They may not see the vital contributions of the supervisor's fundamental planning or goal-setting roles.'[21]

Moreover, there is a possibility that someone with delegated authority may make the decision 'which will vary if only fractionally from what the librarian himself regards as the ideal'.[22] It is always regarded as the responsibility of the library manager to resolve any uncertainties that might be involved in important decisions. Obviously every decision affecting staff is unlikely to please everyone and he should therefore be able to absorb the 'displeasure and sometimes severe hostility'[23] of the junior staff. In spite of the various drawbacks of staff participation, Metcalf strongly recommends that 'several minds ought to be better than one, the stimulation that comes from exploration of new ideas and possibilities is pleasurable'.[24]

Of course, one does not expect the library manager to share responsibility with his colleagues, but some degree of staff involvement is inevitable. Decision-sharing practices are prevalent in many other professions, including industry, social welfare and health-related fields. Some typical library managers tend to apply a diversity of techniques as and when the situation dictates. They delegate temporarily, consult occasionally, share with some and ignore others within the library system. This is no style, but a reflection of the manager's inability to run the library. It is for this particular reason that writers on library management do not advocate any 'alternative to the advisory library committee, which exercises its influence most beneficially'[25] and advise participating actively in discussions related to library issues.

A major criticism directed towards participative decision-making is that it consumes a considerable amount of valuable staff time. But it has been suggested that the time wasted in the process of inadequate consultation and arbitrary decision-making far exceeds the 'supposed time loss incurred by operating within the framework of an operational committee'[26] in the library. The library manager ought to develop a system so that senior staff avail themselves of the chance to contribute to the developmental process. It is undeniably true that where subordinates are part of the decision-making process, they are more likely to help implement policies. As the universities expand, service expectations from libraries grow and give rise to complex issues, and the library managers require accurate and up-to-date information for solving problems. It is certainly difficult 'to make wise decisions unless the relevant facts of the situation to be decided upon have been assembled and assessed'.[27]

The choice of manager in libraries has to be made carefully. Managers should be able to lead, not merely make decisions. A librarian with an authoritative attitude has an excessive dislike for any of his power to be delegated to the staff further down the hierarchy. He must have ingenuity and a broad enough vision to feel comfortable and secure and in no way consider any power-sharing or decision-sharing as a threat to his own job. The individual staff members in libraries are said to be over-controlled and are given little responsibility.[28] One important grievance which contributes to the discontentment of subordinate staff is the lack of consultation, a pervasive problem in most of the university libraries in Arab Islamic countries.

There is an acute shortage of native librarians in rich Arab countries like Qatar, Kuwait and Saudi Arabia. There are fundamental differences in the way various nationalities respond to management. Some expatriates tend to expect and respect a somewhat authoritarian style of management, whereas others prefer to be consulted before decisions concerning them are made and like participative management. Natives of rich Arab Islamic countries favour firm management but, in contrast to Europeans and Asians, have higher and more realistic hopes of progressing to higher positions. Some expatriates from poor countries, holding executive positions in the university libraries of rich Arab Islamic countries, have developed unique styles of management and their attitudes towards their own compatriates and other non-natives working in various junior positions leaves much to be desired. They consider themselves far superior to and far more knowledge-able than their colleagues and subordinates. In such a climate, the question of participative management in problem-solving does not arise. They can never apply managerial skills justly in improving the performance of all subordinates. It is very difficult for the manager to apply different styles of management in the same organization without appearing unjust or unfair.

Motivation and performance

The decision-sharing process helps tremendously to motivate staff to implement projects and 'as a result . . . concern for performance is felt through the organization'.[29] While three stages of planning are identified, namely organizational planning, management planning and development planning, it is the latter which is most closely related to the improvement of job performance. 'The objective of motivating is to create and maintain in all persons working in an organization the desire to achieve the objectives of that organization'.[30] Positive motivators are responsibility, a sense of achievement and the opportunity to utilize specialized knowledge, as well as good salaries, job security and respect. John Adair, in his work, *Training for leadership* (1968), claims that 'motivation is inherent in all human beings' and that the library manager should direct his energies towards fostering job satisfaction, thereby eliminating frustration. No doubt human nature can be motivated, provided appropriate ways and means are found and the management is aware of the psychological approaches which ought to be carefully selected and applied. Abraham Maslow, in his *Motivation and personality* (1954), describes five motivations related to the fulfilment of human needs. There are psychological needs, food, sleep, etc.; safety or security needs; social needs, e.g. prestige or recognition received from both within and outside the organization; self-actualized needs, the opportunity for self-fulfilment and accomplishment through personal growth and development; and esteem or ego needs, i.e. success or self-respect. Here self-fulfilment is at the bottom of the list simply because, 'the more one want is being satisfied, the less its satisfaction matters'.[31] Herzberg exclaims that motivation problems can be alleviated by job enrichment strategies. The positive motivators, as listed in Jones and Jordan's work, include achievement, recognition, the intrinsic nature of the work, responsibility, advancement and professional or personal growth.[32] The first motivator achievement, according to Benge, is not applicable to less developed countries. He believes they do not have achievement values and motivation is largely culturally determined.

> For reasons with which we are all familiar individuals in LDCs have no particular sense of vocation so that it is almost accidental what profession they eventually embrace. (Works on management theory assume that people have chosen their vocation.)[33]

This is in fact an out-dated statement which is no longer valid or applicable to most of the Arab Islamic states, with the exception of poor countries where the choice is limited. In Nigeria, Sudan, Jordan and Pakistan, two of the hygiene factors as motivators, salary and working conditions, are totally absent. (Hygiene factors include interpersonal relationships with colleagues and students; working conditions; availability of non-professional staff to add to trained personnel; staff, status and pay; job security.) There can probably never, at least in the immediate future, be a time 'when the size of the pay packet alone will determine the level of the individual worker's satisfaction'.[34]

A high standard of performance from library staff and a high standard of presentation of service to readers is needed in every university library. The manager, whatever the economic, social and physiological limitations, must 'stimulate and encourage each individual'[35] to perform duties with honesty and efficiency. One personnel management theory assumes that the average person has an inherent dislike of work and will avoid it as far as possible. It is essential to direct, control and even threaten people in order to get jobs done. Some people are very disorganized, unwilling to pull their weight and not prepared to work efficiently. A number of these people from poor countries, who are fortunate enough to have very good salaries and other remunerations in rich Arab Islamic countries, still seem discontented and dissatisfied. A typical example is that of a librarian from a poor country, working at King Faisal University libraries, who was moderately qualified, but was enjoying a salary no less than a university teacher in Saudi Arabia. He was always seen walking around, carrying some papers in his hand and pretending to be working very hard. Such examples are no less numerous in other countries of the developing world.

The library managers should be fully alert to fundamentally lazy people and should not hesitate to terminate their service. We must use our human and technical resources as economically and diligently as possible. The librarian should comprehend the significance of public services and the nature and structure of technical, reference and automated library services. A standardized process for getting jobs done should be evolved. Willard Austen, in 1911, stressed the functional division of labour, by which he meant that some persons were better adapted to doing one kind of work than they were to other kinds and efficiency required the elimination of those not adapted to a particular kind of work.[36] Michael Gorman thinks we should move away from hierarchy in the library.[37] The absurd and damaging idea that there are 'public service types' and 'technical service types' is partly produced by library education. Abandoning such ideas would substantially help the library manager in planning the work in the library as a whole and securing optimum efficiency.

In 1897, Frank P. Hill, in his paper, 'Organization and management of library staff', recorded his experiences, which are equally applicable today in many university libraries in developing countries. The subordinate staff feel that the 'Librarian delights in finding fault . . . . when he is inspecting the library with an attentive ear and observing eye it is for the sole purpose of picking flaws'.[38] He goes on to say, don't be misled, don't be suspicious, such is not the fact. No-one knows better than the librarian that praise and encouragement are good and necessary stimulants. While commenting on enthusiasm, he says that, with staff working in libraries merely for the money, one should expect very little enthusiasm and very little good, downright hard work. The author believes that the majority of expatriates in the university libraries of rich Arab Islamic countries are working for the money and very few have real commitment or are making a genuine contribution to promoting the improvement of libraries. One of the obvious reasons might be their feelings of insecurity, since they are hired on a yearly contract basis and most appear to be unsettled because they do not 'belong here'. They will have to return to their home countries upon the termination of the contract and may encounter unsurmountable difficulties in terms of job prospects, their children's education, housing, supporting their family, etc. Some of the facilities which must be extended to subordinate staff include time off for illness and occasional short absences without salary deductions. Since the library managers are concerned with high productivity, they need to identify the symptoms of stress which are visible especially when there is an excessive workload. Also, if the staff are over-qualified and their talents and expertise are under-utilized, there will be stress signs. Further indications of human stress are related to fatigue, sadness, depression and sensitivity to criticism. Expecting staff to produce more and better work would generate disenchantment.

Communication channels

No managerial skill or technique can be effective without an appropriate structure of communication in the university library system. Whether the type of communication is 'upward, down-ward or horizontal',[39] no barriers should exist and the manager must have both formal and informal contact with the subordinate staff. (See Figure 2.1.)

The establishment of an efficient channel of transmission is vital to the functioning of a university library. It is a system in which information is transferred, and ideas and thoughts are exchanged between people. Verbal communication is used to maintain rapport with individual members of the library staff. Ineffective leadership breeds symptoms of frustration among subordinates. The library manager should 'emphasize coordination rather than supervision'.[40] The manager, by means of communicating with subordinates, can influence activities towards the attainment of goals. Unfounded rumours, opinions and informal discussions among the junior staff lead to unpleasantness and a polluted atmosphere. In a centralized library system the communication lines are shorter between the library manager and the library staff when they both are located in the same building.[41] But in physically diversified units, communication becomes more com-plex. Drucker has recorded three aspects of communication:[42]

1 It is the recipient who communicates, the so-called communi-cator only utters
2 People can only understand within the limits of their experience
3 People as a rule perceive only what they expect to perceive.

A successful manager is one who is a good listener and not only

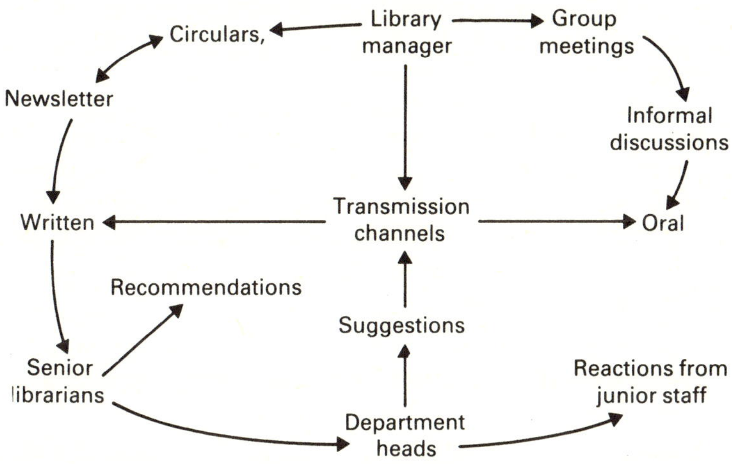

Figure 2.1 *Communication channels*

communicates downward, but encourages upward communication. 'Channels for receiving members must exist.'[43] In most of the Arab Islamic countries, communication up the management hierarchy has not been developed as effectively as the traditional downwards communication.[44]

Oral communication helps to remove any barrier which may otherwise exist. It may be in the form of a regularly scheduled group meeting including senior staff or an occasional general meeting inviting all the professional staff and offering them the opportunity to express their feelings. The library manager might issue instructions to be carried out or a memorandum which should invite comments, suggestions, recommendations and reactions from both the senior cadres and junior library staff. Naturally, written communication is less flexible than verbal, as it allows the staff to speak up and show their approval or disapproval of the manager's ideology. One popular communication channel is the production of a newsletter including 'items of interest about library development'.[45] It may even include information concerning library staff promotions, marriages, engagements, etc. For the purpose of effective communication, the University of Jordan library publishes a regular newsletter. Likewise, the University of Petroleum and Minerals library, Saudi Arabia, issues *Library*

Scene and a number of other periodic publications, including a newsletter for facilitating communication not only with the library staff, but also with the university community at large.

A breakdown of communication is found in many university libraries in Arab Islamic countries. This is exclusively due to the appointment of either incompetent or dictatorial library managers. Syed Hussein Alatas has rightly stated the genus to which such library managers belong.[46] The essential characteristics of a fool are

> that he is not able to recognize problems and if they are told to him he is not able to solve them. He normally does not admit that he is a fool. A man does not become a fool if he does not know everything.

The problem of slow development is often due to the combined effort of the fools and the corrupt. Although people make mistakes, the superbly talented 'Dr Know-all' never permits anyone to contradict his point of view, which he feels determined to inflict upon his subordinates, thereby making them a very miserable and unhappy lot. 'Influencing staff', according to Lloyd, 'rather than exerting power over them is the best method for the manager to discharge his duties.'[47]

Staff training and development

If university libraries are to render an efficient service to support the educational objectives of the university, the professional staff must be forthcoming in using their knowledge and skills. It is only through staff loyalty that libraries can become the educational instrument essential for study and research. But the library manager needs to optimize the use of manpower and create an atmosphere conducive to career development and job satisfaction by fostering in-service training programmes to promote staff competencies. The manager should be aware of and able to identify 'the training needs of each individual librarian'.[48] Needless to say, the objective of in-service training is to enhance the efficiency of the library which organizes it. Inefficient staff require training since their negligence may negate the work of the library. Dr Hisham Abbas, Professor of Library Science ·at the King Abdulaziz University, recommends that 'staff development must

44

be a continuous process, with its objective being to enhance professional capabilities and improve work effectiveness through a well organized programme of self-improvement'.[49] If the quality of staff is the most 'important single factor in providing an effective library service',[50] the subordinate staff must be trained 'to do their job better'.[51] In 1960, it was recognized at the Ahmadu Bello University that there was a clear need to provide staff training and tuition at several levels. The inculcation of correct methods of work can increase the output of library assistants.[52] There are two identifiable categories of staff training: (a) university courses, short courses, seminars, workshops, conferences, symposia and lectures, and (b) staff meetings, individual staff conferences, individual study, correspondence courses, observation, staff assignment and supervision.[53]

What in-service training achieves is discussed by Susunaga Weeaperumer.[54]

(a) It helps to expose the limitations of formal, professional education in libraries
(b) It helps the development of the right attitude to work
(c) It is a means of furthering post-professional studies
(d) It gives an opportunity for the exploration of in-service trainees' special areas of interest.

Any such staff training programmes must be designed by experienced and senior librarians, keeping in view the objectives of the university, the goals of the library and the type of service to be rendered.

The library profession is not a very prestigious profession in many if not all developing countries. An interesting survey was conducted in Taiwan, where sixteen library directors were asked 'when you meet someone for the first time and they ask you what you do for a living, how do you respond?'[55] Four of them said they were librarians or in library work, three said they were librarians, but also taught, four indicated that they were teachers, but also worked in the library, two responded that they were teachers, one said he was a college administrator, while another evaded the question by saying he was an outsider to libraries and hence did not feel he could answer such a question in a representative manner. This attitude is mainly due to the occupational background and non-recognition of the status of our profession. For example, an expatriate from India, who is presently a librarian in one of the faculties in the King Abdulaziz University, was interviewed by a reporter from *Arab News* (a daily newspaper published in Jeddah). He declared that he was a lecturer in library science, chiefly to satisfy his instinct and to identify himself with the teaching staff of the university.

We must attempt to make librarianship a prestigious profession, one of first choice, not of last resort. One factor which makes this difficult is that there is an abundance of opportunities in rich Arab Islamic countries for talented young people to receive training and pursue careers in recognized and remunerative professions, such as medicine and engineering. Librarianship schools should not aim just to fill places, rather they should set high admission standards and high standards for graduation. Even if this means that places remain unfilled, it is better than turning out numerous librarians of doubtful quality. In selecting candidates, great importance should be attached to character – candidates who demonstrate that they make every effort to follow the teachings of the Qur'an and Sunnah, who are of stable and sound moral character.

There is growing concern to abolish the illusion that 'any fool can put a book on a shelf'. At the same time, library managers should not make such a mystique of their profession that they imagine themselves to be more indispensible and important than they really are. Nor should they surround themselves with a protective façade of jargon, for this can make the profession seem ridiculous. They should treat their subordinate staff with respect and consult them before issuing orders. The individual staff members should, as far as possible, be given responsibility for organizing their own work. But they remain accountable to the manager and overall responsibility rests with him. The staff should work together as a team and both initiative as well as loyalty should be rewarded. They should respect the manager, but not feel that they should 'lick his boots'. It is worthwhile to consider the role of the imam in leading prayer; he is chosen by the consensus of the local people because of his seniority and merit, but if he makes a mistake the people have a duty to warn him, and, if necessary, replace him.

Chapter 3

Reference and information services

The accessibility of university library collections without unavoidable inconvenience to the seekers of knowledge is one aspect of the library's service to the reading community. Another aspect is to provide a congenial atmosphere for uninterrupted browsing, personal study and research. Yet another component of user services is to offer practical help to the individual in the location of information. This is to eliminate or at least minimize user frustration in discovering a piece of information or a specific item from a formidable variety of scattered resources.

To meet the needs of diverse university communities, the user services are organized differently in different countries. The University of Petroleum and Minerals library, Saudi Arabia, has an information services division which includes a reference department and an on-line searching department, as well as providing an inter-library loan service, photocopying service and library instructions. A collection use service division of this university library is responsible for overall supervision of the entire operations of the circulation department. In contrast, in many university libraries, e.g. at the National University of Malaysia, the Universities of Calabar and Ilorin, Nigeria, and Yarmouk University, Jordan, all activities related to circulation, reference, readers' assistance and photocopying are grouped under the readers' services division. In some cases, as at the University of Jordan and King Faisal University, Saudi Arabia, circulation and reference departments have been set up to function independently, with partial coordination in fulfilling user requirements.

In order to identify the various dimensions of reference,

information and readers' services, one approach would be to tentatively present the purposes and objectives of various service units in some of the university libraries in the developing countries. At the University of Ilorin library, the aims of the reference service include 'supplying answers to readers' enquiries, helping users find desired information and a lot of bibliographic searching'.[1] The basic function of the reference department at the King Faisal University is to 'help faculty, students, staff and members of the public in the use of the library resources'.[2] At the University of Jordan Library, 'the reference department aids in directing readers by answering their questions, referring them to suitable references and showing them how to use them.'[3] The reference librarian who mans the reference desk at the University of Petroleum and Minerals library, Saudi Arabia, is available to

1 explain how to use the library
2 identify the location of the various library facilities
3 provide assistance in using library resources, including the card catalogues and DOBIS/LIBIS terminals
4 assist in obtaining information from the collections, with special emphasis on the reference collection.[4]

The sources of the reference department help the readers to 'find a definite piece of information and understand where a subject fits into the scheme of universal knowledge'[5] so as to facilitate the search. The reference section of Yarmouk University library gives advice to students in conducting research and using reference materials, e.g. encyclopaedias, and assists in the preparation of bibliographies.[6]

There are two major categories of reference services; firstly, responding to a simple enquiry by referring the user to a particular source, or, secondly, an extensive research enquiry which demands the compilation of a short bibliography or a literature search conducted on behalf of the user. In most university libraries in developing countries, 'to offer an elaborate information service against a background of chronic acquisitions and cataloguing backlogs is . . . to put the cart before the horse'.[7] But the staff of readers' services divisions, in a number of university libraries which the author visited, are occupied with clerical and routine tasks and do not have 'sufficient time to offer extensive reference and information services'.[8] The University of the Punjab library, Pakistan, has a supervised reference section, maintained by a qualified and experienced librarian who appears to be anxious to help the readers use catalogues and locate materials on the shelves. Similarly, the University of Agriculture has appointed a reference assistant who handles all the reference and research enquiries. Reference service includes assistance in using the technical devices, such as periodical indexes, card catalogues, printed book catalogues, Computer Output Microfiche (COM) and showing readers how to use encyclopaedias, abstracts, etc., in pursuit of information. Some universities do not appoint a reference librarian or readers' advisor, e.g. Quaid-e-Azam University, Islamabad, where such work is undertaken by the senior staff at the circulation desk. The readers' advisory service at the University of Qatar has taken the form of producing 'manuals for the use of catalogues and reference sources'.[9] This practice is followed by the majority of university libraries, as will be described later in this chapter.

The extension of reference services involves the provision of research facilities to advanced students, faculty and other users. The University of Khartoum library in Sudan answers serious research enquiries and caters for the needs of research workers from outside the university.[10] A most sophisticated and highly developed on-line searching service is provided by the University of Petroleum and Minerals library in Saudi Arabia. Well over 125 different files in the DIALOG information service and the SDC search service in California may be interrogated via terminals in the central library. On-line searching of over 80 million records permits a subject approach to the contents of UPM's periodical and document collections. Both faculty and postgraduate research workers are required to complete a 'search request' form in which the particular subject or topic to be investigated and the related key words are recorded. Full assistance in preparing a personal profile is accorded to the researcher by the expert member of the library staff. On-line searching services to users are not uncommon in Western countries, for example at the Flinders University of South Australia library, where an on-line information retrieval service in the medical and biological sciences is offered to staff and higher degree students through the MEDLINE network, based at the National Library in Canberra.[11] The searches are carried out each afternoon and data bases covering other topics of possible interest are also accessible.

Borrowing privileges

All university libraries have identical membership categories, such as faculty members, postgraduate students, undergraduate students and non-teaching staff. A recent trend in the Arab Islamic countries is the extension of services to the community at large. The University of Jordan, being the largest library in the country, offers its services to the Jordanian community. Likewise, the University of Petroleum and Minerals Library, Saudi Arabia, in addition to its own university readership, extends borrowing rights to employees of private companies, government departments, ministries, ARAMCO and the students and staff of King Faisal University, which is located in the same province. Similarly, several other university libraries, which include King Saud University, Saudi Arabia, the University of Jos, Nigeria, the University of Qatar, and the National University of Malaysia, permit members of the public to use the library, but borrowing facilities are restricted to those with application forms duly attested by their respective employers, who are willing to undertake the responsibility for the loss of borrowed items. The number of books each member can borrow varies considerably from university to university. In the United Kingdom, 'a typical pattern would be that undergraduates can borrow up to six volumes for two weeks, postgraduates twelve volumes for two months and academic staff twenty volumes for an unlimited period'.[12] The Flinders University of South Australia medical library allows students to borrow up to four books for a period of two weeks. The University of the Punjab in Pakistan also allows postgraduate students four books and undergraduate students three books for two weeks only. This is a common pattern shared by many university libraries in Pakistan. A close examination of the book-borrowing privileges prevalent in a select number of university libraries in Nigeria, Jordan, Saudi Arabia and Pakistan does not reflect a sizeable dissimilarity in their practices. As is evident in Table 3.1, academic staff always appear to be a privileged group of the university community and are allowed to

Table 3.1 *Book-borrowing privileges*

University	Academic staff		Postgraduate students		Undergraduate students	
	No. of books allowed	Loan period	No. of books allowed	Loan period	No. of books allowed	Loan period
Nigeria						
University of Ilorin	6	4 weeks	4	2 weeks	4	2 weeks
University of Calabar	10	2 weeks	10	1 month	5	2 weeks
University of Jos	10	4 weeks	6	2 weeks	4	2 weeks
Jordan						
University of Jordan	No limit	One term	5	2 weeks	3	2 weeks
Yarmouk University	25	One term	5	2 weeks	3	2 weeks
Saudi Arabia						
King Saud University	20	One term	15	1 month	10	1 week
University of Petroleum and Minerals	No limit	One term				
King Faisal University	10	One term	–	–	5	2 weeks
Pakistan						
University of Engineering and Technology, Lahore	10	Academic session	6	1 month	4	20 days
Bahauddin Zakariya University, Multan	12	3 months	4	2 weeks	4	2 weeks
University of Agriculture, Faisalabad	8	3 months	3	2 weeks	2	10 days

borrow over ten titles for a period of two to four months. In Saudi Arabia, where education is given a very high priority, the loan policies for students are very generous compared to those of university libraries in other Arab Islamic countries.

A limited number of books, i.e. four or five, loaned to students in countries other than Saudi Arabia for the relatively short period of two weeks, does not encourage intensive reading. The reduced loan period also results in massive overdue fees, thereby increasing the consumption of library staff time in furnishing recall notices to the defaulters. There are obviously various loan renewal methods, the most common being bringing the books to the library circulation desk and having them restamped, as long as they are not required by another reader.

The actual borrowing procedure varies from one university to another. Most libraries issue readers' tickets to each borrower and then use a multiple slip system, in which case the reader obtains a transaction slip from the circulation desk and fills in his own particulars and the author, title, accession number or location, etc., of the required book. This system is in operation in only a few universities, which include the University of Al-Gezira, Sudan, the National University of Malaysia and the University of Petroleum and Minerals, Saudi Arabia.

Borrower's Number	Accession No.	Date Due
AUTHOR		Location No.
TITLE		
Your Name and Address in BLOCK Letters		

I acknowledge that this book is on loan to me from the University of Ilorin Library in accordance with the regulations in force.

Signature................................   Date................................

Figure 3.1 *University of Ilorin, Nigeria, transaction slip*

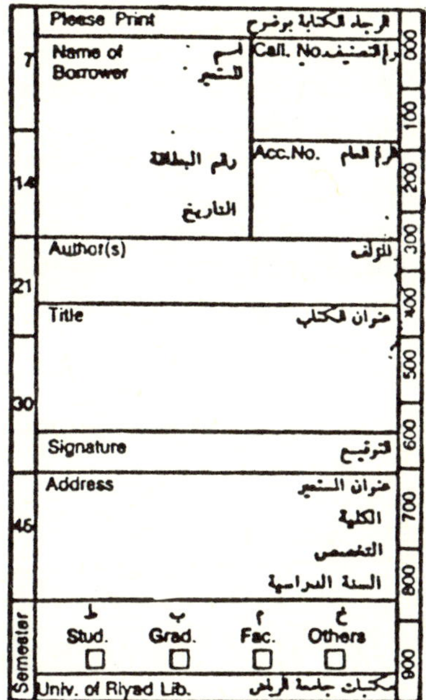

Figure 3.2 *King Saud University library, Saudi Arabia, transaction slip*

Most universities follow either the Brown or the Newark charging system, which are considered more simple to operate and do not entail the readers' efforts and time in completing one request form for each item to be borrowed. In Pakistan, most of the students of the Allama Iqbal Open University reside in different parts of the country and do not have the opportunity or the resources to visit the university library, which is situated in Islamabad. They pursue a wide variety of correspondence courses which require not only a few prescribed textbooks, but also supplementary reading materials. Since there is no developed public library system in the country, they have to rely exclusively on the library resources of the Allama Iqbal Open University, which does not extend a lending facility to distant borrowers. It is, therefore, essential that the university library should seriously consider introducing a postal circulation system, whereby every registered student should be entitled to borrow reading materials from the university library through a postal loan procedure.

Normally, periodicals, theses, government publications, manuscripts, heavily used books and non-print materials are not loaned to the members. Neither are reference books permitted to be taken off the library premises. With regard to the circulation of periodicals, particularly back issues or bound volumes, the policy of university libraries has somewhat relaxed in recent times. There are some universities in Nigeria, including the University of Jos, where all senior staff, graduate students and research workers are allowed to borrow bound volumes of journals (five years old or

مكتبة جامعة اليرموك		
تاريخ الارجاع :		رقم التسلسل :
تاريخ التجديد .		رمز التصنيف :
الجزء :		عنوان الكتاب :
		المؤلف :
		اسم المستعير .
السنة :	الدائرة :	الرقم الجامعي :
التاريخ :		التوقيع :

Figure 3.3 *University of Yarmouk library, transaction slip*

more) for one week.[13] Although current periodicals do not circulate at the King Faisal University libraries,[14] back issues are lent for limited periods to the teaching staff. Also, at the University of Petroleum and Minerals library,[15] bound volumes may be borrowed for one week without further renewal. This university library is an exception, in that it issues, on a non-renewable weekly basis, microfiches, microfiche readers and video cassettes. Films are loaned to faculty members for one week for classroom use only.[16] In addition, it permits the borrowing of back numbers of newspapers for seven days.[17] In contrast, the vast majority of libraries in Arab Islamic countries have clearly specified that periodicals are not allowed outside the library

<table>
<tr><td colspan="2" align="center"><u>UPM LIBRARY</u></td><td colspan="2" align="center"><u>UPM LIBRARY</u></td></tr>
<tr><td colspan="2" align="center">Periodicals Charge-out Card</td><td colspan="2" align="center">Periodicals Charge-out Record</td></tr>
<tr><td colspan="2">Call No. ______________</td><td colspan="2">Borrower's
Name</td></tr>
<tr><td colspan="2">Title ______________</td><td colspan="2">Number</td></tr>
<tr><td colspan="2">Volume ______ Issue ______</td><td colspan="2">Tel. No.</td></tr>
<tr><td colspan="2">Date ______________</td><td colspan="2"></td></tr>
<tr><td colspan="2">Borrower's
Name ______________</td><td colspan="2">Title   :
Vol. No. :</td></tr>
<tr><td colspan="2">I.D. Number ______________</td><td colspan="2">Date   :</td></tr>
<tr><td colspan="2">Due Date:</td><td colspan="2">Date Due:</td></tr>
<tr><td colspan="2"></td><td colspan="2">Remarks</td></tr>
</table>

Figure 3.4 *University of Petroleum and Minerals library, transaction slip*

building. However, there are some university libraries which tend to be generous in lending back issues of periodicals to the teaching staff only, but certain conditions are attached to such transactions. One of the universities in Saudi Arabia allows faculty members to borrow old journals through their respective faculty libraries and not directly from the central library. This typical policy has been put into operation by an expatriate librarian for the convenience of teaching staff.

Several university libraries in Malaysia, Kuwait, Nigeria and Saudi Arabia have introduced a vacation loan system so that the student may borrow a limited number of books and retain them throughout the holidays. However, the retention of materials without proper renewal is not advocated. The materials may be renewed by telephone, as this method saves the precious time of the readers who may not have the means to come to the library personally, especially if it is situated at a reasonable distance from their faculty or residence. Books at the University of Petroleum and Minerals library can be renewed through a postal system which requires the use of a special form designed by the university library. One has to fill in the classification number, author/title, the borrower's name, ID number and full postal address. The circulation department, upon receipt of the form, renews the books mentioned on the form and returns it to the borrower after recording the new return date.

SEARCH RECORD

UPM LIBRARY

1st Search   Date : ————

Reserve Slip

Date:

Catalog   ——
Circulation file   ——
Stacks   ——
Reshelving   ——

Call Number :

Author :

2nd Search   Date : ————

Title   :

Catalog   ——
Circulation file   ——
Stacks   ——
Reshelving   ——

When this book is returned please inform:

3rd Search   Date : ————

Dr./Mr.

Catalog   ——
Circulation file   ——
Stacks   ——
Reshelving   ——

Telephone:

Address

If not found after 3 searches send slip to Head, Circulation.

Figure 3.5 *Search record, University of Petroleum and Minerals library, Saudi Arabia*

The staff of the circulation department usually searches the catalogues, circulation records and bookshelves to establish whether the library has purchased the item and, if it is not on the shelves, whether it has been issued to another user. Once the search is completed and it is discovered that the item is on loan to another borrower, a letter is normally sent to him, requesting him to return the item on or before the return date.[18] Once the book is retrieved, the prospective borrower is notified by means of a letter or postcard. He is supposed to contact the circulation department within three days or, in some universities, within a week; the date by which he ought to collect the reserved item is usually indicated

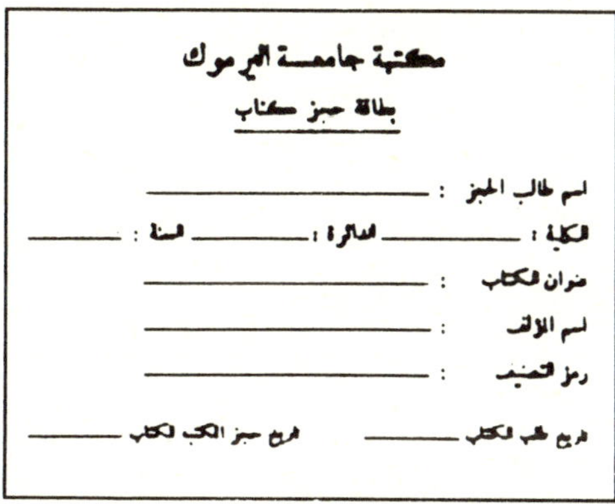

Figure 3.6 *Reservation slip, Yarmouk University library, Jordan*

Reserved for you

AUTHOR

TITLE

CALL NO. ___ DATE REQUESTED

This book is now in the library and will be reserved for you until

___ P.M. ___ 19 ___

Notice mailed ___ Telephone ___

MEDICAL LIBRARY
KING FAISAL UNIVERSITY
DAMMAM · SAUDI ARABIA   By ___

Figure 3.7 *Reservation slip, Medical Library, King Faisal University, Dammam, Saudi Arabia*

on the notification posted to him. If he fails to respond within the specified period the book is either reshelved or loaned to another reader.

The retrieval of books from students and staff is an arduous, painful, and time-consuming operation. Although the issuing of overdue reminders is not compulsory, university libraries do send one to three recall notices asking borrowers to return the materials without further delay. This is the most lenient policy, and is pursued by very few university libraries in Arab Islamic countries. The imposition of fines is a widespread practice which seems to act as a deterrent for most, if not all, the users. The University of

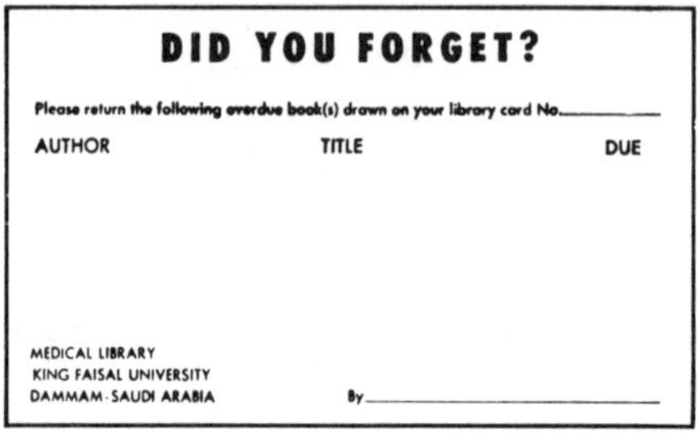

DID YOU FORGET?

Please return the following overdue book(s) drawn on your library card No.________

AUTHOR				TITLE				DUE

MEDICAL LIBRARY
KING FAISAL UNIVERSITY
DAMMAM-SAUDI ARABIA			By________________________

Figure 3.8 *Recall notice, Medical Library, King Faisal University, Dammam, Saudi Arabia*

Engineering and Technology Library in Lahore, Pakistan, has a borrowing procedure which underlines the fact that the retention of books by members beyond the prescribed time limit entails a fine of 25 paisa per volume per day. If the book is reported lost by the reader, he is required to pay the full price of the book. 'If one volume of a set is injured or lost, and it is not available separately, the whole set has to be replaced or paid for.'[19] Other penalties which the university library may impose upon the defaulters include (a) a fine of up to 50 rupees (£2.50) per book and (b) suspension from/cancellation of library membership.[20] There are other university libraries in Pakistan which charge a very nominal fine, such as the Bahauddin Zakariya University, or no fine at all, such as the Allama Iqbal Open University Library. In Saudi Arabia, the University of Petroleum and Minerals Library charges

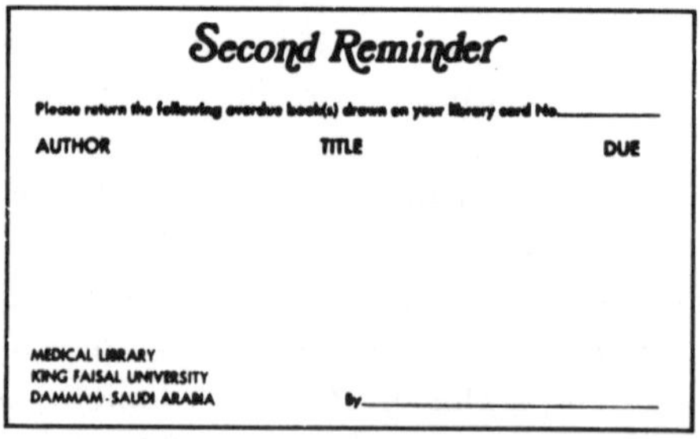

Second Reminder

Please return the following overdue book(s) drawn on your library card No.________

AUTHOR				TITLE				DUE

MEDICAL LIBRARY
KING FAISAL UNIVERSITY
DAMMAM-SAUDI ARABIA			By________________________

Figure 3.9 *Second recall notice, Medical Library, King Faisal University, Dammam, Saudi Arabia*

1 Saudi Riyal per day, up to a maximum of 20 Riyals (£3.35), or the replacement cost of the item, whichever is larger.[21] Those who damage books have to pay 15 per cent of the current price of the book. King Saud University library, Riyadh,[22] imposes a fine of a ½-Riyal per day for overdue books. In Nigeria, the university libraries do charge fines for overdue books which range from 5 Kobo, as at Ilorin,[23] to 10 Kobo, as at Jos.[24] At the University of Calabar library,[25] the fine for recalled books is 20 Kobo per day, with the same fee for periodicals.

Fines are not an effective option in most university libraries in Arab Islamic countries. According to Thompson,[26]

1 It is expensive, especially of staff time; it is, as the Americans say, spending dimes to collect nickels
2 If the fines mount up too quickly on a book, it is self-defeating, because the fact that there are such fines to pay becomes a further reason for not returning the book
3 Fines create an atmosphere of antagonism out of all proportion to their doubtful success in ensuring the prompt return of books; to uninformed minds the library begins to look like a money-grabbing organization
4 It should always be remembered that the readers who abuse their borrowing privileges are in the minority, and it is a bad policy to gear the whole system to accommodate them rather than to suit those who, by and large, conduct themselves responsibly
5 Since the library's users are not any way financially uniform, a fine system cannot work equitably.

Mutilation and losses

The imposition of fines is undesirable since it leads to theft and illegal borrowing. In poor Arab Islamic countries, students either cannot afford to purchase books which are very costly or the works are not easily available in the local bookshops. In Pakistan the librarian used to be held responsible for any book losses. Once it so happened that a librarian decided to take up senior position in another library, but was not released from his present position until he had paid off the total cost of missing or lost books.[27]

Regulations concerning mutilation and losses are fairly strict in the majority of university libraries. In Pakistan, the rules of the University of the Punjab specify that readers and members should not damage, mark or write upon any book. Those who violate this rule are required to pay the fine determined by the librarian.[28] Harvey and Lambert, during their visit to Pakistan libraries in 1968, observed that the penalty for lost items was not seriously imposed.[29] In fact, at some universities in Pakistan, the defaulters are required to replace the damaged material with a new copy or to pay double the prevailing market price.[30]

In Saudi Arabia, the penalty for damage or loss of materials at the University of Petroleum and Minerals library is 150 per cent of the list price of a particular book. In Nigeria, at the University of Ilorin, all cases of stealing, mutilation or defacement of library books are regarded as serious offences and dealt with severely. In other instances the student found guilty of cutting, seriously damaging or converting a library book to his personal property is punished very severely; this includes him being referred to the university executive body to be sent down from the university temporarily or permanently. Even in the United Kingdom, library thefts remind librarians of the vulnerability of the collections for which they are responsible. There is a movement towards more rigorous security measures.[31]

Thompson believes that fines are no solution to the problem and that it is better to 'rely on persuasion for the return of overdue books. Two or three reminders bring most books back.'[32] Experience suggests that book losses may be minimized if a number of courses of action are adopted.

1 The extension of lending facilities, i.e. the number of books each user can borrow should be increased and the loan period should be extended
2 All belongings, e.g. bags, cases, baskets, etc., must be deposited in the cloakroom and not allowed into the library
3 Heavily used works should be shelved behind the circulation desk
4 Shelves should be rearranged so as to permit more effective supervision
5 The installation of a Diver Detection Device or other anti-theft security system

6 The extension of opening hours
7 The regulations should specify that theft is not only a social, but a major crime in Islam
8 The provision of cheap photocopying services.

Opening hours

The deliberate removal of books from the library is certainly an offence, but the motives of these thefts must be considered. Appropriate steps must be taken to eradicate these causes and relieve the frustration that tempts readers to steal materials. As we notice from Table 3.2, opening hours in a vast number of

Table 3.2 *Library opening hours*

University library	*Opening hours per week*
University of Petroleum and Minerals, Saudi Arabia	96 (103, exam period)
Ahmadu Bello University, Nigeria	101
Technological University of Malaysia	94
University of Agriculture, Pakistan	93
National University of Malaysia	90¼
Universiti Sains, Malaysia	92½
University of Agriculture, Malaysia	91
University of Khartoum, Sudan	89
King Saud University, Saudi Arabia	87 (106½, exam period)
King Faisal University, Saudi Arabia	86
University of Benin, Nigeria	86
University of Calabar, Nigeria	79½
University of Engineering and Technology, Pakistan	78
University of Kuwait	76
Yarmouk University, Jordan	75
University of Qatar	72
NED University of Engineering and Technology, Pakistan	72
Islamic University, Pakistan	72
University of Al-Gezira, Sudan	65
Omdurman Islamic University, Sudan	57

university libraries in Arab Islamic countries are fairly long, compared with several Western university libraries. This obviously enables students to study in the library for long hours. In particular, the introduction of a semester system has resulted in the increased use of libraries. Most university libraries in Saudi Arabia, Malaysia and Nigeria are kept open for 80 to 106 hours per week. The longest opening hours are those of King Saud University library, Riyadh, Saudi Arabia, during the examination period.[33] In the beginning of each academic semester, the library remains open for 73 hours weekly, in the middle of the term, this is extended to 80 hours, and in the last part of each semester, the library is kept open for 106½ hours. Similarly, the University of Petroleum and Minerals library observes a 96-hour weekly schedule, which is extended to 103 hours during the examination period. In Nigeria, the longest opening hours are those of the Ahmadu Bello University library, but, unlike other university libraries in Islamic countries, it is open all day on Friday without being shut for the prayers. The University of Agriculture, Faisalabad, Pakistan, is open for 93 hours a week. However, several other universities, which include Bahauddin Zakariya, Allama Iqbal Open, Islamia and Quaid-e-Azam, have opening hours which range from 35 to 55 hours per week. Surprisingly, the University of the Punjab, Lahore, the oldest and biggest research library in the country, slashed its opening hours in 1980. The university authorities thought that it was kept open too long (70 hours per week) and curtailed its hours to 42 hours weekly.[34] In Malaysia, most of the university libraries are open for over 90 hours weekly. The National University of Malaysia[35] observes these opening hours:

Monday–Thursday	8.15 a.m. to 11.30 p.m.
Friday	8.15 a.m. to 12.15 p.m.
	2.45 p.m. to 11.30 p.m.
Saturday–Sunday	8.15 a.m. to 4.30 p.m.

In the United Kingdom, the University of Nottingham library[36] remains open for 73 hours a week and several other university libraries, which include the School of Oriental and African studies, University of London,[37] the University of Birmingham and the University of Sussex, remain open for less than 70 hours per week. Similarly, in Australia, most university libraries are open for 55 to

70 hours weekly. The Flinders University of South Australia library is kept open for 68 hours per week during term time and 40 hours a week during long vacations.[38]

In Arab Islamic countries, the extensive opening hours in many libraries present an excellent opportunity to the users to work on their assignments, pursue research projects or prepare for examinations on the library premises. However, all libraries must make provision for readers to pray according to the scheduled times during the day. Libraries should close at the time of *Adhan* and the readers and staff go to the mosque for the *Salaat*. Very large, or even medium-sized libraries, however, might have their own mosques inside the library, as is the case with King Abdulaziz University library, Saudi Arabia, and the National Library of Malaysia. It is not good enough for people to claim that reading is more important than praying or that the library staff should pray by themselves, postpone prayer, combine prayers or pray in shifts. It is clear from the Holy Qur'an and Sunnah that we all have to pray at the prescribed times, and, unless there is a very good reason to the contrary, that we should pray in *Jama'at*.

Reprographic services

The photocopying service is the most frequently requested element of user services in university libraries. Materials such as reference works, rare books, theses, periodicals or heavily used items which are not normally loaned may be photocopied, adhering strictly to copyright laws, and supplied to students. Ten years ago very few libraries in most Arab Islamic countries possessed photocopying machines. As Cosmas Enu described the Nigerian situation in 1972, 'a very few libraries have photocopying machines'.[39] Now the picture is relatively improved, since several universities in Nigeria, e.g. Ahmadu Bello, Ibadan, Jos, Calabar and Ilorin, have installed photocopiers and make copies of portions of books or periodical articles at subsidized rates, provided that copyright laws are not contravened. Some even permit the copying of personal documents or private notes. In addition, certain libraries are responsible for giving bindery services to the users, provided the bindery unit is not over-burdened with the library's official work.

In Pakistan, the University of Engineering and Technology library permits readers to photocopy all library materials at a nominal cost. It has three photocopiers – UBIX, Copystar and Nashua 1220-S. The next in importance is the copying service at the University of Agriculture, where students make extensive use of these machines. There are now over one hundred different models of copier which use the electrostatic principle available throughout the world. They range from large, high-volume machines, e.g. the UBIX 450, which can cope with all the photocopying requirements of university libraries, to small, table-top machines which can still turn out a dozen copies a minute. In the process of reprography, the electrostatic method is becoming increasingly popular, since its two branches, xerography and electrofax, are widely used in libraries.[40] The former is suitable for the production of book catalogues, library guides, and subject bibliographies, at a cost much lower than that of the prolonged procedure of printing, which is far more expensive if a limited number of copies are desired. In view of copyright restrictions, the libraries do not operate self-service, coin-operated machines. Also, the use of the machines by a special assistant helps to avoid wear and tear, and the machines are less likely to be damaged. Especially in Kuwait, Jordan and Saudi Arabia, hundreds of thousands of pages from documents are photocopied every day for the library-users. Almost all university libraries make a very nominal charge for each exposure and a free service is extended to those working on officially approved projects. The most sophisticated photocopiers have been installed at universities in Kuwait, Qatar and Saudi Arabia, at the King Saud, King Abdulaziz and Petroleum and Minerals universities. As early as 1973, the University of Kuwait library developed an excellent audio-visual and reprographic unit which contained four Apeco photocopying machines and a Xerox plate-maker. Now it has replaced these with some of the most advanced machines currently available on the world market.

Unlike many university libraries in Western countries, Arab university libraries have set up photographic, audio-visual or learning resources laboratories through which microfilming, slide production, transparencies, photo-images and other related services are provided free to the teaching staff and at a very low cost to the library members. In the United Kingdom, only very few university libraries, which include the Senate House, University of London, the University of Reading and the University of Southampton, provide a photographic service. Usually, it is the photographic department of the university, located on the library premises, which provides such a service. Thompson believes that there is no essential reason why such a service should be part of the library.[41]

Whatever photocopier or other audio-visual machines or equipment are acquired, it is pertinent to have facilities for support, maintenance and continuous operation. In some countries, adequate equipment supplies and repair services are non-existent for certain models; these must not be purchased and slightly more expensive ones, which carry guarantees and have established offices with technical staff, should be preferred.

Education in library use

Providing a user education service is undeniably an essential ingredient of readers' advisory work, particularly if it is organized on both a formal and an informal basis. In Arab Islamic countries, undergraduate students are not accustomed to exploring, discovering and retrieving information from library resources to complement their studies in the first year of university education. In these countries, the students are either completely unaware of the library services or else waste their time in fruitless searching: 'university libraries are static institutions, more concerned with storing books and other documents . . . . they passively await the approach of the potential user, instead of actively drumming up business.'[42] Obviously, many students waste their precious time wading through volumes of periodicals for articles they could reach in half a minute by using the index. The Nigerian, K. K. Oyeoku, rightly said that if we are to produce good research students we must produce graduates who can use libraries effectively. He proposed in 1966 that a fully-fledged course of at least six lectures, with sufficient practical work, should be established in all university libraries.

With regard to the survey of library use by Saudi Arabian students, Dr Saleh Ashoor reached the conclusion that either the students had never used any type of library prior to entering the university or that they simply studied their text books.[43] Dr

Abdulaziz Al-Nahari believes that 'university libraries are little used by students because of the general lack of student interest'.[44] It follows that to persuade students to use the libraries and to arouse interest in them demands a constructive 'user education programme'. In developing such a programme the Readers' Advisory Service Unit of the University of Sussex library stressed two major themes:[45]

1 That the modern library is not to be thought of merely as a collection of books, but rather as an active communications complex, demanding – but also rewarding – the expenditure of time and effort in mastering techniques of access
2 That as the human component in this system the librarian himself provides an indispensable access point.

It goes without saying that library orientation programmes contribute to the growth in library use. Just as the chemistry laboratory is designed for the exclusive use of chemistry students, the library is a laboratory developed and equipped for the benefit, utilization and experimentation of the entire university community. Readers should be introduced to the

(a) techniques of using catalogues
(b) characteristics of the literature of their disciplines
(c) methods of searching indexes and abstracts
(d) document-scanning skills
(e) shelf arrangement and book location
(f) use of bibliographical and reference works
(g) non-print media resources and use of hardware
(h) special collections, e.g. theses, manuscripts, report liera-
      ture, government publications, etc.
(i) photocopying, binding and other services available for
      students

User education programmes in various university libraries include some, if not all, of the points cited above. In Nigeria, for example at the Ahmadu Bello University library, in 1965, the students were offered a 'learn to learn' course.[46] There were eleven groups of twenty to thirty students and each group received five hours instruction in the course of eight days. The course consisted of how to use the catalogue and how classification works, and finally each student received a booklet entitled 'How to use the Library'. One of the successful aspects of the course was the demonstration of finding books through library card catalogues. Surprisingly, this course was organized and taught by the teaching staff of the English department.

The attitude of university teaching staff to library instruction varies from enthusiasm to mild antagonism. There are those who, having found out how to use libraries by using them themselves and by applying their own intelligence to the problem encountered, believe there is no need for such instruction. Others feel that if such instruction is given, it should be given by them, instead of by the library staff.[47] The teaching staff of the English department of Ahmadu Bello University expressed their views regarding library instruction over twelve years ago and claimed that they were capable of giving such instruction to students. In the Arab Islamic world, however, the librarian is considered responsible not only for preparing user education programmes, but also imparting instructions to students. Only in universities where a library school exists are a number of either optional or compulsory courses, such as research methods, taught by the library and information science teachers. Alternatively, library instructional courses are planned and designed by the staff of the Readers' Services Departments of university libraries. The University of Jos library aims to become a 'teaching library' and offers formal and informal courses in library use so that students may become 'better exploiters of the library resources'.[48] Informal guidance is mainly confined to postgraduate students.

In Saudi Arabia, 'four out of seven university libraries offer instructions in the use of the library'.[49] The duration of such instruction is one day. At the University of Petroleum and Minerals library, library instruction is an inter-departmental operation conducted by the reference librarians at two levels, the first for beginners and an advanced course for first-year students. Since the library has a very active reference department and staff are motivated to assist users in locating books or information on the shelves or through computer terminals, user education has become an ongoing activity. The Universities of Kuwait and Qatar have also organized short instructional courses for newcomers. The University of Jordan library, however, is more productive still, since its programme comprises a special slide show which is shown to students at the beginning of the academic year.

Almost all university libraries produce a wide variety of library publications which reinforce and supplement instructional programmes. Library guides, handbooks, literature search handouts, all such materials must be produced skilfully and the needs of the user community should not be overlooked. If library services are to be developed, far greater emphasis has to be placed on the exploitation of what might be termed the 'secondary strategies'[50] of library resources. The increased potential benefit of the library services thus created will, however, only be appreciated if both student and academic staff can be fully acquainted with the library's objectives in education, research and the pursuit of general interests.

Chapter 4

The selection and acquisition process

Choosing materials simply means selecting with the utmost care, insight and capability the material that would match the library's objectives, the student population's existing and anticipated needs and the curriculum.

'A well-selected collection may attract more students to the library, encourage reading beyond curricular requirements, and provide a helpful stimulus to those who want to improve their reading ability.'[1] In the selection process close cooperation between academic staff, library staff and administrative staff is vital. Lack of such cooperation results in a haphazard collection which quickly becomes out of date or fails to serve the long-term interests of the institution. Selection policies should be determined in conjunction with the educational aims and research activities of the university. The potential value of a library is reflected in its comprehensive collection, built over a period of time, to serve the actual and anticipated requirements of library users. In short the selection policy should be based on the following points:

1 it should be geared to meet the present and future needs of students and staff
2 students should be encouraged to recommend materials for the library
3 all the faculty members should be persuaded to choose materials in their areas of specialization
4 one-man selection in any particular subject field should be avoided
5 gaps in the selection process should be filled in by competent senior library staff

> 6 subject specialist librarians should be empowered to liaise
> with the faculty members in choosing books

Overall responsibility for the formulation and implementation of the selection policy must rest with the chief librarian. He should further delegate powers to the chief of technical services or acquisitions and encourage subject specialist librarians to share in the selection process. Those who may shoulder such responsibility must possess:

(a) an adequate knowledge of the subject
(b) sufficient knowledge of the curriculum
(c) a knowledge of the range and level of courses
(d) the capability to evaluate reading materials
(e) the capability to visualize readers' needs
(f) the sound judgment to select appropriate books
(g) a familiarity with the bibliographical tools
(h) an awareness of book-reviewing journals
(i) a familiarity with trade catalogues
(j) contacts with publishers and bookdealers

If the selection is carried out by the faculty members alone, there will be numerous problems in the development of a comprehensive collection for the benefit of all concerned. They may not have the time to select materials on a regular basis and may even lack knowledge of a wide variety of bibliographies and printed book catalogues. The chief librarian, however, should 'make available to the faculty the machinery for suggesting additions within his field'.[2] He should develop a mechanism whereby bibliographical information about published and unpublished material is brought to the notice of the faculty members. This requires the librarian to be completely familiar with the constant changes introduced in the syllabus and with the inception of new departments in the university.

Selection practices

Selection policies and practices vary considerably in different universities in different countries. In the United States, although official responsibility lies with library staff, teaching staff normally have overall control of material selection. Recently, the library staff's share in the selection procedure has been steadily increasing. In West Germany 'each university lecturer has books bought for his own use by the library'.[3] Also, separate funds are available in some universities for the purchase of research materials.

In the USSR, books are chosen in accordance with government directions; one basic objective is the right collection for the right people. A vast amount of literature in university libraries is predominantly political, propagating communism and Russian ideology. Normally, university libraries receive depository copies free of charge, but a selection is also made from publishers' catalogues. If a certain book is in great demand, multiple copies are acquired upon the recommendation of the faculty members. Non-Russian materials are chosen by the Department of Acquisitions of Foreign Literature, and are further scrutinized by the Council of Professors.

In Saudi Arabia, at the University of Petroleum and Minerals library, faculty members participate to the extent that one-quarter of the recommendations are advanced by them. 'These items usually express a specific need for a title. This makes it the most reliable procedure and explains why library policy is designed to increase cooperation on the part of the UPM community.'[4] The remainder of the selection is conducted by the chief librarian and senior library staff. Non-teaching staff and students do not have a noticeable share in the process. At the King Saud University, Riyadh, not only faculty members and library staff may recommend additions to stock, but non-teaching staff and students are also encouraged to participate. At the King Faisal University, Dammam, faculty members select most of the materials except reference and general works, which may be chosen by the chief librarian or the faculty librarians.

All the aforesaid university libraries have a written selection policy. At other universities in Saudi Arabia, including Ummal-Qura University, Makkah, and King Abdulaziz University, Jeddah, it is mainly the faculty members who have the major responsibility for choosing materials and forwarding their suggestions to the central university libraries.[5] However, the chief librarian and the deans of library affairs are empowered to decide whether the materials should be purchased. Observations suggest that the library staff of both these university libraries have taken a great deal of trouble in choosing and building up excellent collections of indexes, abstracts, bibliographies and general reference works. Most of the faculty libraries in the King Abdulaziz University make decisions with regard to the materials recommended by the faculty members through the Selection Committee. This is composed of heads of department or senior professors from each department.[6] In some faculties the librarian complains that the teaching staff do not take an adequate interest in selection of materials, in spite of repeated requests.

The process of choosing books at the University of Jordan is carried out with the help of faculty members, each in his respective subject or area of specialization.[7] Likewise, at the University of Yarmouk, a major proportion of additions are based on the selection made by the teaching staff.[8]

The situation is somewhat different in Nigeria, where, at the University of Ibadan, 'all academic staff and students are free to recommend books and journals for purchase'.[9] But student recommendations are expected to be channelled through the heads of department to ensure that relevant items are sent in. The selection policy of the University of Ilorin is that

> suggestions of books and periodicals for addition to the library
> are welcome. These should be made on recommendation slips
> available from the loans desk. Readers should make sure that
> the book is not already in the library before making a
> recommendation.[10]

At the University of Lagos library, a selection panel is responsible for interpreting the policies laid down by the Book Selection Committee.[11] The Committee is responsible for:

(a) determining interests and mapping out related subject
    areas of importance
(b) establishing the depth of coverage, bias, variety of the
    collection and extent of duplication of items
(c) editing the stock
(d) establishing priority in subject coverage
(e) allocation of book funds by subject priority.

No university library in Pakistan can claim that it has a balanced stock or a satisfactory, up-to-date and exhaustive specialized collection. Haider once remarked that 'in recent years the university libraries have come to feel the inadequacy of their resources to meet the needs of the growing instructional and research programmes of the universities'.[12]

To select materials for a university library, the librarian must be familiar with the course syllabus, the users, the techniques of selection and the strengths and weaknesses of the existing book stock. The practice of choosing materials varies greatly from university to university in Pakistan. At the University of the Punjab, the library staff select books from publishers' booklists, and their choice is submitted to the chairmen of the teaching departments for final approval. The librarian of the university has the power to select reference and general books. For the selection of books on a particular subject it is necessary to seek the approval of the departmental heads concerned. This is mainly done to avoid unnecessary duplication of materials. Although the chairmen rarely disapprove, they do not normally recommend books in addition to those selected by the senior library staff. Theoretically, the materials are selected by the library with the aid and advice of the academic staff. In practice, the academic staff take little interest in advancing their suggestions for additions to the stock. At the University of Engineering and Technology, Lahore, the chairmen of departments assume sole responsibility for choosing books from the publishers' catalogues. The marked lists are sent to the library for placing orders.[13] If the university librarian selects certain books, he has to have them approved by the chairmen of the respective department before they can be ordered. In this case, the selection is mostly in the hands of the teaching staff. The Islamia University library, Bahawalpur, has a more user-oriented selection policy, in that the teaching staff select most of the books in cooperation with the librarian, and students also recommend books quite frequently. The same practice is followed by the Quaid-e-Azam University, Islamabad, where student recommendations are given serious consideration. The University of Agriculture, Faisalabad, is one of the few universities in Pakistan to have appointed a number of librarians who fully participate in selecting materials. Book selection is, therefore, carried out jointly by the academic staff, the university librarian and the senior members of the library staff. Unlike their opposite numbers at Islamia University, Bahawalpur, the students of the University of Agriculture rarely suggest books for the library, and neither do the students of the University of Engineering and

Technology. Book selection at the Bahauddin Zakariya University, Multan, is made exclusively by the teaching staff, though the librarian and library staff offer assistance in the selection process. A survey of the departmental libraries of the University of the Punjab shows that, in twenty-one libraries, selection is made exclusively by the heads of department or directors of the institutes. Only in nine departmental libraries are the librarians also involved in the selection process. Similarly, at the University of Engineering and Technology, Lahore, and at Quaid-e-Azam University, Islamabad, selection is carried out by the chairmen of the departments or the senior faculty members who send their recommendations to the librarians.

Over fifty years ago, F. Drury, a distinguished librarian, put on record the following guidelines with respect to the selection of books:[14]

1 so apportion the library funds as to obtain books of higher quality for the greatest number of people
2 secure any book which the library can use with advantage
3 fix upon a policy of selection and stick to it until it has been proved wrong
4 select books that represent any endeavour aiming at human development – material, mental or moral

Many university libraries in developing countries may have formulated selection policies, taking into consideration Drury's stated guidelines. The question arises as to how far such policies are implemented in practical terms. In Nigeria, for example, it is the policy of the library of the University of Ibadan 'to acquire all printed materials required by students, at all levels, to pursue their courses, to provide adequate materials to enable research students and faculty members to carry out their research projects successfully'.[15] The significant aspect of the selection policy of King Faisal University, Dammam, is that the library should strive to acquire all the relevant materials required to accomplish the university's stated goals. The selection procedure is designed to build a strong and well-balanced collection geared to the service objectives of the library. The objectives of the King Abdulaziz University library, Jeddah, reflect the acquisition policy.[16] Hassan Hashim Hetimish, in his unpublished report, 'The policy of acquisitions in the central library', (Jeddah, King Abdulaziz

University, 1983), states that:

1 the library should own and make available all materials related to the Middle East and Palestine questions
2 the library should own and make available all materials related to Islam, Islamic history and the Islamic world
3 the library should own and make available all materials related to the Kingdom of Saudi Arabia
4 the library should own and make available valuable manuscripts in Arabic and other Islamic languages in order to preserve the Arab and Islamic heritage

As university libraries grow larger, book selection becomes increasingly complex. Where academic staff members feel that they alone are competent to choose books in their subject field and are reluctant to relinquish this responsibility to librarians, they may select books which are helpful in the pursuance of their research or teaching in the classroom, but fail to relate their selection to the needs of the university as a whole, within the framework of budgetary limitations. There is an obvious danger that a faculty member might unwittingly select books inappropriately. His enthusiasm and interest in his subject might induce him to expect that the library will purchase all the required books for him. One faculty member may well recommend a large number of books in a relatively small sub-division of his subject. This would certainly result in an unbalanced development of the library collection. As selection is the most important and highest professional task of the librarian, it must be recorded that librarians, particularly those who are subject specialists with a knowledge of bibliographic tools and modern selection aids, can help to ensure a judicious and valuable selection. Apart from the Western-qualified university teachers, faculty members are not interested in reading book reviews and publishers' catalogues; neither are they well-trained bibliographically. They are not in constant and inevitable contact with bibliographical tools, announcements of publications and other book selection aids to inform them of every important new publication.[17] Danton, on the other hand, suggests that

Faculty participation in book selection is the major asset of current American policy and practice, and it should be greatly strengthened and increased rather than otherwise. Members of the faculty will read different books and journals, visit and work in different libraries, go to different meetings, serve in visiting capacities at various other institutions, and talk to different colleagues, than will any group of librarians. From these numerous contacts, the interested, persuadable Professor who is assured that his ideas will be welcomed, will inevitably bring valuable suggestions for augmenting the library's holdings.[18]

In many developing countries, the majority of faculty members are not anxious to take the trouble to make useful suggestions for additions to stock. They are also not capable of determining which bibliographies would be suitable for developing the collection. A renowned Pakistani librarian, Fazal Elahi, remarked: 'I know of teachers coming to my room and drawing up lists of books to be purchased for their departments in less than one hour, by marking hurriedly items from publishers' announcements'.[19]

This is not untypical, even today, and the faculty members either recommend too many books or they take little interest in the selection procedure and recommend to students only those books which are already available in the library.

Choosing non-print materials

There are several reasons for procuring non-print materials in university libraries. Such materials are acquired to support teaching and research and to supplement the traditional printed material. These non-print materials are sometimes termed 'learning resources'. These materials should be closely connected to the curriculum.

In the selection of non-print materials, the major responsibility rests upon the chief librarian or the audio-visual librarian who should know the audience and the non-print media very well. He should know the distributors and producers who can be trusted. A picture is worth a thousand words, and the librarian may hire or buy the media that have a subject interest for the audience served. The librarian should decide, for example, whether to purchase a film on the history of Jeddah or buy ten books about the history of Jeddah. One may think that ten books offer more information than just one film. However, there is a possibility that the books contain repetitive information on the subject, in which case, the film would be ideal for the audience.

In Saudi Arabia, almost every university has a modern educational technology centre and an audio-visual unit, either as part of the university library or operating independently and extending its services to all the faculties of the university. At the University of Petroleum and Minerals, audio-visual materials and services are provided through the media centre.[20] At the King Abdulaziz University, there is a well-organized Centre for Educational Technology, equipped with sophisticated hardware and manned by qualified staff. They provide an excellent service to faculty members in the production of a wide range of audio-visual materials to aid teaching programmes in the university.

In Jordan, both the University of Jordan and Yarmouk University libraries have established audio-visual departments and adequately cater for the needs of readers.[21] In Sudan and Pakistan, university libraries provide minimal audio-visual services and, due to lack of finances in some universities, audio-visual units do not exist. In contrast, in Nigeria and Malaysia, at universities such as the National University of Malaysia, the audio-visual division occupies an entire floor—with small viewing theatres and a microfilm laboratory.[22]

The evaluation of materials

It is logical to periodically review the existing stock and the deficiencies of collections should be regularly recorded. It is not possible to build up a comprehensive collection without proper evaluation of library resources. A number of points ought to be scrutinized for the effective implementation of a carefully conceived selection policy. Dr Wellard has mentioned seven processes from the public library angle, but four of these are equally applicable to an academic library.

1 what subjects are most read?
2 what subjects are readers most interested in?
3 what groups and individuals read what books?
4 what titles are read and by whom?

In fact, an analysis of the available collections would assist the librarian in devising an appropriate acquisition policy. 'A library's acquisition policy may represent anything therefore from the purely fortuitous to the most rigorous selection, but these practices themselves constitute a policy of sorts.'[23] It would be useful to consult two very important works in the preparation of policy statements. The work of Elizabeth Futas provides a selection of a number of policy statements from university and other libraries.[24] The second is 'Guidelines', produced by the American Library Association.[25]

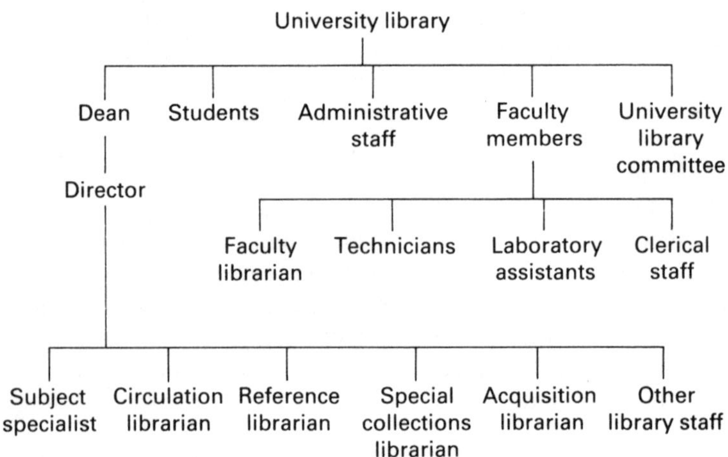

Figure 4.1 *Participants in the selection process*

To sum up, collections should be developed in relation to the university curriculum, teaching methods, and the composition of the reader population to be served. A rich and up-to-date collection of books, periodicals, and other reading and non-print materials is the first requirement for a good library. Second is a high calibre of staff. The most effective technique for bridging the gap between library and classroom is to develop a comprehensive collections that will adequately meet the research, educational, informational and recreational needs of students and academic staff. A useful collection is best built if the faculty members and librarian work together in the early stages of syllabus development so that the courses of study can be safely integrated with the provision of books and other learning resources.

Collection development tools

In some developing countries, such as Nigeria, 'inadequate bibliographical tools often prevent libraries from learning of the existence of many new publications'.[26] In the application of a selection policy, the libraries require a comprehensive and up-to-date collection of four types of selection tools:

(a) for choosing reference materials
(b) for choosing books
(c) for choosing periodicals and continuations
(d) for choosing non-print materials

The library's inability to obtain newly published selection aids hinders the selection process.[27] In the (a) category, Walford and Winchell provide splendid guides to standard reference tools with a brief description of their contents.[28, 29] Another very useful work is Eugene P. Sheehy's *Guide to Reference Books* (9th edn, Chicago, American Library Association, 1976). In category (b), the selection of books, are both current and retrospective bibliographies including *Books in Print* (USA), *British Books in Print*; *Subject Guide to Books in Print* (New York) and *Cumulative Book List* (London). National bibliographies include *British National Bibliography* (London); *Bibliographie de la France* (Paris); *Deutsche Bibliographie* and *Deutsche Nationale Bibliographie*.

In a retrospective selection of books in the fields of sociology, politics, chemistry, zoology, medicine and English literature, the following works would be of utmost importance:

1 *International Bibliography of Sociology*, 5 volumes, 1954–61, Paris, Unesco
2 *International Bibliography of Political Science*, 8 volumes, 1954–61, Paris, Unesco
3 H. C. Bolton, *Select Bibliography of Chemistry*, 1492–1902, Washington, Smithsonion
4 B. Dean, *Bibliography of Fishes*, 3 volumes, 1916–23, New York, American Museum of Natural History
5 *Catalogue of the Library of the Surgeon General's Office*, 62 volumes, 1880–1961, Washington, US National Library of Medicine

6 F. W. Bateson (ed.), *Cambridge Bibliography of English Literature*, 600–1900, 5 volumes, Cambridge, Cambridge University Press

This is merely a selection and not an exhaustive list of bibliographical tools.

Reviewing periodicals and newspapers

Reviews of books appear in literary periodicals, commercial journals and newspapers.[30] There are reviews which come to our notice through a number of journals. Some of the periodicals, e.g. *Kirkus*, include reviews six weeks in advance of publication. *Kirkus* started publication in 1933 and is issued twice a month in the USA by Virginia Kirkus Service Inc. Both *Books to Come* and *Forthcoming Books* are published by Bowker. The former is issued six times a year and the latter is bi-monthly. They give reviews of books in advance of publication. The following periodicals review books after publication:

> *Sunday Times*, London (weekly), contains detailed and comprehensive reviews of newly published books;
>
> *Sunday Telegraph*, London (weekly), comprises analytical reviews of currently published works. The reviews are written by experts in the subject fields;
>
> *Times Literary Supplement*, London (weekly), is a very widely-known reviewing magazine which carries reviews of literary and other academic publications;
>
> *Book Review Digest*, New York (monthly) is an index of reviews appearing in non-technical periodicals. Over one hundred reviewing periodicals are indexed;
>
> *Book Publishing Record*, New York (monthly), commenced publication in 1960 and includes entries similar to the American Library of Congress catalogue cards. It is arranged by subject, according to Dewey, and gives author as well as title indexes;
>
> *British Book News*, London (monthly), started in 1940 and gives reviews of the most useful books on a variety of subjects;
>
> *ASLIB Book list*, a monthly issued from London by Aslib, contains recommendations of currently published books on science and technology;
>
> *Bookseller*, London, is particularly recognized as an informa-

tive weekly which carries evaluative reviews. Its Spring and Autumn issues are specifically produced for export markets.

In addition to these reviewing sources which every university library must subscribe to, there are specialized periodicals in various subject fields. For instance, in the field of sociology, there is the *British Journal of Sociology*, a quarterly published in London by Routledge & Kegan Paul. In the area of geography, some of the notable reviewing journals are: *Geography*, London (quarterly), George Philip & Son; *Geographical Review*, New York (quarterly), American Geographical Society; *Geographical Magazine*, London (monthly), IPC Magazines; *Geographical Journal*, London (monthly), Royal Geographical Society.

So far discussion has been directed towards reviewing journals mostly containing reviews of English books. It would not be inapposite here to describe some of the Arabic journals which provide reviews of Arabic books published in different countries. Table 4.1 gives a selected rather than an exhaustive list of Arabic journals which regularly include appraisals and critical reviews written by Arab scholars. Every university library in Arab Islamic countries anxious to build up a collection of Arabic works should consider subscribing to these journals.

Some Arab daily newspapers which periodically publish reviews of books are *Al-Nadwa*, *Al-Ayam* and *Al-Sahafa*, Sudan; *Okaz*, *Al-Madina* and *Al-Riyadh* from Saudi Arabia; *Pakistan Times* and *Dawn* from Pakistan.

Non-print media tools

In Western countries, librarians acquire media for examination prior to purchase. Unlike books, non-print materials are very expensive and in many instances are not adequately reviewed. Extra care is needed in choosing such media, since these have to be geared to the existing and forthcoming needs of a large audience. Also, a fair proportion of non-print media is not reviewed at all. Reviews of these items rarely mention the availability of similar materials in the same field. Cassettes, for example, may contain useful material, but the quality of recording might be poor. A number of widely-known and reputable journals present reviews, and include the following: *Media and Methods*, published monthly by North American Publishing Co., Philadel-

Table 4.1 *Reviewing journals*

Journal	Publisher	Place of publication	Frequency
Al-Adeeb	Adib Library	Beirut	Monthly
Joharat Al-Islam	M. Salahuddin Al-Mustavi	Tunis	Monthly
Al-Abhas	Centre for Arabic and Middle Eastern Studies	Beirut	Quarterly
Al-Arab	Darul-Yamama	Riyadh	Monthly
Risalat Al-Ilm	Ministry of Educatrion	Amman	Bi-monthly
Mujalat Al-Arabi	Ministry of Information	Kuwait	Monthly
Mujalat Al-Faisal	Darul-Faisal	Riyadh	Monthly
Al-Ta awan al-Sanai	Gulf Industrial Consultancy Organization	Qatar	Quarterly
Al-Maktaba	Qasam Muhamad Rajab	Baghdad	Monthly
Mujalat-al-Aloum al-Idariyah	International Institute of Administrative Science	Cairo	Twice-yearly
Risalat al-Makataba	Jordan Library Association	Amman	Quarterly
Al-Aklam	Ministry of Culture and Information	Baghdad	Monthly
Al-Aloom al-Qanooniyat wal-Siyasiat	Faculty of Law and Policies	Baghdad	Monthly
Al-Mujalat al-Arabia al-Idariyah	Arab Organization of Administrative Science	Amman	Quarterly

phia, which contains articles and reviews of educational films, filmstrips and recordings; and *Media Review Digest*, a quarterly published by Pierian Press, Ann Arbor, Michigan, which includes over 50,000 reviews of various media. The reviews are indexed yearly, covering what appears in more than 200 periodicals.

Examples of non-print media are cassettes and videotapes. Cassettes have built-in reel-to-reel audio-tapes that the reader can place in a tape recorder. They are available from 30 to 120 minutes in length and are blank or pre-recorded. Videotapes are intensively used in university teaching in many developing countries. They come in two main sizes, 16 mm and 8 mm. Videotapes are easier to check and have longer life than films. Pre-recorded videotapes are less expensive than 16 mm films; some are even 50–70 per cent cheaper than films. Also, video equipment is more flexible and easy to operate. It is very convenient for duplicating tapes or transferring films onto tapes. On the other hand, video equipment is relatively more expensive than the average film projector. A very notable selection source is *Video and Cable Guidelines for Librarians*, produced by the American Library Association.[31]

Periodicals and continuations

Unlike books, no critical evaluation of periodicals is published. One of the possible methods of evaluation is to obtain a specimen copy of a periodical and compare it with other available journals in the same field. Also, one may seek the advice of subject specialists, prior to placing subscription orders for a particular title. Extra care is needed, since the subscription has to be paid in advance for one year or an even longer period. To discover the source of periodical publications, the date of inception and the number of periodicals in each subject, it is vital for every university library to have *Ulrich's International Periodicals Directory* (17th edn, New York, R. R. Bowker, 1977). The periodicals are listed under broad subject headings and a name and subject index is included. In addition, there is *Ulrich's Irregular Serials and Annuals* (New York, R. R. Bowker, 1976). It comprises well over 30,000 periodical titles, and updated issues are published at irregular intervals. Another source is *Magazines for Libraries* (3rd edn, New York, R. R. Bowker, 1978), listing around 6,000 periodicals according to subject, with annotations under each title. Other sources for obtaining detailed information concerning periodical titles, publishers' addresses, etc. may be obtained through *Bowker's Serial Bibliography*, the *British Union Catalogue of Periodicals*, *Faxon's Librarians' Guide to Serials* and the *World List of Scientific Periodicals*.

Some publishers send leaflets announcing new serials. Foreign suppliers which specialize in supplying back runs of periodicals include: Dekker Nordemann (Ireland) Ltd, An Elsevier Company, Shannon Industrial Estate, Co. Clare, Ireland and Routledge & Kegan Paul, 14 Leicester Square, London WC2H 7PH (journals published by RKP only).

A guide to periodicals in various subject fields can be found in Sheehey's *Guide to Reference Books*, published by the American Library Association in 1976. Also useful are the *Reader's Guide to Periodical Literature*, the *British Humanities Index*, the *Current Technology Index* and several other indexes and abstracts in a wide variety of disciplines. For Islamic countries, Professor Pearson's *Index Islamicus* is invaluable. An alternative method is to acquire union lists of periodicals produced by universities, institutes of technology or other professional bodies in Arab, African and Asian countries.

Publishers' and bookdealers' announcements

Although reviews are the best sources of selection aids, publishers' announcements are an essential and simple way for librarians to keep informed of available and forthcoming works. 'It must be stressed that catalogues are used for publishing information only. Any critical claims in the catalogues are treated as sales promotion, not as evaluative opinion.'[32] It is beyond doubt that trade catalogues and publishers advertisements are 'our first glimpse at books to come. Later a variety of reviews from a number of sources either confirm our feelings or prompt us to reevaluate them'.[33]

There are a number of announcement services provided free of charge by Western suppliers. For instance, Bumpus, Haldane & Maxwell Ltd, in England, regularly send, to libraries on their mailing list, advance announcement cards giving complete bibliographical details about each item along with an indication of readership level, e.g. for undergraduates, research and reference, vocational and general. Also included are annotations and a classification number. A similar service, in an improved format, is extended by Blackwell, Oxford, and Blackwell, North America, who send six copies of each item, and give the readership level, but no annotations. Such services eliminate much of the time and effort which the librarian must devote to the preparation of book orders. The Library of Congress card service is another tool for selecting materials. Publishers' catalogues are continuously updated; some comprise a simple list of newly published items, whereas others give short notes on each title. Another increasingly popular service is the issuing of leaflets, each consisting of detailed information about the authors' credentials, the work's market or readership, brief description, contents, format, price and publication date.

For the selection of rare works, there is the British *Annual Directory of Booksellers Specialising in Antiquarian and Out of print Books*. Another useful volume, published in the United States, is *The Antiquarian Booktrade, an international directory of subject specialists*.[34] In addition to *Clique* and *AB Bookman's Weekly*, journals containing information relating to rare, out-of-print and second-hand works, the *British Museum Catalogue of Fifteenth-Century Books* can help in identifying rare materials. However, the works listed in the *British Museum Catalogue* are not for sale.

Other selection aids

Experience suggests that a number of potentially significant selection aids come from a variety of sources:

1 the catalogues compiled by professional bodies solely for their members, e.g. the Library Association, London, and the British Institute of Management
2 most faculty members in both the developed and developing countries prepare course outlines and append a reading list for students
3 faculty members sometimes produce a list of useful and required works and send it to the library for purchase
4 subject bibliographies compiled by specialists in the field or subject specialist librarians
5 printed catalogues of different university libraries

6 announcements on radio and interviews with authors of currently published works
7 visits to local bookshops and established publishers, as well as national bookdealers
8 attending book exhibitions held locally, nationally and internationally
9 examining exchange lists received from other libraries on a reciprocal basis
10 bibliographical records of unanswered reference enquiries prepared by the reference librarian
11 lists of unfulfilled lending requests due to non-availability of works in stock
12 a record of orders unfulfilled because they were out of print, out of stock, not yet published and similar reasons

Regarding book exhibitions, one of the most notable is held annually at Frankfurt. The Frankfurt Book Fair has been organized every year since 1948–9. The biggest exhibitors are from West Germany, the United Kingdom, the United States, France, the Netherlands, Italy and Switzerland.[35] Other notable fairs are the London Book Fair and the Riyadh Book Fair. There are fairs organized by university libraries, such as the University of Qatar library which has been arranging and inviting publishers from Arab states since 1972.[36]

Ordering procedures

Once it has been established that the selection of materials with the aid of selection tools is a responsibility shared by the library staff and the library users, the next step is the preparation of orders. The acquisition department receives requests for items to be obtained in a variety of forms and from a variety of sources. Figure 4.2 illustrates the selection and ordering procedure in a university library; Figure 4.3 shows classification and cataloguing procedure. A survey carried out concerning the ordering methods in university libraries in various developing countries indicates slight variations. For instance, the University of Khartoum in Sudan uses an order form containing columns, such as names of the supplier, order number, date, number of copies, author, title, place and date of publication, publisher, price, reader, department and remarks. There are notes on the verso of the order form for the bookseller.

1 Please address parcels, invoices and correspondence to the librarian, University of Khartoum, Sudan.
2 Please quote the order number overleaf in all correspondence and on the invoice. Do not refer to the name of the reader and department, as these particulars are for use in the library.
3 Please send two copies of the invoice. If the consignment is large please send one copy by printed post and include the other in the parcel.
4 Please enclose the duplicate of this order with the work (if it is immediately available) or with the invoice. If the work is at present unobtainable please return the duplicate after placing a cross against the cause of non-delivery. A work on order from abroad should not be reported as such, but only if it proves to be unobtainable.
5 A work that is at present unobtainable will remain on order unless you report 'out of print – order cancelled'; you report 'not traced, further particulars required' (We shall re-order it if we find additional particulars.); it has been ordered from a secondhand catalogue, and you report 'already sold'.

King Faisal University libraries, Dammam, have designed multiple order slips both for Arab and English materials. Likewise, King Abdulaziz University libraries have also prepared order forms to facilitate the ordering procedure. Also, Yarmouk University library, Jordan, has produced six varying colours of self-carboned order slips.[37] Since the establishment of Yarmouk University Bookshop, all orders are placed with the bookshop; this minimizes correspondence with national or international bookdealers. Some libraries maintain 'direct contact with book-sellers in the United Kingdom, Europe, USA, Asia, the Middle East'.[38] In the University of Petroleum and Minerals library, Dhahran, the 'majority of new books are purchased through wholesalers',[39] who match their subscription profile with a large number of materials they acquire from 3,000 publishers. An alternative method is to place a standing order, particularly for serials, continuations and other publications issued at certain intervals. These 'are received automatically'.[40]

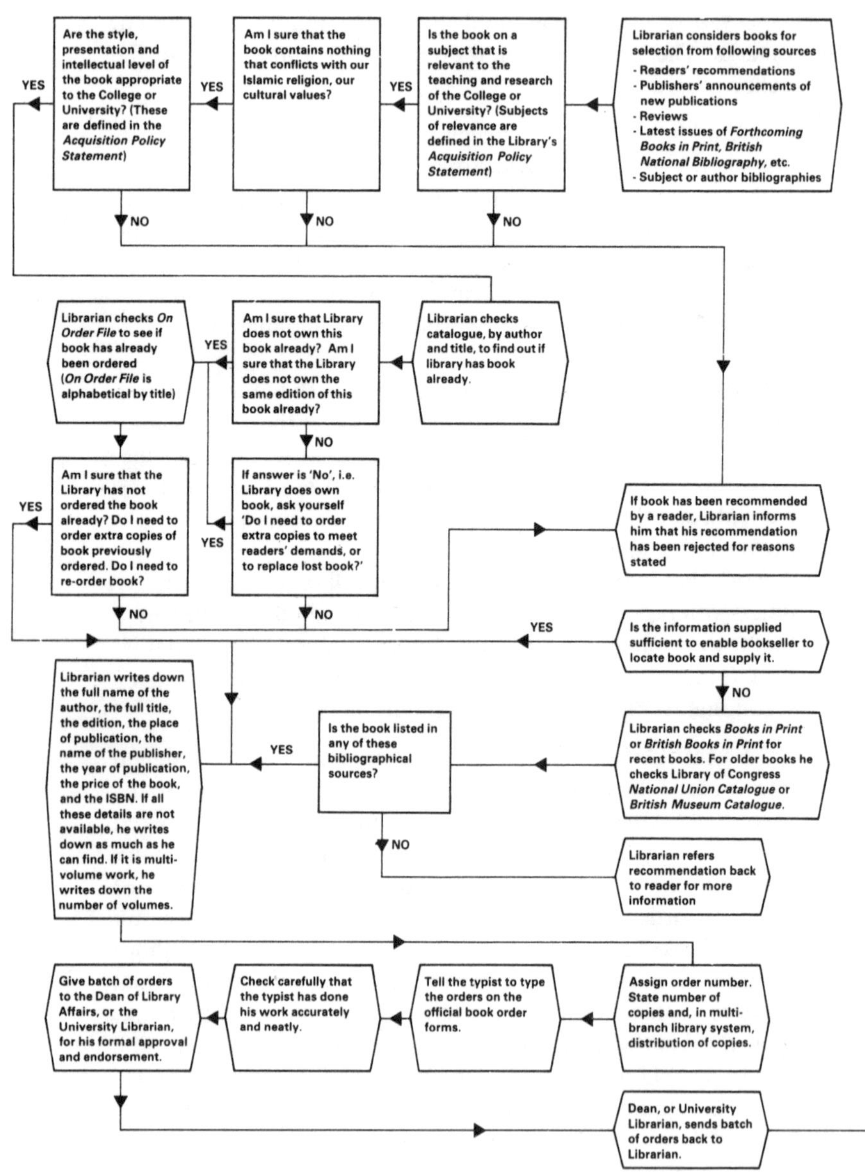

Figure 4.2 *Book selection and ordering procedure*

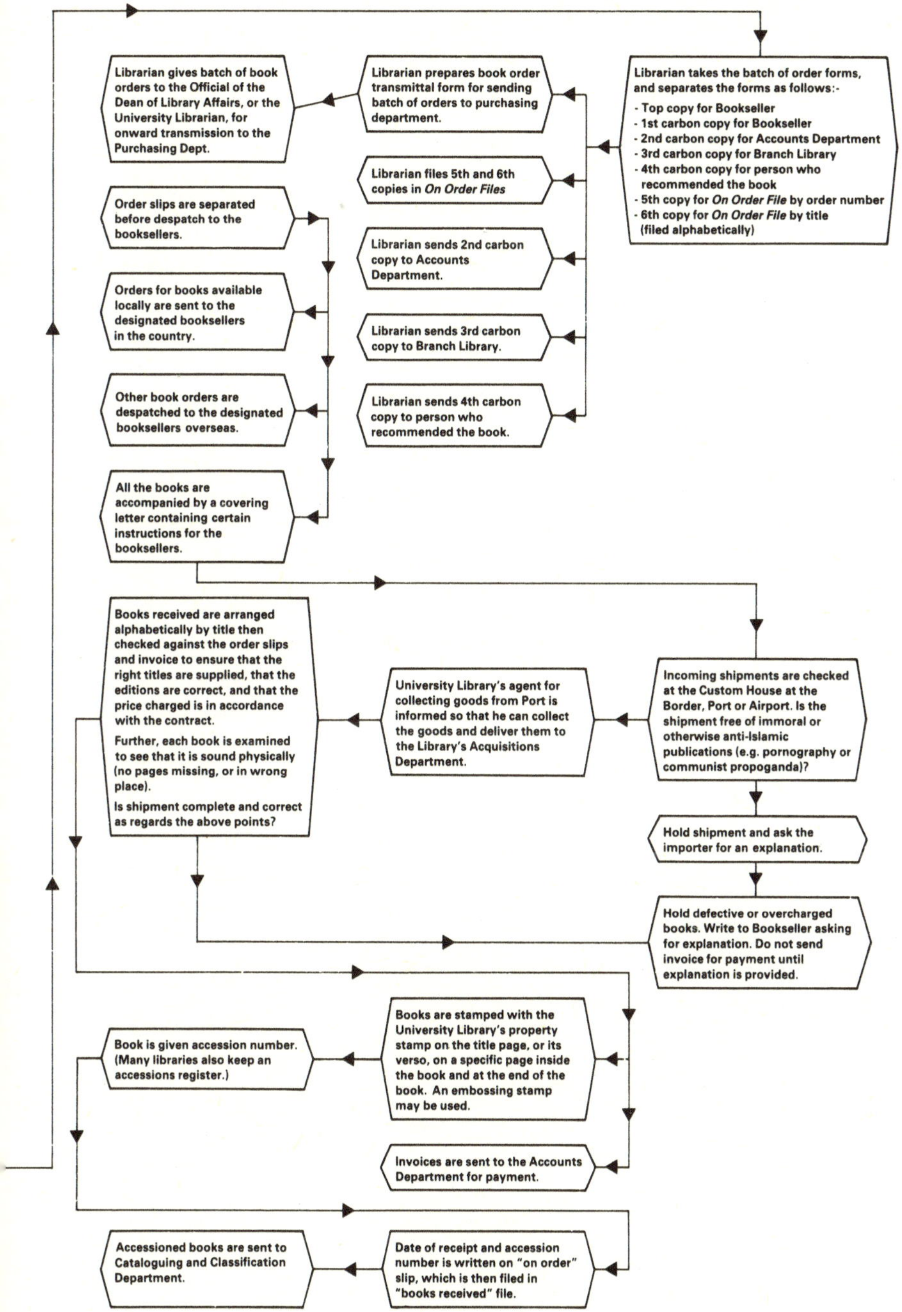

Librarian gives batch of book orders to the Official of the Dean of Library Affairs, or the University Librarian, for onward transmission to the Purchasing Dept.

Librarian prepares book order transmittal form for sending batch of orders to purchasing department.

Librarian takes the batch of order forms, and separates the forms as follows:-
- Top copy for Bookseller
- 1st carbon copy for Bookseller
- 2nd carbon copy for Accounts Department
- 3rd carbon copy for Branch Library
- 4th carbon copy for person who recommended the book
- 5th copy for *On Order File* by order number
- 6th copy for *On Order File* by title (filed alphabetically)

Librarian files 5th and 6th copies in *On Order Files*

Order slips are separated before despatch to the booksellers.

Librarian sends 2nd carbon copy to Accounts Department.

Orders for books available locally are sent to the designated booksellers in the country.

Librarian sends 3rd carbon copy to Branch Library.

Other book orders are despatched to the designated booksellers overseas.

Librarian sends 4th carbon copy to person who recommended the book.

All the books are accompanied by a covering letter containing certain instructions for the booksellers.

Books received are arranged alphabetically by title then checked against the order slips and invoice to ensure that the right titles are supplied, that the editions are correct, and that the price charged is in accordance with the contract.

Further, each book is examined to see that it is sound physically (no pages missing, or in wrong place).

Is shipment complete and correct as regards the above points?

University Library's agent for collecting goods from Port is informed so that he can collect the goods and deliver them to the Library's Acquisitions Department.

Incoming shipments are checked at the Custom House at the Border, Port or Airport. Is the shipment free of immoral or otherwise anti-Islamic publications (e.g. pornography or communist propoganda)?

Hold shipment and ask the importer for an explanation.

Hold defective or overcharged books. Write to Bookseller asking for explanation. Do not send invoice for payment until explanation is provided.

Book is given accession number. (Many libraries also keep an accessions register.)

Books are stamped with the University Library's property stamp on the title page, or its verso, on a specific page inside the book and at the end of the book. An embossing stamp may be used.

Invoices are sent to the Accounts Department for payment.

Accessioned books are sent to Cataloguing and Classification Department.

Date of receipt and accession number is written on "on order" slip, which is then filed in "books received" file.

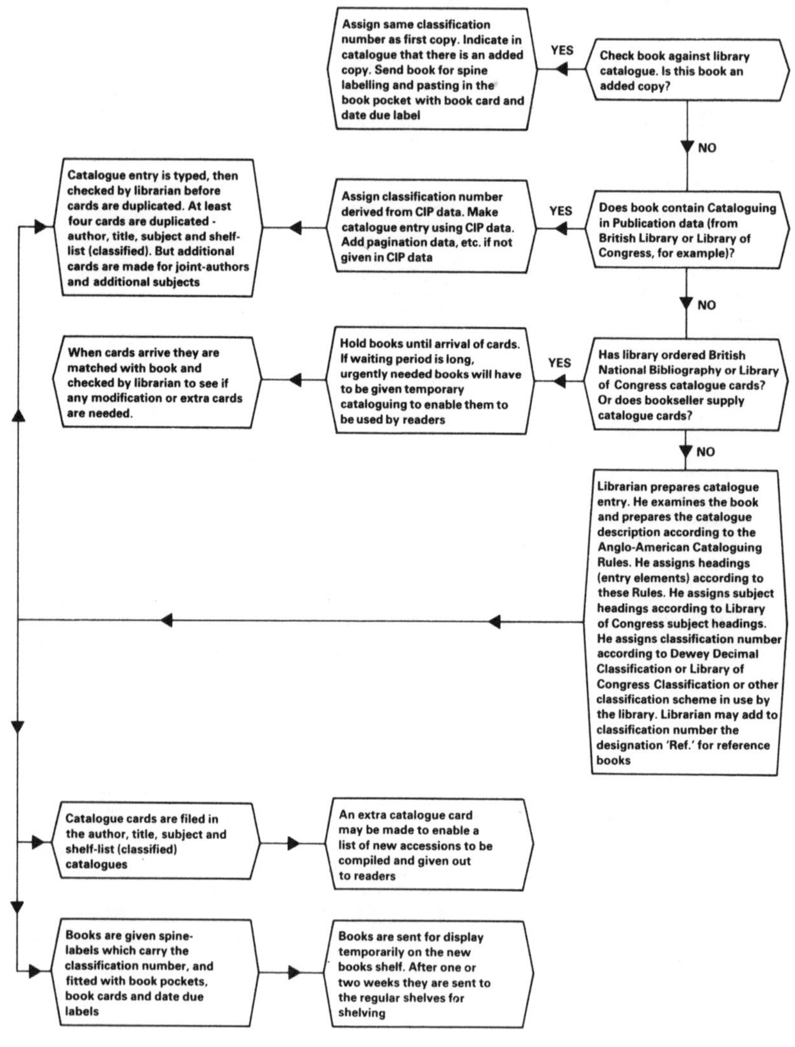

Figure 4.3 *Cataloguing and classification*

90

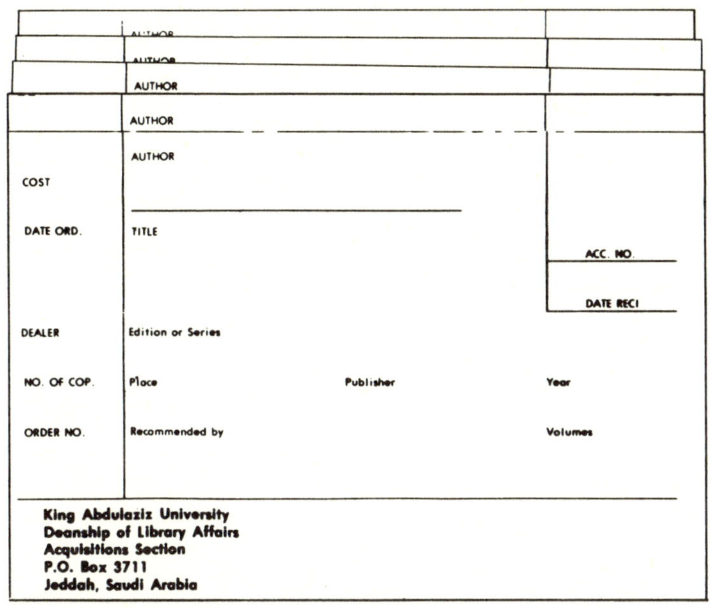

Figure 4.4 *Multiple acquisition slip, King Abdulaziz University library, Jeddah, Saudi Arabia*

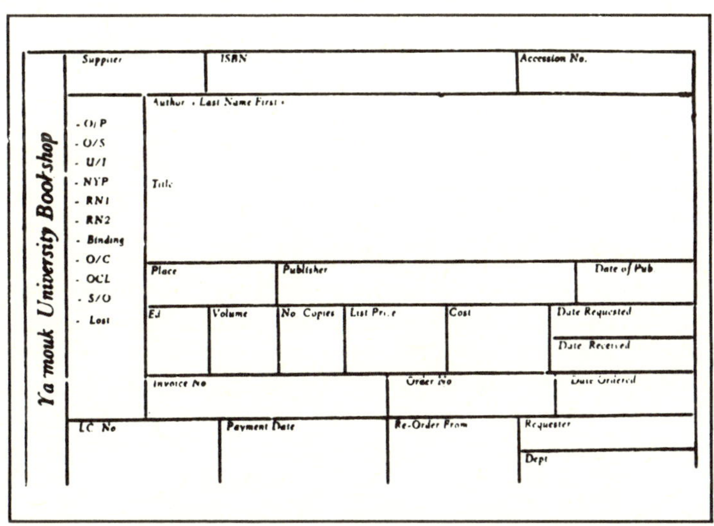

Figure 4.5 *Multiple acquisition slip, Yarmouk University, Jordan*

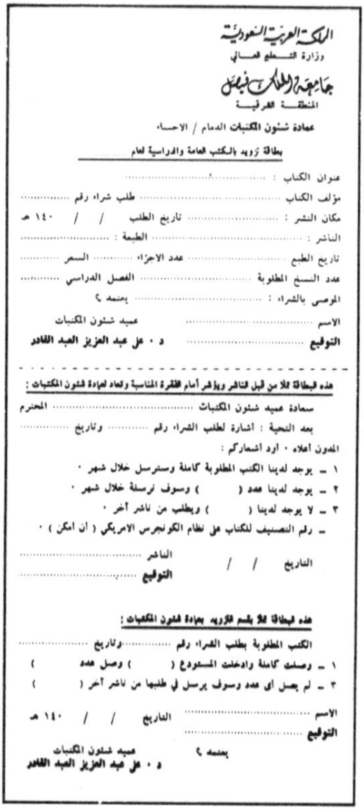

المملكة العربية السعودية
وزارة التعليم العالي
جامعة الملك فيصل
المنطقة الشرقية

عمادة شئون المكتبات الدمام / الاحساء

بطاقة تزويد بالكتب العامة والدراسية لعام

عنوان الكتاب : ....
مؤلف الكتاب .... طلب شراء رقم ....
مكان النشر : .... تاريخ الطلب / / ١٤٠ هـ
الناشر : .... الطبعة : ....
تاريخ الطبع .... عدد الاجزاء .... السعر ....
عدد النسخ المطلوبة .... الفصل الدراسي ....
الموصى بالشراء : .... يعتمد ؟
الاسم .... عميد شئون المكتبات
التوقيع .... د · علي عبد العزيز العبد القادر

- -

هذه البطاقة تملأ من قبل الناشر ويؤشر أمام الفقرة المناسبة وتعاد لعمادة شئون المكتبات :

سعادة عميد شئون المكتبات .... المحترم
بعد التحية : اشارة لطلب الشراء رقم .... وتاريخ ....
المدون اعلاه · اود اشعاركم :
١ ـ يوجد لدينا الكتب المطلوبة كاملة وستترسل خلال شهر ·
٢ ـ يوجد لدينا عدد ( ) وسوف نرسلة خلال شهر ·
٣ ـ لا يوجد لدينا ( ) ويطلب من ناشر آخر ·
ـ رقم التصنيف للكتاب على نظام الكونجرس الامريكي (ان امكن) ·

التاريخ / / الناشر ....
التوقيع ....

هذه البطاقة تملأ بقسم التزويد بعمادة شئون المكتبات :

الكتب المطلوبة بطلب الشراء رقم .... وتاريخ ....
١ ـ وصلت كاملة وادخلت المستودع ( ) وصل عدد ( )
٢ ـ لم يصل اي عدد وسوف يرسل في طلبها من ناشر آخر ( )

الاسم .... التاريخ / / ١٤٠ هـ
التوقيع ....
يعتمد ؟ عميد شئون المكتبات
د · علي عبد العزيز العبد القادر

Figure 4.6 *Acquisition slip for Arabic materials, King Faisal University, Dammam, Saudi Arabia*

Problems in acquisition

It is important to follow up an unfulfilled order after an appropriate period. For example, at the University of Khartoum library, at the end of each academic year, an order file is examined and outstanding orders which exceed three years are cancelled and the bookdealer is duly informed.[41] In the majority of developing countries, a substantial proportion of the books purchased by the university libraries 'emanate from Europe and America'.[42] This is specifically true in the case of the University of Ibadan library. In some instances, delays of four to six months in the receipt of materials have been experienced. After several months have elapsed, the libraries receive disappointing information that the

Order No	ISBN		LC Card Number
Order No	ISBN		LC Card Number
Order No.	ISBN		LC Card Number
Order No	ISBN		LC Card Number
Order No.	ISBN		LC Card Number
Order No.	ISBN		LC Card Number
Order No	ISBN		LC Card Number
List Price	Author		
Date Ord.	Title		
Date Rec'd			
Vender	Edition or Series		Vols
Copies	Place	Publisher	Year
Class No.	Recommended By	Faculty	Cost
Library	King Faisal University Libraries Box 1982 Dammam, Saudi Arabia		

Figure 4.7 *Multiple acquisition slip, King Faisal University library, Dammam, Saudi Arabia*

item is out of stock, out of print or not yet published. The library has no alternative but to cancel the order or to request the bookdealer to continue searching through the second-hand dealers. A five to six months' period to acquire most European publications is not uncommon for Indian medical libraries.[43] Some publishers state that the missing issues of periodicals should be claimed within a specified period, which is, in fact, 'shorter than the period the magazine normally takes to arrive'.[44] Other problems occur when duplicate materials are received, some due to error on the part of bookdealers, others due to duplicate orders. For instance, the inability of inexperienced or inefficient staff members in the acquisition department to prepare orders, without detailed bibliographical checking and verification, results in the submission of the same order more than once. If a work is written by more than one author and a second order is prepared under the name of a different author, or under the editor, or under the first part of the author's name, complications in tracing duplicate orders are bound to arise. Likewise, multiple orders for the same series may be sent under different titles within the series. Moreover, imperfect and unwanted titles received in the shipment have to be returned promptly to the supplier and simultaneously a request has to be made for the credit notes, so as to inform the accounting department, who are then able to settle the account and free money for further purchases within the financial year.

The payment of bills is a major cause for concern for many university libraries in developing countries. At the University of Ilorin library, Nigeria, various overseas dealers held up shipments for several years due to the non-payment of bills. This problem has not lessened, as the university authorities

> agreed to request the Nigerian universities officer in London and in Washington to settle the various debts . . . . with the settlement of these debts, the various dealers now felt obliged to resume shipment and forward books they had hitherto been withholding.[45]

In many developing countries, complicated foreign exchange regulations, import restrictions and postal and customs formalities have greatly hindered the growth of university library acquisition programmes. Although methods of placing orders vary from university to university in Pakistan, Sudan, Jordan and Nigeria, most universities order through local dealers who have a licence to import books. In Pakistan, a Unesco coupon scheme was introduced in 1950, but suspended in 1954. Under the scheme book-dealers were issued licences to acquire books from the USA.[46]

In an interview with Hassan Hashim Hetimsh, Head of Technical Services, King Abdulaziz University libraries, Jeddah, a number of problems which are usually encountered in the course of receipt of shipments came to light. These are equally shared by the Acquisitions Department of King Faisal University libraries, Dammam, and both the university libraries in Jordan. The shipment is sometimes received without the original invoice, the invoice arrives long before the shipment or the shipment from overseas vendors is partially received. It becomes extremely difficult to process the invoice. To facilitate the checking procedure, the vendors are requested to state the invoice number and the airline bill number on each carton of books. Since university libraries are located at a distance of thousands of miles from the vendors, bookdealers and warehouses, lack of or inefficient

94

communication creates further problems in acquisition work. It has been suggested, in rich Arab countries, that there must be direct telephone link to contact the publisher or vendor inside the country and abroad; this would overcome numerous difficulties. Alternatively, a telex must be installed in the technical services department; this will help to place rush orders and to inform the dealer about the urgency of certain orders which need expediting. This practice is followed in several developed countries but may not be feasible in poor developing countries where running and operational costs of a telephone and telex machine would be an additional burden upon the limited library funds.

In spite of the fact that Pakistan is signatory to the Unesco Agreement on the Importation of Educational, Scientific and Cultural materials,[47] the import restrictions imposed by the Pakistan government have impeded the efforts of booksellers to ensure prompt supplies of books to libraries. Curiously, the government's import laws make no provision for the procurement of filmstrips, tapes and other audio-visual aids. The licensing system, suspended in 1954, was re-introduced in July 1967 and licences for the import of books were also issued directly to educational institutions. By ordering through foreign suppliers, the universities were required to make payment in advance by letter of credit, but previously they used to get books from local dealers on credit.[48] For those who place orders with overseas vendors, as in the case of some Nigerian, Kuwait, and Saudi Arabian university libraries, the period to settle the invoices is ninety days, although some publishers permit an additional period of grace. In Nigeria, it sometimes takes much longer to pay the vendors due to arduous procedures. So the 'dilatory practices have resulted in the cancellation of certain journal subscriptions by some publishers and dealers. Others have withdrawn their ninety days grace period . . . . still others cease to send any publications to Nigeria without pre-payment.'[49]

In Saudi Arabia, some university libraries, such as University of Petroleum and Minerals library, are fortunate in that they receive most of the ordered materials within eight weeks from the USA and three months from the UK and other European countries.[50] Moreover, their mechanism of settling invoices is very efficient indeed and they keep their overseas vendors happy by making payment within reasonable time limits. In some other universities, the clearance of invoices through lengthy administrative channels is very time-consuming, thereby causing inconvenience for the vendor and giving rise to an unhealthy relationship between the library and the bookdealer. In the acquisition process, one sometimes has to place a rush order without additional expense, as has happened frequently at King Faisal University libraries. This type of service by the bookdealer promotes goodwill.

Acquisitions through gifts, exchange and legal deposit

So far, acquisition, whether by standing order, blanket order or direct order, has been discussed. It is simply paying for the materials acquired from a university bookshop or through an overseas agent. Now other methods which do not involve financial remittances or transactions are underlined.

Gifts are the most popular and simplest method of acquiring materials for libraries. There are donors who present their collections in their own lifetime, e.g. the Dr Abdullah Naseef collection has been presented to the King Abdulaziz University library, Saudi Arabia, while Dr Naseef is still president of the university. There is a potential gift when the owner of a collection dies, and his relatives approach the university librarian and offer to sell the collection at a very nominal price. Such a collection of 18,000 volumes was that of Dr Henry Carr, which was purchased by the University of Ibadan library after his death.[51] This type of gift is not very common in Islamic countries, where people hardly think that the university library might be willing to make an offer. Sometimes, owners deposit materials with the library and retain the right to withdraw them whenever they may wish. Other people not only give reading materials to the library, but also donate sums of money for the purchase of materials. Many Nigerian university libraries, except Lagos,[52] have benefited tremendously by the receipt of important gifts:

> of the £1.2 million given to the Ahmadu Bello University in the form of the United Kingdom Educational Grant, the libraries have spent on books and back sets of journals approximately £29000. . . . the library has received . . . £4000 worth of books from the Government of the Netherlands. . . . the Government of the Lebanon has given 2000 books in Arabic and French.[53]

During 1980 the University of Ilorin library, Nigeria, received several donations, which included 400 titles donated by members of the Faculty, College of Engineering, Michigan Technical University, USA. The Irish embassy in Lagos gave some titles on Irish life to this university library.[54]

In Pakistan, the earliest donation to the University of the Punjab, Lahore, came from H. M. Percival, who contributed 6,500 volumes in 1911. Many other gifts from prominent personalities, Maulana Muhammad Hussain Azad, Professor Siraj-ud-din Azar and Dr A. C. Woolner, have been added to the library collections. The University of Karachi library has continuously received gifts comprising individuals' comprehensive collections – the Shamsul Islam, Imtiaz Muhammad Khan, and Quaid-e Azam collections are a selection from over a dozen special collections. They have also been presented with cash donations from Glaxo Laboratories, Pakistan Mineral Development Corporation, Pakistan Tractor Corporation and State Life Insurance Corporation of Pakistan.[55]

In Saudi Arabia, King Saud University library, Riyadh, has acquired many collections of rare books contributed by prominent citizens.[56] One of the notable collections is that of Al-Sheikh Omar Bin Hasan Al-Sheikh which is arranged according to Dewey Decimal classification.[57]

From the above discussion, it is apparent that individuals or relations of scholars within the country, small business establishments, professional associations, government agencies, foreign embassies, visiting scholars from other countries and international organizations are potential sources and donors.

Some university libraries are actively engaged in exchange programmes. The University of Jordan has entered into exchange agreements with other institutes; such exchanges help to strengthen and enrich university library collections. In Saudi Arabia, King Abdulaziz University library subscribes to a number of periodicals which include *Radiance* (50 copies), *Impact* (50 copies), *Muslim Scientist* (10 copies), *Musallatut Arabia* (200 copies), *Al Jawhid* (200 copies) and *Alam al-kutb* (200 copies). All these additional copies are sent to other Islamic institutes around the world purely as gifts.

Especially for university libraries in poor Islamic countries, certain organizations supply reading materials free of charge to libraries requesting them. The Asia Foundation, established in

1954, is a non-profit, philanthropic organization which has offices in San Francisco and Washington, as well as resident offices in fourteen Asian countries. It sends American books and professional periodicals to those organizations in Asia which need them. Books are sent to Asian countries for the use of students, scholars and businessmen and to libraries for anyone's use. Also, there is the Darien Book Aid Plan, set up in 1945 and based in Connecticut. The purpose of this association, which is a women's voluntary organization, is to build a foundation of peace, understanding and friendship by free distribution of books and periodicals. They supply reading materials to individuals or organizations, such as universities, in over one hundred foreign countries. They emphasize that requests for materials should include complete details of name, size, level of reading group, postal address and categories of subjects. Freedom House/Books USA was formed in 1962 in New York by Edward R. Murrow. It was created to supply American books to people in Asia, Africa and Latin America. Franklin Book Programmes is also a non-profit educational corporation. It was founded in 1952 in New York and has offices in Cairo, Kabul, Islamabad, Tehran and in other developing countries. They provide funds and give training and assist in the planning and production of books and related materials.

The second method of acquiring materials without financial transactions is to obtain them on an exchange basis. This involves hard work in preparing lists of materials available for exchange, entering into regular correspondence with the outside world, sending out advertisements to journals, such as *Unesco Journal of Information Science*, *Library Association Record*, London, *Library Journal* and several other journals which carry exchange announcements. Every acquisition librarian ought to have the latest edition of the *Handbook on the International Exchange of Publications* (Unesco, Paris). It describes methods of exchange, rules, regulations and agreements for the exchange of materials, transportation procedure and customs.

Finally, university libraries may obtain materials from all the publishers in the country, provided they have been designated as legal depositories. They can also acquire materials from international organizations, if they have been chosen as depositories for their publications. For instance, the University of Jordan is a depository for United Nations, WHO, FAO, World Bank and Unesco publications. In Nigeria, the University of Ibadan library became a depository library in 1950 and continues to receive two copies of every work published in the country. In Saudi Arabia, Jordan and Kuwait legal deposit laws have not been enacted. In Qatar, however, a legal deposit law has been drafted in accordance with the guidelines of the Arab League Educational Cultural and Scientific Organization.[58] It was expected to be approved in 1983/4. There are no national libraries in Kuwait and Jordan, so the University of Kuwait library and the University of Jordan library have been endeavouring to fulfil the role of national libraries by acquiring materials and compiling bibliographies.[59]

A comprehensive collection at Ibadan University library, Nigeria, is the result of a legal deposit law. A fine is imposed for failing to deposit two copies at the National Library and one at Ibadan University library.[60] Obviously, the library is faced with a number of problems relating to the provision of space, labour, personnel, finance and regulations of legal deposit.[61] However, the national library, as a legal depository, actively operates and participates in exchange programmes. It offers federal government documents for exchange, and requests Africana, periodicals and reading materials in the social sciences and humanities.[62]

Choosing publishers and bookdealers

In almost all developing countries, publishing is not a well-established trade, simply because the readership at university level is not large enough for the publishers to make a reasonable profit. In Arab Islamic countries, over 95 per cent of books are published in Arabic. In Malaysia, most of the books produced locally are in Bahasa, which is the official and national language of the country.[63] In Nigeria, there are not enough well-stocked bookshops to meet the acquisitional needs of university libraries.[64] In Pakistan, as in most other Islamic countries, bookselling is actually a mixture of publishing and bookselling, and the majority of bookshops have to import books, particularly from the USA and Europe.[65] It is, therefore, pertinent for university libraries to give serious consideration to choosing vendors who can provide an efficient service.

In the book trade, both publishers and booksellers claim that they make low profits due to the rising costs of paper, printing, etc. Experience shows that they never reveal the true figures and the publisher reserves the right to increase his prices at short notice. The bookseller can quote remarkably high prices, thereby enabling him to offer a considerable discount to his customers. In the past, publishers were reluctant to supply books directly to libraries and, therefore, orders had to be placed with booksellers. With the increasing competition in the book trade, publishers are now eager to sell their product directly, bypassing the bookseller. The acquisitions librarian must be concerned that the book fund is utilized as economically as possible and must ensure the reliable supply of currently published works. In the UK, the prices of books are fixed by publishers individually and the bookseller is required by law not to sell any such books at less than the published price. Obviously, the publishers themselves may sell books directly at a reduced price. Though publishers do not offer any discount, they tend to deduct 5 per cent of the value of the books from the air-freight charges. In the case of textbooks, a 10 per cent deduction is made from the air-freight charges. It is a tricky business since one can never be certain about the price fixed by the publisher. It was reported some years ago in Dammam that on occasions four times the price quoted in *British Books in Print* for a particular book was charged. Terms and conditions of publishers differ greatly from one to another. The author conducted a survey in 1977 at the King Faisal University library, Dammam, and discovered considerable variations in the discount offers, supply time and other aspects.

The Press Agency of Kuwait publishes a large number of Arabic books and seems willing to give a 20 per cent discount on books published by others. It can also offer 20 per cent discount on English-language books published by Prentice-Hall. Heffer's, 20 Trinity Street, Cambridge, England, is bound by the 'Net Book Agreement' and cannot sell books at a reduced rate. They can, however, allow concessions on the air-freight charges which will be equivalent to 10 per cent of the invoice value of the books. They can despatch books available from their huge stock within seven to ten days. They cannot supply Library of Congress or BNB catalogue cards along with the books. Cassell Ltd, a London publishing house, is prepared to offer 20 per cent straight discount on their own publications. They guarantee delivery within six weeks. Walter J. Johnson, 355 Chestnut Street, Norwood, New Jersey 07648, USA, allows 10 per cent, subject to the type of publication, and gives a three-month period for settling invoices. Vendors who can supply catalogue cards include John Menzies Library Services, PO Box 17, 24 Gamble Street, Nottingham, England, and John Smith and Sons, 57–61 St Vincent Street, Glasgow.

Faxon in the USA and Blackwell and John Menzies in the UK supply periodicals to a number of university libraries in the Middle East. They all supply at the published price and offer no discount. Blackwell's handling or service charge per periodical is £3, whereas Faxon's cost is 4½ per cent of the price of each title.

Clearly it is necessary to select vendors only after extremely careful assessment of all aspects of the relevant acquisition situation, i.e. price and other terms such as payment date and shipping charges; services offered such as cataloguing and renewal facilities; and supporting information such as lists of new and backlist titles arranged in convenient forms.

Last but not least, the Publishers International Directory (Bowker, New York) is an essential tool for a university librarian; it contains details of international bookdealers in well over sixty countries.

Chapter 5

Size of collections and finances

Collection criteria

Different standards have been developed in different countries on different occasions for judging the adequacy of university library collections. A well-known formula, quoted in several books and research articles, was devised by Verner Clapp and Robert T. Jordan in 1965.[1] It quantitatively measures collections: volumes per student, per faculty member, per master's and doctoral field, per undergraduate honours programme, methods of instruction, availability of good study places and proximity to other libraries. R. Marvin McInnis attempted to test the validity of this formula and discovered that it was merely a rough guide for collection development.[2] Rogers and Weber, on the other hand, commented that it does not recognize book needs between, say, 'history and engineering, rather it assumes a universe of subjects will be covered by the academic community and thus the differences among subjects even out as do the differences in the use of the library by individuals'.[3] Alan Cartter's measurement is based on total book stock, annual additions to stock and current periodical subscriptions.[4] Likewise, Melvin Voigt describes a formula for establishing a yearly acquisition rate of books: the number of books for undergraduate students, for graduate disciplines, and for research work in the university.[5] Several examples and formulae related to the adequacy of collection size can be found in Lancaster's *The Measurement and Evaluation of Library Services*.[6] It must, however, be emphasized that 'in some of the operation's research applications, models are based on assumptions which cannot be verified by librarians in their day-to-day experiences with library users'.[7]

A more practical formula for determining the size of collections is as follows: let us say that 10,000 is the minimum number for books covering the subject of psychology. Of these, probably 10 per cent or less 'represent the truly active material in the field, the current important new works of wide interest, plus the backlist of basic and case works'.[8] If there are seventy subject fields in which the library is to possess materials, one must multiply $70 \times 10,000$ and get a total collection of 700,000 volumes. Accepting 10 per cent as an accurate estimate, one is left with a basic collection of 70,000 volumes. The categorization of subject fields creates certain complications. If we take engineering, 10,000 books or, still less, 10 per cent of that number, 1,000 volumes would be totally inadequate to support study and research in this vast discipline, which comprises in itself several subject areas, e.g. architecture, mining, mechanical, electrical, chemical, petroleum and industrial engineering. Also, the quantity and 'range of materials being published which are relevant to the academic program it is supporting'[9] may vary tremendously, so it would be difficult to acquire an equal number of materials for all the disciplines.

The Republic of China Library Association has prepared standards for university library collections. It suggests 50,000 volumes for each subject taught, an additional thirty volumes for each student and an additional 500 volumes for each higher degree student.[10] If there are fourteen subjects or faculties, a basic collection of 700,000 volumes would fulfil these criteria. No university library in an Arab Islamic country, except King Saud University in Saudi Arabia, seems to have developed such a collection. Table 5.1 reveals that the National University of Malaysia, which was set up in 1979, has 350,000 volumes in stock. It has 123,000 titles in microform and 2,600 audio-titles. Many collection standards do not take into account the increasing trend of acquiring materials in microform for economy of space. Another university, with 320,000 volumes, is the Universiti Sains Malaysia, serving 3,132 students and 412 faculty members. The University of Malaysia is the oldest in the country and has approximately 600,000 volumes in stock, serving 9,000 students and 1,200 staff.

The University of Kuwait library has built up a very comprehen-

Table 5.1 *Size of collections, 1983*

University	No. of students	No. of teachers	Total volumes
Jordan			
University of Jordan	8,970	580	280,000
Yarmouk University	3,263	153	83,000
Kuwait			
University of Kuwait	17,033	608	383,991
Malaysia			
National University of Malaysia	5,745	860	350,000
Technological University of Malaysia	3,582	410	143,537
University of Agriculture, Serang Selangor	4,110	507	160,123
University of Malaysia	9,000	1,200	600,000
Universiti Sains Malaysia	3,132	412	320,000
Nigeria			
Ahmadu Bello University	15,731	1,176	279,618
Rivers State University of Science and Technology	3,186	302	50,323
University of Benin	4,000	200	100,000
University of Calabar	2,798	292	70,000
University of Jos	3,686	281	80,000
Pakistan			
Islamia University, Bahawalpur	598	88	60,000
Islamic University, Islamabad	59	7	11,000
NED University of Engineering and Technology, Karachi	1,828	100	56,393
University of Agriculture, Faisalabad	3,062	388	110,000
University of Engineering and Technology, Lahore	3,070	207	72,000
University of Baluchistan	2,286	157	60,000
University of the Punjab, Lahore	7,794	386	310,000
Qatar			
University of Qatar	2,642	n.a.	100,000
Saudi Arabia			
Islamic University, Medina	1,055	85	85,000
King Abdulaziz University	14,609	992	210,000
King Faisal University	350	99	30,000
King Saud University	21,000	1,644	330,000
University of Petroleum and Minerals	3,200	602	192,606
Sudan			
Omdurman Islamic University	1,585	192	80,000
University of Al-Gezira	n.a.	n.a.	14,000
University of Khartoum	8,777	675	350,000

sive collection of 383,991 volumes, but it has to cater for the needs of over 17,000 students and 608 staff members. The oldest university in the table is the University of the Punjab, possessing 310,000 volumes and serving a reader population of nearly 8,000 students and 386 teaching staff. The university has thirty-four teaching departments which have their own departmental libraries, totally independent of the main university library. Most of the departmental library collections are far less than adequate. A survey of the book stock of thirty departmental libraries conducted by the author revealed that one library falls in the range of 1,000 to 2,000 books, four libraries have 2,000 to 5,000 books in stock, three libraries have less than 6,000 volumes, four libraries have less than 7,000 volumes, six libraries have less than 10,000 volumes, three libraries possess less than 12,000 volumes, one library has less than 15,000, one library contains less than 20,000 volumes, and two libraries have between 30,000 and 35,000 volumes. The book collections of two libraries fall in the range of 35,000 to 45,000 and just one library has in stock over 60,000 volumes. There are altogether twenty universities in Pakistan, of which four were established between 1979 and 1981. Among the respondents to the author's questionnaire, four universities have a total book stock which does not exceed 72,000.

The University of Jordan, established in 1962, with a present student population of 8,970 and 580 faculty, has developed a collection of 280,000 volumes within a span of twenty years, to which it consistently adds 15,000 volumes annually.[11] Yarmouk University library in Jordan, set up in 1976 and serving just over 3,000 students, has collected 83,000 volumes so far. Rivers State University of Science and Technology, Nigeria, also serving around 3,000 students, has acquired 50,323 volumes. Thus, comparing the number of students of the two universities shows a great contrast in the size of their holdings. In Nigeria, Ahmadu Bello University has a readership of 15,731 students and 1,176 teaching staff and its bookstock, as reported in October 1982, is 279,618 volumes. In Saudi Arabia, King Saud University has 21,000 students, including 5,000 female, and the library book stock is 330,000. Surprisingly a figure of 7.9 million books was reported in the *Arab News*, an English-language daily newspaper published from Jeddah, on 7 May 1983. The accuracy of this information is questionable, since Dr Abdullah Isa, a Saudi expert on university libraries, put the figure at only 298,632 volumes in 1981–2. King Abdulaziz University, with over 14,000 students enrolled, has built up a collection of only 210,000 volumes. If one considers the date of establishment, one observes that King Faisal University, Saudi Arabia, and Yarmouk University, Jordan, were founded in 1975 and 1976 respectively, but the stock of the former is merely 30,000 volumes whereas the latter comprises 83,000 volumes. Although the date of inception is indicative of the annual acquisition rate, it has no bearing on the strength of collections, which is greatly dependent on the number of students, staff, subjects, faculties, departments and, finally, the availability of materials within a particular subject field.

Amongst the most fortunate universities, with few budgetary limitations, is the University of Kuwait library, which now boasts of 383,991 volumes collected within seventeen years, one of the highest stocks for universities in Islamic countries.[12] The University of Qatar, which commenced its activities in 1973, has a present student intake of 2,642 and a total collection of 100,000 volumes. The University of Khartoum, set up in 1945 with a modest collection of 13,000 volumes,[13] now contains 350,000 volumes. This Sudanese university appears to have made remarkable progress during the last six years. Colin Steel reported in 1976 that its holdings were 255,000 books, but in November 1982 it reported an increase of 95,000 volumes. Serving a readership of well over 8,000, the University of Khartoum library has been adding approximately 16,000 volumes yearly. Other university libraries in Sudan are not so fortunate and this is reflected in their inadequate stock. This is due to the overall economic condition of the country and the meagre resources allocated to libraries.

Apart from the main libraries of various universities in different countries, several universities have faculty libraries. In most cases their stock does not exceed 10,000 volumes. At the King Abdulaziz University, the faculty libraries include: arts (4,000 volumes),[14] medicine (8,000 volumes),[15] science (5,000 volumes) and engineering (10,000 volumes).[16] The faculty libraries at King Saud University, Riyadh contain collections ranging from 10,000 to 30,000 volumes.

In most of the Arab universities, especially in prosperous countries, there is an increasing trend to maximize use of educational technology and to avoid total dependence on traditional printed materials for learning, teaching and advancement. It is this shift in emphasis which has brought about a considerable change in the building of comprehensive collections of non-print media in several university libraries. In Saudi Arabia, the University of Petroleum and Minerals library has acquired 60,000 reels of back issues of journals and newspapers, dissertations on microfilm, about 8,000 16 mm film cassettes and other forms of non-print media.[17] In addition, there are over 250,000 microfiches consisting of specialized research reports drawn from two main sources, namely the National Technical Information Service and the Educational Resources Centre.[18] Likewise, the King Abdulaziz University library has 60,000 microcards, 5,000 microfilms, 300 cassettes and other audio-visual materials totalling well over 67,000 items.[19] King Saud University library has in stock over 17,000 audio-visual items[20] whereas King Faisal University library has a very small collection of non-print materials. At Umm al-Qura University in Makkah the stock of non-print media includes 6,000 items of microfilms, 16 mm films and filmstrips.

The University of Qatar library has developed an audio-visual section consisting of microforms of back numbers of journals and some doctoral dissertations. The University of Kuwait library's audio-visual collection consists of 34,102 items. Similarly, in Jordan, the University of Jordan library contains a comprehensive stock of microfilms, microfiches, slides, etc., and Yarmouk University library has only a very small collection of non-print materials.

In Pakistan and Sudan, hardly any university library has developed a sizeable collection of non-print materials. But in Malaysia almost all university libraries include audio-visual or special collection units; the Universiti Sains Malaysia library is at the top of the list, with an existing stock of 100,000 microfiches, microfilms, 16 mm films, slides, cassettes and other forms of non-print materials.

As librarians, we are responsible for developing university library collections and conserving knowledge and ideas, 'whether they appear in books, maps, pictures, recordings, films or any one of a dozen or more forms'.[21] The most significant aspect of collection-building is the great importance of non-print media; they must be accepted as invaluable tools to assist the teaching and learning process in universities. Better still, we should develop practical guidelines for judging the size of collections and implement them effectively, instead of setting ideal standards and goals which might well be 'purely theoretical' and far from the real situation.

In Saudi Arabia, Dr Abdullah S. Isa, who is considered an authority on university library standards, succinctly states that the university library must have a basic stock of 130,000 volumes and should acquire annually 25 volumes per student, 160 volumes per faculty member, 600 volumes per undergraduate major field, 6,000 volumes per master field and 26,000 volumes per doctoral field.[22] At present, four university libraries in Saudi Arabia, namely UPM, Umm al-Qura, King Abdulaziz and King Saud, meet the basic stock criteria, but no university is meeting the requirements, as far as annual additions per student and per subject field at master and doctoral level are concerned. Also, all the university libraries in Malaysia and Kuwait, one university in Jordan, three in Nigeria, one in Sudan and three university libraries in Pakistan meet the basic figure suggested by Dr Abdullah S. Isa, who believes that these should be considered minimum standards. In the United Kingdom, however, the average bookstock of a university library is approximately 500,000 volumes, except those of Oxford and Cambridge university libraries which have more than 3,000,000 volumes.[23] In spite of this, the Association for University Teachers in the United Kingdom comments that existing collections, by any reasonable standards, are woefully inadequate.[24]

Periodical subscriptions

Periodical literature, both primary and secondary, is of immense value in the pursuance of higher degrees and research programmes in the university. Periodicals, as compared with books, provide up-to-date information and access to current fields of knowledge, and bring to light the results of research, whether ongoing or concluded in different parts of the world. In developing countries, engineers, scientists, medical experts and research scholars subscribe to one or more journals issued by professional organizations or specialized agencies, and also look to the library to provide numerous journals within their spheres of interest. The university libraries, therefore, bear the responsibility of making available these advances in human knowledge, in the form of periodicals and other non-book materials. According to Guy R. Lyle, these journals are invaluable and indispensable tools for the library.[25] In recent years, the rate of inflation and the rising costs of paper, printing, publishing and distribution have resulted in a sharp increase in a vast number of periodical subscriptions. It seems that some libraries in Islamic countries are subscribing to more than 3,000 journals (see Table 5.2).

Table 5.2 *Periodical subscriptions*

University	*No. of periodical subscriptions*
University of Kuwait	5,024
University of Khartoum	5,000
University of Agriculture, Malaysia	4,400
National University of Malaysia	4,000
University of Benin, Nigeria	4,000
Technological University of Malaysia	3,927
King Abdulaziz University, Saudi Arabia	3,780
University of Petroleum and Minerals, Saudi Arabia	3,670
Ahmadu Bello University, Nigeria	3,667

Several other university libraries in Malaysia, Nigeria, Jordan and Saudi Arabia subscribe to journals ranging from 2,000 to 2,800. In Pakistan and Sudan the situation is not very promising. The two well-established university libraries in Pakistan, namely the University of Karachi[26] and the University of the Punjab, acquire 454 and 350 titles respectively. The average university library in Britain subscribes to about 4,000 periodical titles.[27] There are some university libraries in Pakistan and Sudan where subscription lists do not exceed even 100 titles. Perhaps these university libraries should vigorously pursue gift and exchange policies and make direct contact with the university libraries of developed countries and rich Islamic countries so as to explore the avenues of acquiring current and back-issues of periodicals. One such example is that of the University of Al-Gezira, Sudan, which receives 103 journals in medical and health-related fields, all paid for by the World Health Organization.

Budget preparation

Budget preparation is an intellectual exercise, based on the librarian's capability to evaluate and analyse the requirements of the university library, calculate the library's probable income and forecast expenditure for a specific period. The institution of new disciplines, expansion of departments and faculties, growth in student population and initiation of diverse research programmes render the formulation of budgets more complex. It is appropriate to explain the different types of budget and their implications for the decision-makers or planners.

The line budget is fairly easy to prepare, as it simply involves adding 10 per cent for reading materials and 5 per cent for personnel costs to the previous year's budget and then submitting the estimates to the higher authorities for approval. It does indicate the number of works to be purchased and other inputs to the library, but it does not reflect on 'how the resources will be allocated and utilized'.[28] Moreover, it does not show what results are to be achieved. In budgetary planning, one should ask 'how successfully resources have been utilized in the past and what services are needed in the future to reach the desired output'.[29] The line budget does not consider the provision of services to users at all and simply estimates the amount of money required in addition to operational costs.

The service-oriented budget delineates the various functions and services to be performed for the readers. For example, it will take into account the number of photocopies produced for faculty members and students, distribution of library bulletins, preparation of bibliographies for research students and staff and binding of back-runs of periodicals. The total cost for the provision of these services helps the librarian tremendously in justifying his budget estimates. The university libraries which regularly compile library statistics and show, in their widely circulated annual reports, not only the library's inputs, but also the services the library performed for readers, are successful in convincing the higher authorities to apportion more funds to the libraries. One such example is the University of Ilorin library, Nigeria, whose annual report gives not only the figures representing the total annual acquisition of various reading and non-print materials, but also records other information, as shown in Table 5.3.[30] W.

Table 5.3 *University of Ilorin library, Nigeria, services, 1980–1*

Volumes borrowed and consulted for	1980–1
Home reading	10,656
Reserved collection	9,840
Books and journals	28,467
Reprographic services	
Official requests	9,883
Others	14,019

Summers uses the term 'performance budget' rather than service-oriented budget, which he believes may be amalgamated with the line budget, especially where data to back up the librarian's claim are concerned.[31]

Another very popular type of budget is called the Planning Programming Budgeting System (PPBS). The formulation of this kind of budget demands foresight, thorough awareness and understanding of the objectives, setting up criteria for the evaluation of measures to achieve those objectives and suggesting alternative programmes to accomplish goals with the highest benefits and minimum expense. As the various choices are considered, resources are allocated to priority areas. In establishing priorities, one has to decide 'which services to cut or reduce'.[32] So the librarian should compile a list of priorities underlining the areas where relatively more finances are needed and point out those where possible reductions may be made. However, if we carefully allocate all costs and precisely determine the unit costs of giving information, reference, reprographic and lending services, as well as other types of library service, we will discover that the most practical approach for minimizing costs would be to increase the utility of the available materials and services. In any case, a reduction in services must not have any impact on the quality of services rendered. With the Planning Programming Budgeting System, the major drawback is that it 'does not show the other alternative courses of action considered or the reason for their rejection'.[33] For instance, for the cataloguing of materials, there is no indication of the costs and benefits of alternatives, such as original cataloguing, cooperative cataloguing, centralized cataloguing or the cataloguing performed by a commercial firm. This process of budget formulation is considered a complicated one.

Planning

It is ideal to entrust the task of budgetary planning to a particular section within the library. Almost all university libraries in Islamic countries plan their financial estimates on a yearly basis; this is largely due to the fact that governments allocate funds to universities at the beginning of the financial year. The requirements of university libraries vary greatly especially with regard to:

(a) the acquisition of print and non-print materials for fulfilling an unanticipated demand
(b) employing extra staff on a temporary or permanent basis
(c) purchasing equipment and furniture to accommodate an increased student population
(d) other running costs

In addition to the above requirements which are changeable, budgetary planning must take into account any mechanization of library activities which is in the pipeline. As far as the approval of budgetary estimates is concerned, the university librarian must demonstrate his ability to persuade the higher authorities to provide the desired funds without substantially curtailing them. University libraries need two types of funds: (a) operational funds and (b) capital grants. Operational funds are needed for staff salaries, subscription to journals, stationery and the repair of furniture and fittings. Capital grants are required for the books, buildings and furniture. The older universities need more operational funds, since they have larger academic programmes and more students and staff. On the other hand, new universities require huge capital grants because they have to start everything from scratch, i.e. the construction of buildings, purchase of equipment, books and furniture.

The university librarian may, if he wishes, instruct the departmental or faculty librarians to submit a written statement of their requirements a few months before the end of the financial year. These should be incorporated into a unified university library budget by the section responsible for planning and preparing budget estimates. The university library committee, which is usually composed of distinguished members of the university, would then look into financial needs and presumably suggest certain modifications or reductions in the budget estimates. The

112

librarian's first successful achievement would be to secure the library committee's formal endorsement of his well-prepared budget. In Pakistan, for example, after the approval of the library committee, the budget is submitted to the finance committee of the university, which forwards its recommendations to the senate. All university budget estimates are published after the final approval of the senate. The university budgets, in published form, are then submitted to the finance department of the provincial government. If the preparation of the university budget is done carefully and far enough in advance, and keeps within the prescribed limits of the approved five-year plan and budget estimates, the finance department does not reduce the figures. If a reduction has to be made, the University Grants Commission (Pakistan) is consulted; this body is empowered to assess the needs and demands of the universities. No university can be sure how big a grant it would get and when it would be available.

University libraries in poor Islamic countries have not escaped the drastic reductions in their budgets caused by the world-wide economic recession. French university libraries have also suffered badly; 'the combined effects of chronic neglect and the economic situation have led to a dramatic running down of library services'.[34] On the contrary, in Saudi Arabia, financial allocations have risen greatly over the last few years. Table 5.4 shows the annual budgets of four universities.

Table 5.4 *Saudi Arabian library budgets, 1979–81 (in Saudi Riyals)*

University	1979–80	1980–1
King Saud University	2,136,400,000	3,128,345,200
King Abdulaziz University	932,250,000	1,269,787,800
University of Petroleum and Minerals	799,546,400	920,867,200
King Faisal University	350,800,000	540,817,600

The new budget in 1979–80 represented an 18.75 per cent increase over spending targets for the previous year.[35] In 1980–1, SR 5,402 million was set aside for the Ministry of Higher Education and the universities. King Saud University received approximately half of the total grant, i.e. SR 3,128,345,200.[36] In Saudi Arabia, education at all levels is totally free and therefore libraries have no source of income. The allocation for the King Saud University library for 1980–1, specifically for the acquisition of materials, was $3 million,[37] by far the highest figure in the history of the Islamic world. The same situation concerning financial allocation prevails in Kuwait and Qatar and to a far lesser extent in Jordan and Malaysia. In rich Arab Islamic countries, there is virtually no visible source of income for universities or university libraries.

Sources of income

In some less prosperous or poor universities, in countries like Pakistan, Sudan and Nigeria, income is drawn from the following channels:

>   student tuition fees
>   support fees
>   magazine fees
>   library membership fees

The university allocates a proportion of its income to the library, in addition to the major contribution made by the government. In addition, there are library fines, and grants made by certain national or international foundations. In 1978, Bahauddin Zakariya University, Multan, received an allocation of 900,000 rupees (£45,000) under the Hungarian Barter[38] and 600,000 rupees (£30,000) under the West German Loan.[39] Out of this special aid, the vice-chancellor of the university granted 500,000 rupees (£25,000) for the purchase of library materials, which greatly helped to enrich the university library resources. Another source of income consists of donations from individuals, both in money and materials. The University of Karachi, on the occasion of its Silver Jubilee, was not only granted cash gifts from a number of commercial organizations, but Kruddson Ltd gave a complete set of the McGraw-Hill *Encyclopedia of Science and Technology* to be placed in the library.[40]

Likewise, the University of Juba library in Sudan, which only had a stock of 4,000, mostly out-of-date books in 1977, received gifts in cash from a number of foreign agencies.[41] The British Ministry of Overseas Development gave £3,500 and Unesco offered $6,000 for the purchase of reading materials. There were even plans for the erection of new library buildings with cash from the European Economic Community. In 1978–9, Professor C. Work of the College of Engineering, Michigan Technological University, USA, donated a useful collection of materials to the University of Ilorin library.[42] Ahmadu Bello University library, Nigeria, in the first few years of its inception, received capital benefits from a variety of sources. Foreign organizations which offered cash included[43] the United Kingdom Government, who gave a grant of £2,100,000, out of which the library received £46,905; US AID, who provided £33,000 for the Institute of Administration; the Ford Foundation, who gave £9,000; and the British Council, who gave £1,000. In addition, the Nigerian Chamber of Mines gave £5,000 to the university library. In accepting gifts, especially of materials, university libraries might perhaps wish to consult the policies formulated by the American Library Association[44] and also the *Statement on Appraisal of Gifts*, prepared by the Association of College and Research Libraries in the United States.[45]

Budgetary formulas

In preparing budget estimates, a variety of formulas are applied for calculating the cost of staff salaries, books and serials, cataloguing, acquisition, including shipping charges, binding of materials, stationery and equipment, and other contingencies. For instance, Dix believes that two-thirds of the annual expenditure of the university library should go to cover the cost of acquisitions, cataloguing and making books available to readers, and the remaining third covers 'the cost of everything else we do to make the existing collection perform its appropriate function'.[46] To calculate personnel requirements, the number of man-hours per unit of work should be multiplied by the number of units of work. This should be divided by the number of hours one staff member works in a year and the number of personnel needed is given.[47] A more simple method to work out the annual cost of materials is as follows:

No. of books to be purchased × average cost per volume = total cost

No. of periodical subscriptions × average cost per issue = total cost
No. of issues per year × cost = total cost
Shipping charges: 10 per cent of publication price
Cataloguing (if done commercially): 10 per cent of publication price

Whatever formula is used, the librarian should balance the limited, or even unlimited funds in some cases, against variables of cost, rate of inflation and user needs.[48] The budget of the university library should indicate estimated expenditure under individual heads, such as salaries, furniture and equipment, stationery/supplies, postage, travel, sundries/electricity, cleaning, etc., books and periodicals, back-runs of journals, audio-visual materials, printing and photocopying, binding and computerization.

Although small university libraries can survive without computers, large libraries with adequate finances at their disposal would facilitate user services and relieve staff from spending considerable time on routine operations by introducing automation. In some university libraries, the librarian is supposed to justify each year why he should be provided with ample funds. In this situation, it would not be inapposite to consider the zero-base budgeting formula, which involves preparing a 'decision package' for each activity each year, giving purpose, description, benefit, consequence of not performing the activity, performance measures, analysis of costs, alternative levels of efforts, alternative methods of performing the activity.[49] The librarian should prepare a separate package for each alternative level of effort and for each alternative method of performing the same activity and then review all packages and decide at which point the costs outweigh the benefits.

The allocation and distribution of funds

What percentage of the total university budget should be allocated to the library? It depends on several factors, e.g. the economic condition of the country, availability of total funds, sources of income, whether or not the library is placed high on the list of priorities of the university and, above all, the attitude of the higher authorities towards the library. With regard to the distribution of university budgets, it is heard in the university circles of some developing countries that the

> availability of funds and resources of a particular university depends more often on the contacts and influence of some members of that university and the responsive and friendly attitude of the authorities towards them rather than on the actual needs and the academic merit of the institution itself.[50]

Returning to the question of percentages, it was proposed at the Meeting of Experts on the National Planning of Library Services in Latin America[51] that 5 per cent of the total university budget should be allocated to library services. In the United Kingdom, the Report of the University Grants Commission in 1967 submitted that the annual cost of library provision in a university of medium size should not fall below about 6 per cent of the total university budget.[52] In 1967, when a Seminar on Standards for West African Libraries was held at the University of Ibadan, J.O. Dipeolu, librarian of the University of Ife, suggested a figure of 4 per cent for West African university libraries.[53] But John Dean, who has a great deal of experience of African university libraries, proposed at least 6.5 per cent.[54] In 1973 the National Universities Commission in Nigeria recommended 5 per cent, whereas the Ratcliffe Report rejected this figure outright; Ratcliffe observed that in 1974 the Ahmadu Bello University library was allocated less than 5 per cent. Ratcliffe recommended not less than 8 per cent for the next ten years.[55]

In 1977–8, a survey of budgetary allocations of university libraries in Pakistan revealed that almost all university libraries were granted insufficient funds. The percentages were: the University of Engineering and Technology library, Lahore, 2.8 per cent; Bahauddin Zakariya University library, Multan, 6.6 per cent. The highest percentage is 6.6, which was the result of special aid given by the French government under the French Economic Assistance Programme to Pakistan.

Dr Abdullah S. Isa, in his doctoral dissertation, recommended 6 to 8 per cent of the university budget to be given as a recurring grant for university libraries in Saudi Arabia, but he also proposes that 'a one time block grant of $2,000,000 to $4,300,000 should be made available to each university library in the initial years for development of basic collections'.[56] Aguolu also believes that 'there is considerable justification for a block grant to be made to all new university libraries by the Nigerian Government'.[57] Elizabeth Moys has put forward a number of arguments for an initial grant:

1 the library must obtain, as quickly as possible, a good basic collection, without which both teaching and research will be seriously hampered
2 very expensive material, such as sets of journals, encyclopedias and bibliographies, are among the early essentials
3 many of these are available only on the second-hand market, and will be unobtainable if funds are not immediately available
4 all too frequently the students cannot afford to buy enough books for themselves and the library must provide some duplicate copies
5 prices rise continuously, and therefore it is cheaper to buy as soon as possible

Moys's arguments are valid, but in poor Islamic countries hardly any new universities have been awarded block grants; however, overseas governments or charitable foundations have frequently offered cash donations or reading materials to libraries.

The annual budgets of university libraries in different countries vary considerably, as is evident from Table 5.5. There is certainly no relationship between the foundation date of a university library, student enrolment, existing collections and financial allocations. One of the major factors which contribute to the allocation of library funds is the government educational policies of each country and the significance attached to education and libraries in the progress of the nation. It is apparent from Table 5.5 that most of the university libraries listed either maintained their level of budgetary allocation during 1981–2 and 1982–3 or managed to have their funds increased. The biggest increase and the biggest budget is that of the University of Qatar library, followed by the University of Kuwait library. In Nigeria, the Ahmadu Bello University library, the University of Calabar library and Rivers State University of Science and Technology received substantial allocations which is a reflection of Nigerian

118

Table 5.5 *University library budgets, 1981–3 (£)*

University library	1981–2	1982–3
National University of Malaysia	750,000	700,000
Universiti Sains Malaysia	600,000	700,000
Technological University of Malaysia	652,074	677,409
University of Agriculture, Malaysia	360,375	453,250
University of Petroleum and Minerals, Saudi Arabia	716,660	716,660
University of Qatar	8,638,692	2,875,730
University of Kuwait	2,898,692	9,077,626
University of Jordan	384,335	526,665
Yarmouk University, Jordan	400,000	n.a.
University of Al-Gezira, Sudan	33,000	88,000
Ahmadu Bello University, Nigeria	600,000	5,000,000
University of Calabar, Nigeria	1,164,456	1,549,949
Rivers State University of Science and Technology, Nigeria	695,021	1,090,053
University of Jos, Nigeria	724,626	618,662
NED University of Engineering and Technology, Pakistan	13,809	13,952

government policy to promote higher education in the country. All university libraries in Malaysia have annual allocations which are considered adequate to run the libraries efficiently and provide effective services for readers. Surprisingly, one university, namely the Universiti Sains Malaysia, had its annual grant increased from £600,000 in 1981–2 to £700,000 in 1982–3, whereas the National University of Malaysia library's annual allocation was reduced from £750,000 in 1981–2 to £700,000 in 1982–3. Since Jordan is not among the wealthy Arab nations, the library budgets are far smaller than those of neighbouring states. In Saudi Arabia, financial grants for the King Saud University libraries, the University of Petroleum and Minerals library and King Abdulaziz University libraries are relatively higher than for the other four universities in the kingdom, but still not adequate for expanding university libraries, where an insufficient number of qualified librarians adversely affects the quality of services to readers. At present, both Pakistan and Sudan are amongst the poor Islamic countries and meagre library funds have greatly retarded any sincere effort to promote the development of university libraries.

Once the funds are allocated to the university, the amount has to be divided, while maintaining a proper balance between the money to be spent on salaries and reading materials as well as other overheads. The British Standing Conference of National and University Libraries proposed that 50 per cent should be spent on reading materials and the same on staff salaries. According to Standards for College Libraries in the United States, 35 to 45 per cent should be allocated for buying reading materials and 50 to 60 per cent for personnel.[58] Roger and Weber believe that 60 per cent is normal for staff salaries in university libraries.[59] It would simply mean that the remaining 40 per cent may be spent on books, periodicals, binding, stationery, travel costs, equipment and other contingencies. In view of this, the library is likely to be left with less than 20 per cent to spend on reading materials. In contrast, in 1980–1, the University of Petroleum and Minerals library, Saudi Arabia, spent only 20 per cent on staff salaries and 30 per cent on books and other print and non-print materials. The rest was spent on other components, such as travelling, supplies, stationery, equipment, etc. The Australians, Wainwright and Dean,[60] have recommended that at least 10 per cent of the annual funds to be spent on monographs and serials should be provided for non-book materials, but that this provision must not be at the expense of funds for monographs and serials. In developing countries, however, it is not practicable to allocate such an amount from within the library bookfund which in many cases is either inadequate or just about sufficient to keep up with the purchasing of an unprecedented influx of printed literature. In any case, special allocations will have to be sought if the university library is planning to build up a comprehensive collection of non-print materials. Alternatively, those libraries with incredibly high budgets and a very high percentage of bookfunds at their disposal may utilize a fair proportion of the allocation for acquiring audio-visual materials.

In Table 5.6 'Percentages of university library budget reserved for bookfunds', several factors come to light as we examine the variations from one country to another. It appears rather difficult to apply standard criteria for fixing the percentage of library

Table 5.6 *Percentages of university library budget reserved for bookfunds, 1981–3*

University	1981–2	1982–3
Ahmadu Bello University, Nigeria	83	80
King Abdulaziz University, Saudi Arabia	n.a.	79
University of Qatar	69	n.a.
University of Jordan	59	63
University of Calabar, Nigeria	63	63
University of Jos, Nigeria	62	n.a.
Universiti Sains, Malaysia	58	50
National University of Malaysia	50	43
University of Agriculture, Malaysia	40	n.a.
University of Al-Gezira, Sudan	21	49
University of Kuwait	29	31.4

budgets to be utilized for the procurement of reading materials. In Malaysia, a certain amount of consistency is observed, as the bookfund percentages range from 40 to 58 over the two-year period. The variations in Nigerian universities are greater; 60 to 83 per cent of the total library budget is reserved for reading material. Many other university libraries in Saudi Arabia, Qatar and Jordan spent well over 60 per cent of library funds on the acquisition of materials.

The university libraries in Pakistan have been very hard-hit by high inflation, economic stringencies and a very low per capita income. In 1980–1, at the oldest university in the country, the University of the Punjab library could only spend 22 per cent of its extremely limited budget on books and periodicals. The book-funds of two professional university libraries, the University of Engineering and Technology, Lahore, and the University of Agriculture, Faisalabad, in 1980–1 were 19.8 per cent and 40 per cent respectively.

University libraries are also faced with the problem of improper utilization of their budgets. Should the universities with decentral-ized libraries allocate money to each department or faculty library? Should the central library retain a part of the budget for general and reference collections and for journal subscriptions? Perhaps it is advantageous if purchasing is centralized as this permits flexibility and leaves open the option to disregard certain unnecessary requests for materials and to simultaneously attempt to fill the apparent gaps in those subject areas which have hitherto been neglected. On the other hand, the bookfund may be divided between materials essential for supporting research programmes and materials required to aid teaching and learning in the university. Some might wish to further sub-divide the amount fixed for research materials between the faculties either according to the areas of ongoing research or the number of higher degree students and teaching staff. Whatever method is applied to the distribution of available funds, great care should be exercised in making optimum, accurate and precise utilization of resources for the benefit of all concerned.

Chapter 6

Planning and designing buildings

The planning of new library buildings from scratch, the extension of existing premises and the adaptation of old structures pose a diversity of problems for the university librarian. Especially in tropical countries like Saudi Arabia, Sudan, Malaysia and Nigeria, the librarian needs to be conversant with the climatological, sociological, environmental and physiological implications that considerably affect the planning and designing of university library buildings. In addition, he ought to have a thorough knowledge of the following elements:

   (a) objectives of the university
   (b) depth and range of courses taught
   (c) student body and expected growth over twenty years
   (d) future plans for new departments or faculties
   (e) financial limitations
   (f) the collection and its growth rate over twenty years

There are enormous demands on the librarian to plan an ideal and functional building, particularly in Western countries where 'most buildings fail in some serious way, and they fail because the client is unable to state clearly what he needs in terms that the architect can grasp and manipulate intellectually'.[1]

The construction programme

Evidently the librarian is required to prepare an initial 'construction programme' and provide detailed outlines of both the exterior and interior of the proposed building. At this stage, he may be confronted with various issues beyond his ability and power to solve them. For instance, he may not be fully acquainted with the architectural and engineering aspects of library design, such as acoustics, ventilation systems, lighting, floors, ceiling and wall materials, furnishings and fittings. Moreover, he is not a final authority in the university, he may not have the influence to have his ambitious 'construction programme' rubber-stamped and approved by the university governing body.

One must not overlook the saying of C. A. Cutter, who stated in 1881 that 'the architect is the natural enemy of the librarian'.[2] Librarians believed that 'architects were opinionated, unfair, and unreasonable, whilst architects thought that librarians did not know what they wanted'.[3] Although the situation has changed over the last hundred years, architects still feel that very few librarians are capable of negotiating with them. In poor developing countries like India, it has happened very frequently that 'final plans of the university library buildings have been approved and the buildings have been constructed even before the appointment of a fully trained and qualified librarian in the university'.[4] In 1977, J. A. Fab Akhidime commented that several Nigerian libraries were being planned and built without the professional advice of librarians. Obviously, there was widespread suspicion of libraries, librarians and their motives and many powerful people did not realize the potential importance of libraries in education.[5] Library buildings have not escaped criticism, even in Australia, where the well-known Munn–Pitt survey, carried out in 1934, made a relentless remark about the inadequacy of university library buildings.[6] Conversely, there are Arab Islamic countries, like Saudi Arabia, Jordan, Malaysia, Nigeria and Qatar, where some university librarians have been deeply involved in the pre-planning stages of university library buildings. In Jordan, where Yarmouk University library was erected in 1979, the librarian was given the opportunity to put forward his ideas.

Likewise in Malaysia, at the Universiti Sains Malaysia library, built in 1982, the chief librarians of both of these universities made valuable contributions to the building programmes. Syed Salim Agha, chief librarian of the University of Agriculture, Serang Selangore, Malaysia, which was erected in 1974 and extended in 1982, actively participated in the preparation of the library extension programme. The specialized knowledge and interest of these distinguished librarians in Malaysia is evident from the fact that they read papers on Malaysian University library buildings in a workshop on university library buildings in Southeast Asia, held in Singapore, 22–6 November 1977.

In the past, librarians in Nigeria had little say in the planning process. Recently, the attitude of the university authorities appears to be changing, as it is apparent that the librarians at the University of Calabar, the University of Jos and Rivers State University of Science and Technology, whose library buildings are under construction, have taken part in the preparation of their library building projects.

It would be unfair to deprive professional Arab Librarians of their due share in the planning and writing of library building programmes. In Saudi Arabia, Dr Abbas Tashkandy cooperated with the planning committee in designing the multi-storey King Abdulaziz University library building which was completed in 1977. This functional building adequately meets the needs of library users. However, in view of the unprecedented rate of growth of the student population, a new and vast library complex is being planned.

The University of Kuwait library building, constructed in 1966, was planned by a notable professor of library science, Dr Ahmad Badr, who was then director of the library. However, he emphasized, in his book written in Arabic on university libraries, that cooperation between the university librarian and the library building consultant is of the utmost importance.[7] Another distinguished Arab writer and professor of librarianship at the King Abdulaziz University, Jeddah, Dr Mohammad Fathi Abdulhady, visited the United Arab Emirates as an expert in 1980 and advised them about the establishment of a university library. He produced a detailed report on the planning of a university library which was published in 1981.[8]

The University of Qatar library, which was housed in a building erected in 1973, has, during the past couple of years, become unable to cope with the large increase in users and materials. A. M. El-Tilbani, director of libraries, has helped the architect, library consultant and other members of the planning committee with the new library building, which is now under construction.

In some Arab Islamic countries which are not fortunate enough to have petroleum and mineral resources, such as Sudan and

Jordan, the development of new library buildings has been very slow. The University of Jordan library, built in 1972, has ceased to function adequately owing to lack of space for readers and materials. Recently an extension to the library was begun.

A number of university librarians from Nigeria, Sudan, Saudi Arabia, Qatar, Jordan and Pakistan reported in January 1983 that their university library buildings do not adequately meet the needs for housing materials and staff. Some of these libraries occupy buildings not specifically designed to house libraries. A number of these were built during 1965–75. Dr Abdullah Isa categorically stated, in his Ph.D. thesis, that in Saudi Arabia 'most of the existing library buildings are becoming inadequate'.[9] In the Third Development Plan, 1980–5, the Saudi Arabian Central Planning Organization specified that the universities were planning new campuses which would include large, permanent library buildings.[10]

One wonders if John Dean's comment that 'we are still building libraries which are quite inadequate for their purpose simply because we have produced no reasonable standards of practice'[11] ia valid today. It is also relevant to consider a very significant point made by Peter Hoare, Chief Librarian, University of Nottingham, England, in his paper on 'Consideration of some planning factors and standards relating to university libraries in tropical developing countries'. While discussing seating, space, staffing and other standards he concludes that the 'standards generally applied to such libraries are often based on those created for different environments'.[12]

To begin with, in tropical countries like Sudan, Saudi Arabia, Kuwait, Jordan, Qatar, Malaysia and Pakistan, the university librarians will have to be thoroughly aware of the climatic and social conditions of these countries. Secondly, they should be aware of the standards documented by librarians within these Arab Islamic countries. Thirdly, he should have formal or informal contacts with those distinguished librarians who have successfully devised library building programmes which have been implemented. Finally, he should have access to some of the existing building plans, designs and drawings of some of the other university libraries in these countries.

The librarian will have to independently prepare a building plan in the form of a written programme which should specify in considerable detail the required reading rooms, seating, stock areas, staff areas, audio-visual and computer, as well as information technology areas. It would be ideal to incorporate some sketch drawings. The librarian might well seek help from the deputy librarian, or any other member of the library staff who has specialized knowledge and the ability to assist in the writing of a building programme. This is, of course, the responsibility of the librarian. A thoroughly planned, carefully conceived and intelligently devised programme should reflect his professional knowledge and experience and achieve the objectives of the library – to be housed in a building that would conveniently accommodate users, staff and materials. With his well-prepared programme, he may or may not be able to convince the university's higher authorities. It is therefore advisable to form a planning team.

The planning council

The planning council should consist of the following personnel:

1 vice-chancellor/vice-president or director-general
2 dean, preferably of the faculty of engineering or architecture
3 university librarian/dean of library affairs
4 a senior professor in the area of curriculum planning and research
5 architect
6 consulting architect
7 library consultant
8 interior designer

Ellsworth believes that the librarian should be chairman of the planning team.[13] Gelfand states that, if the university librarian does not have experience in planning a library building, a library consultant should be appointed member of the planning council.[14] It is appropriate to suggest that the vice-chancellor or director-general should be chairman of the planning team. At least one dean from any faculty, college or institution of the university should be a member of the council. The dean of the faculty of engineering or architecture would be preferable, since he could act as a consulting architect or engineer to the council. A survey carried out in all the universities in the eight countries studied here, indicates that several universities have architecture or engineering faculties. The appointment of the dean of one of these disciplines to the planning council eliminates the need to appoint a consulting architect or engineer. Among these univesities are the King Faisal University, Dammam,[15] King Abdulaziz University, Jeddah, University of Petroleum and Minerals, Dhahran, King Saud University, Riyadh,[16] University of Kuwait,[17] Yarmouk University, Jordan,[18] University of Khartoum, Sudan,[19] and many universities in Nigeria, Malaysia and Pakistan. Universities without any such specialist would be better to have a consulting architect. A professor from the faculty of education or someone involved in curriculum planning would prove an ideal member of the council. An architect is a must for the planning council, but a library consultant is not, provided the librarian has previous experience of planning a library building. It would not be inapposite to list here some of the prominent university librarians who have had experience in planning library buildings and could possibly act as library consultants, especially in developing countries.

1 Dr Abbas Saleh Tashkandy (formerly dean of library affairs), professor of library science, King Abdulaziz University, Jeddah, Saudi Arabia, Dr Abbas was fully involved in the planning and designing of the King Abdulaziz University library building
2 Dr Ahmad Badr, professor of library science, King Abdulaziz University, Jeddah, Saudi Arabia. Dr Ahmad, as director of libraries, University of Kuwait, planned the building without needing the advice of a library consultant
3 Syed Salim Agha, chief librarian, University of Agriculture, Serang Selangor, Malaysia
4 Haji Mohammad Darus, chief librarian, Technological University of Malaysia, Jalan Gurney, Kuala Lumpur, Malaysia
5 Edward Lim Huck Tee, chief librarian, Universiti Sains Malaysia
6 K. Mahmud, university librarian, Ahmadu Bello University, Zaria, Nigeria
7 B. U. Nwafor, university librarian, University of Jos, Jos, Nigeria
8 J. A. Omhu, university librarian, Rivers State University of Science and Technology, Port Harcourt, Rivers State, Nigeria

J. A. Martin gives a very useful checklist for planning new medical library buildings and it could be taken as a guide for librarians who might be involved in the future planning of their libraries.[20]

1 consider function of parent institution and role of library
2 survey use of library
3 study work flow patterns and spatial relationships, i.e. staff accommodation
4 search literature for new service approaches, techniques or equipment
5 visit new libraries
6 develop concise programme of needs
7 develop preliminary layouts
8 select architect
9 select planning team
10 review (6) with all likely helpers
11 employ consultants on (6)
12 review architect's initial plan
13 equipment lists and specifications
14 review specifications (bidding)
15 select move coordinator
16 plan move

Librarian and architect

It largely depends on the university librarian to advise the university authorities whether a consulting architect and a library consultant need to be appointed. It would use up a fair proportion of the building funds to pay both or one of these, especially if they were hired from outside the university. However, collaboration between the university librarian and the architect is inevitable, so great care must be taken in choosing a competent and experienced architect to shape the future of the university library building. It must be borne in mind that 'no two building programmes for university libraries can ever be completely identical, even though the total surface area may be the same'.[21] The university librarian who himself prepares a building programme, without the assistance of a library consultant or consulting architect, should be able to interpret his entire scheme to the architect. In 1950, while additions to the library of the University of Connecticut were planned, an unhealthy atmosphere developed; the president of the university had to order the director of the library 'not to inflict himself on the architect'.[22] However, the architect's capabilities are limited by his understanding of the functions of the library building he is required to design.[23] The librarian should provide him with clear specifications concerning the space requirements for various library units, the type of materials to be housed and where reading rooms, work rooms, toilets, etc., should be located. In 1899, Frank Hill reported that 'the active, progressive and liberal architects and librarians were very near together on vital points'.[24] In 1981, Dr Abdullahi Mohammed, head of the department of library science, Ahmadu Bello University, Zaria, Nigeria, commented that 'it calls for compromise and maturity of thoughts, ideas and positive disposition between the two'.[25] Herbert Ward, in his paper, 'Building libraries and services worldwide', which he read at the Library Association National Conference in Brighton in 1978, stressed the point that good library building requires the close cooperation of both architect and librarian.[26] The librarian would also need frequent consultation with an interior designer, if one is available. To communicate effectively, both with the architect and the interior designer, he should expand his knowledge by extensively reading literature on library buildings. Apart from books on the subject, it would be pertinent to browse regularly through such periodicals as *Interior Design* magazine, *Architectural Digest* and *Library Journal*.

The librarian should not 'worry about providing specific suggestions or coming up with a design',[27] but he must specifically state his requirements and make sure they are comprehended by the architect.

More precisely, he should explain and give surface dimensions for each of the following units:

(a) bookstacks
(b) special materials
(c) circulation
(d) general services
(e) seating capacity
(f) library personnel
(g) lighting requirements

The bookstacks unit

In many university libraries in developing countries the shortage of space is accentuated because of the large number of books which are either redundant or of purely research value. Diana Rosenberg, chief librarian of the University of Juba, Sudan, rightly complained that the library occupied just one room of the university, housed in a former army barracks.[28] She noticed that a large number of 4,000 books donated to the library were out of date or of little relevance to the courses. In response to the author's questionnaire, 60 per cent of the respondents from Sudan, Jordan, Qatar, Nigeria, Saudi Arabia and Pakistan reported inadequate space in their university libraries for the storage of reading materials, Malaysia being an exception, where four out of five university librarians expressed satisfaction with regard to the adequacy of space for the storage of collections. All these Malaysian university library buildings were erected between 1974 and 1982. Sessa and Galvin, in an unpublished report entitled 'An evaluation of size and functional aspects of the library building of the University of Petroleum and Minerals, Dhahran, Saudi Arabia', written in 1976, underlined a very significant point: the campus architects paid little attention to the desired amount of space for seating and collections.

The university library building should be a symbol of contemporary tropical architecture, centrally located in the campus and permitting easy access to all departments and colleges of the university. Some university library buildings, including the University of the Punjab, Pakistan, University of Jordan, King Faisal University, Dammam, University of Juba and Omdurman Islamic University, Sudan, and the University of Calabar, Nigeria, are overcrowded and the bookstacks are far too close together. In certain cases, too many desks have been placed virtually adjacent to the stacks and some desks even block the circulation routes. They appear very haphazardly placed. The fault does not rest with either the architect or the librarian, because most of these quarters which house libraries were never planned as library buildings.

Planning of the stack areas will be dictated by:

(a) the organizational structure of the library collections
(b) the total existing stock and annual rate of growth, multi-

plied by the number of years for which the building is planned
(c) the average size in centimetres of materials, since oversize materials may not be intershelved
(d) the size of shelves to be purchased

If the library is to be arranged by subject, a position will have to be chosen for the stacks, on each floor of a multi-storey building, and the required area should be worked out accordingly. The University of Jordan, for instance, has two stack areas, one in the basement, comprising philosophy, psychology, religion, social sciences and fiction and another stack area on the upper floor, containing works on languages and literature, pure and applied sciences, geography, history and fine arts. Likewise, the University of Petroleum and Minerals library, Dhahran, Saudi Arabia, has stack areas on the third floor dealing with humanities and social sciences and on the fourth floor, where pure and applied science materials are shelved. In Nigeria, the University of Jos has a number of stack areas in the library which are organized according to subject.[29]

The next vital step in calculating the area to be occupied by shelves is to ascertain the number of existing books. If the present stock is, say, 50,000 volumes and the annual addition is 5,000 volumes, the library would require to accommodate 150,000 volumes over a period of twenty years. It should be noted here that, in view of the varying thickness of volumes, ten books on average would occupy a 1-foot space on a shelf three feet long. The size of volumes is also an important factor when calculating shelving capacity. An observation suggests that over 85 per cent of the bookstock of university libraries in Saudi Arabia (King Faisal, King Abdulaziz, Petroleum and Minerals), Jordan (University of Jordan, Yarmouk University) and Pakistan (University of the Punjab, University of Engineering and Technology, Lahore, University of Agriculture, Faisalabad, University of Karachi and Quaid-e Azam University, Islamabad) consist of works between 23 cm and 28 cm in height. At some university libraries, such as the University of Ilorin[30] and University of Calabar,[31] Nigeria, King Abdulaziz University, Jeddah, Saudi Arabia and the National University of Malaysia,[32] indexes, abstracts, bibliographies and reference works, normally grouped as oversized, are not intershelved with the lending stock. This permits economy of space and caters for an increased number of volumes to be shelved in the stacks.

The height of the bookshelves and the number of shelves in each stack, whether single or double-faced, is another factor influencing space requirements. Metcalf suggests a range 66 feet long, divided by 6-foot high, double-faced bookstacks, seven shelves high, each stack 3 feet wide and 9 inches deep, placed at a distance of 4 feet 6 inches from bookstack centre pole to bookstack centre pole, which would house fifteen volumes per square foot.[33] If the stack shelves were more than 9 inches deep, as is the case at King Abdulaziz University library, Saudi Arabia, the centre pole spacing would be increased, thus considerably reducing the number of volumes per square foot. Some libraries, such as the University of Jordan, have free-standing double stacks placed on load-bearing floors. Each stack contains seven shelves. At the King Abdulaziz University library, Saudi Arabia, each stack consists of six shelves, each shelf 3 feet wide, 10 inches deep and 12 inches high. Single-faced bookstacks, as on the ground floor of the University of Petroleum and Minerals library and at the Islamic University, Medina, Saudi Arabia, used because of the lack of overall storage space, do not help to resolve or minimize the problem of accommodating constantly growing collections. Another undesirable practice, that of having only three 3-foot long shelves in each stack, even for the housing of oversized reference works, as at the King Faisal University library, Dammam, and the University of Jordan, further complicates the problem of using storage space economically.

Henderson also agreed with Metcalf, in that where 'minimum ceiling height is 7 feet 6 inches, fifteen volumes of average size per square foot of floor space' is an established practice in many libraries.[34] Mason suggests 250 books per standard double-faced section of 7 shelves; one double-faced section will average 18 square feet in the stacks.[35] John Harvey, who has visited Pakistan,[36] Afghanistan, Turkey and Kuwait,[37] acted as director of the Iranian Documentation Centre, Tehran, and later taught library science in a library school in Tehran, proposed, for Iranian university libraries, the following criteria for measuring space for books:[38] 150,000 volumes of average size should require 0.19 square feet per volume; 150,000 additional volumes need 0.22 square feet per volume. He goes on to suggest that, as the collection increases, less square feet per volume would be required.

However, the following is a more practicable formula:

Measure the distance between columns. Multiply length by width to find out square feet. If, in the bookstack layout, the space is 10 feet × 10 feet, one module will comprise 100 square feet.

Count the number of double bookstacks which can be placed in the space available and multiply by 2 to calculate total single-faced stacks. Work out the linear feet of shelves in each stack. Say all stacks are 3 feet wide and 6 shelves high.

Each single stack will contain 18 linear feet.

Linear feet × total single-faced stacks = total linear feet.

Total linear feet × number of shelves in each stack = number of volumes in one stack.

$$\frac{\text{Number of volumes}}{\text{Square feet}} = \text{number of volumes per square foot.}$$

To avoid getting involved in mathematical calculations, it is appropriate to use already established formulas which have been recognized all over the world. Henderson,[39] Mason[40] and Metcalf[41] have provided guidelines with regard to book storage space areas in libraries. The author suggests that a university librarian planning for the housing of 400,000 volumes would require a 26,680 square foot space.

To achieve economies in shelving space, the following courses of action may be taken:

1 university libraries should consider having separate storage space for infrequently consulted works
2 compact shelving may be introduced
3 multiple copies of works may be transferred to the faculty libraries or departmental reading rooms
4 if finances permit, bound volumes of serials may be replaced by such materials in microfiche form
5 mobile shelving may be introduced

F. J. Hill believes that maximum use of space is obtained by more effective use of normal shelving.[42] In addition to planning space for stacks, the location of bookstacks should be carefully chosen; it should be the easiest place to get to in the library

134

because this is where the majority of users end up.[43] Finally, the librarian should decide on the type of shelving suitable for housing all kinds of materials. Normally, adjustable steel shelving, which is fireproof and more durable than wooden shelving, is ideal for university libraries. Uniformity in size and pattern would make the shelving aesthetically pleasing. Metal shelving of light grey or sandstone colour, which can be dismantled and re-erected to suit library needs, is recommended for university libraries.

The special materials unit

The librarian involved in planning new buildings, renovation or remodelling of existing structures or contemplating extensions will have to bear in mind the new technologies, computerization, the increasing use of audio-visual materials in education and special collections, such as rare documents, government publications, manuscripts, archives, theses, maps, etc. These all need to be housed and made accessible to readers. All respondents to the author's questionnaire indicated one or more of the above-mentioned materials in their university libraries.

In calculating the space requirements for periodicals, allowance must be made for the back issues of future subscriptions, as well as the back issues of present subscriptions still to be acquired. Allowing for an eventual, say, 60,000 volumes, 4,000 square feet of space will be needed. Here, an allocation of 1 square foot for every fifteen volumes is taken as a standard. Special collections of such materials as maps pose a diversity of handling and storage problems. The Technological University of Malaysia and the University of Malaysia, King Abdulaziz University, University of Petroleum and Minerals and King Saud University in Saudi Arabia, the University of Jordan, the University of Kuwait and many university libraries in Nigeria and Pakistan have substantial map collections. Some university libraries have transferred map collections to their respective faculty or departmental libraries, whereas others are encountering difficulties in organizing maps and making them accessible to users. University librarians should prepare a description of the materials – atlases, folded maps, aerial photographs, etc. – and the number of items acquired annually.

They should be aware of the square feet needed for each number of maps. One recorded figure is 2,000 square feet per 100,000 maps, using five-drawer map cases stacked with 100 maps per drawer.[44] The librarian should also communicate to the architect the approximate weight of each full map case which, according to one estimate, weighs around 200 pounds per square foot.

There has been a growing trend towards learning by means of non-print materials, such as films, slides, video-tapes, audio-tapes and cassettes. The use of microfilms and microfiche is already well-established in university libraries. For instance, the University of Petroleum and Minerals library, Dhahran, possesses 34,000 reels of microfilm (back issues of serials), 12,300 16 mm films, cassettes, etc. and 262,000 microfiches (report collection).[45] The Universiti Sains Malaysia has 100,000 items of audio-visual materials.[46] The University of Kuwait has over 34,102 items of audio-visual materials including 16 mm films.[47] In Nigeria, the Universities of Jos[48] and Ilorin[49] have small collections of microfilms, microfiche, and slides, and the University of Calabar is planning to set up an audio-visual unit.[50] The University of Jordan has a photography laboratory which contains modern photocopying machines and a set of microfilming equipment. The King Abdulaziz University, Jeddah, also has, on the first floor of the building, a separate unit which contains six microform reader/printers, one microviewer, one microfilm reader and a substantial collection of audio-visual items shelved in steel cabinets. It is estimated that 'an ordinary microfiche cabinet with 9 drawers, 4 sections per drawer jam packed, holds 36,000 fiche. A more reasonable figure would be about 30,000 fiche.'[51]

It is apparent that, in the planning process, space has to be allocated for necessary pieces of equipment, and for storage of the materials. It is estimated that 800 square feet of space would be required for an audio-visual unit in libraries. In any case, adequate viewing and listening facilities must be provided. Provision should be made for the storage of heavy and bulky items, such as film reels, film shipping cartons or film inspection machines. An audio-visual room should be designed with a suitable sound and visual atmosphere. In the absence of media technology centres in universities, the library audio-visual unit should be equipped with slide copying machines and facilities for the production of transparencies and other items.

The circulation unit

In this area the activities of issuing books for loan and discharging them when returned, issuing books from the reserved collection of prescribed set texts and control of readers entering and leaving the library are carried out. It follows that this area should be adjacent to the door of the library, and, as far as possible, screened in such a way as to minimize disturbance to readers in the quieter reading areas of the library. If the circulation system is computerized, a system which the University of Petroleum and Minerals library, Saudi Arabia, intends to initiate,[52] the space requirement for the housing of computer discs, for related equipment and for carrying out operations will be doubled. Libraries already having spacious circulation areas may not need additional space to install a mechanized system. However, no university library in Malaysia, Qatar, Sudan, Jordan, Kuwait, Nigeria or Pakistan has so far automated its circulation system.

Whether the system is manual or automated, the library would need counter units, preferably made of light mahogany. These can be ordered through reputed suppliers. The standard size of units used in several university libraries is either 3 foot or 6 foot long, 2 foot 9 inches high and 2 foot deep. The total area required for circulation units should be around 800 square feet.

The general services unit

This should include an area for praying in the libraries of Islamic countries, especially if there is no mosque in the vicinity of the university library. It may sound irrelevant or funny to Western and non-Muslim readers, but provision for students to pray on the library premises must be considered an essential ingredient of any planning programme. Even today, the King Abdulaziz University library, Jeddah, King Faisal University library, Dammam and the Faculty of Engineering of King Abdulaziz University have excellent facilities for readers to say prayers in the libraries at the fixed times of the day. At least 500 square feet of space should be planned for this activity, which is compulsory in Islam.

Planning for an exhibition area also falls in this unit. The concept of an exhibition area is a fairly recent development in university library planning. This particular area, which would be situated beyond the circulation desk, would have display cases for models, sculptures, plans, paintings, drawings, calligraphy and other examples of the work of students and faculty members. The exhibition would be changed at regular intervals and new items displayed. Exhibits from outside organizations, both local and national, could be mounted. For this purpose, 500 square feet of space would be required. The University of Petroleum and Minerals and King Abdulaziz University libraries in Saudi Arabia have exhibition areas, where various exhibitions are organized. Similarly, the University of Jordan library has a good-sized hall where exhibitions of cultural interest to both students and members of the general public are held.

The general services unit should also comprise an area for current periodicals and newspapers. The display area should be fitted with appropriate display stands. Another 300 square feet of space will be required for this area.

The seating capacity unit

The librarian should identify the categories of actual and potential users and the seating requirements for postgraduate and under-graduate students, research scholars and faculty members, and administrative and technical staff. In addition, he should specify seating for both smoking and non-smoking reading areas, relax-ation areas, cubicles for students preparing doctoral dissertations, and study carrels for students who prefer privacy. Other special-ized reading and study areas with audio-visual carrels and seating for map users will have to be provided. Seminar rooms, a library instruction room, a photocopying room and a typing room fall in the sphere of the seating capacity unit. The reading areas must be located at a reasonable distance from the circulation and reference units, where the movement of users may be a distraction to readers, who must be guarded against auditory and visual interruptions. A building designed on an open-plan basis would permit subsequent changes to be made in the reader areas. A number of small reading areas are preferable to a single large reading area.

The University of Ilorin library, Nigeria, has a number of reading rooms located on the ground and first floors of the library building. There are five reading rooms:

Reading Room A	located to the right on the ground floor of the new building; has forty-eight reader places
Reading Room B	to the right of the old building; has sixty reader places
Reading Room C	to the left of the old building
Reading Rooms D and E	to the right, on the first floor of the new building; seating for research students and faculty members only

The University of Jordan library is housed in a three-storey building; a further three floors are under construction. It has reader accommodation around the bookstacks. Also, there are carrels which are specifically reserved for research students and faculty members. Similarly, the University of Ilorin library provides a carrel room located on the first floor of the building.

The floor plans of the University of Petroleum and Minerals library indicate that reading accommodation is available on the first and third floors (see Figure 6.1). The second floor houses the offices of the Dean of Library Affairs, the Technical Services Department and Library Administration. On the third floor, the humanities and social sciences collections, back sets of periodicals and microforms are stored, and seating for readers is provided. Likewise, the fourth floor houses the pure and applied sciences collections and also has reading areas (not shown in Figure 6.1). On the first floor, three reading areas are located, two near the current periodical display units and one among the Arabic reference bookstacks.

The floor plan of the University of Jos library, Nigeria (see Figure 6.2), Bauchi Road Campus, shows four sets of readers' tables in between subject collections. The most significant feature of the interior design is that the subject specialist librarian's offices are located near the reader accommodation, which makes it convenient for readers to seek advisory services from the library staff. The plan shows that the desks of the law librarians and the social sciences librarian are located in the proximity of the reading area. However, one reading area, which appears to be surrounded by catalogue cabinets and the circulation desk, is unlikely to have a quiet atmosphere and be absolutely free from the frequent

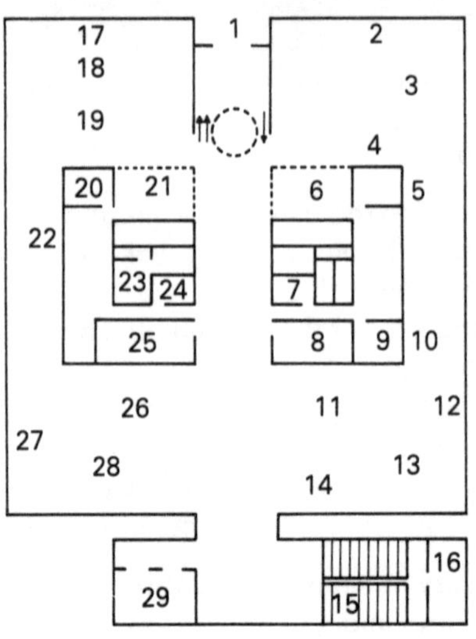

(a) First floor

1 Entrance
2 Reference collection
3 Indexes and Abstracts
4 Computer terminals
5 Business directories
6 Reference desk
7 WC
8 Director General Educational Aids
9 Reference Librarian
10 Standards
11 Current periodicals
12 Reference collection
13 Reading area
14 Reference works
15 Stairs
16 Smoking area
17 Arabic reference collection
18 Reading area
19 Newspapers
20 Head of Circulation
21 Circulation desk
22 Theses
23 Stairs
24 WC
25 Media centre
26 Current periodicals
27 Middle East Collection
28 Reading area
29 Elevator

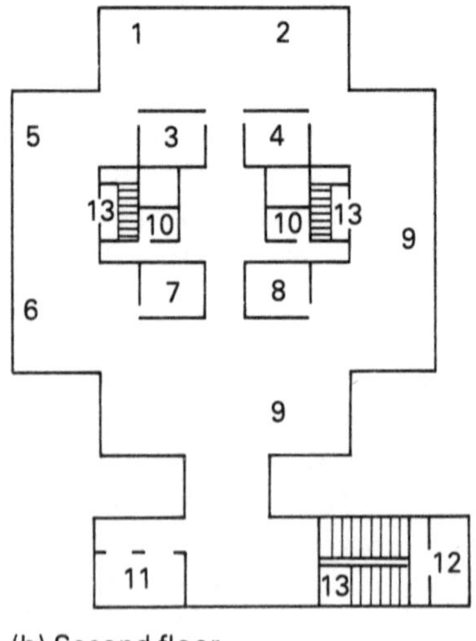

(b) Second floor

1 Accounting dept
2 Monographic acquisitions
3 Dean's office
4 Conference room
5 Acquisitions dept
6 Periodicals dept
7 Systems room
8 Searching dept
9 Cataloguing dept
10 Toilets
11 Elevator
12 Smoking area
13 Stairs

Figure 6.1 *Floor plans, University of Petroleum and Minerals library, Dhahran, Saudi Arabia*

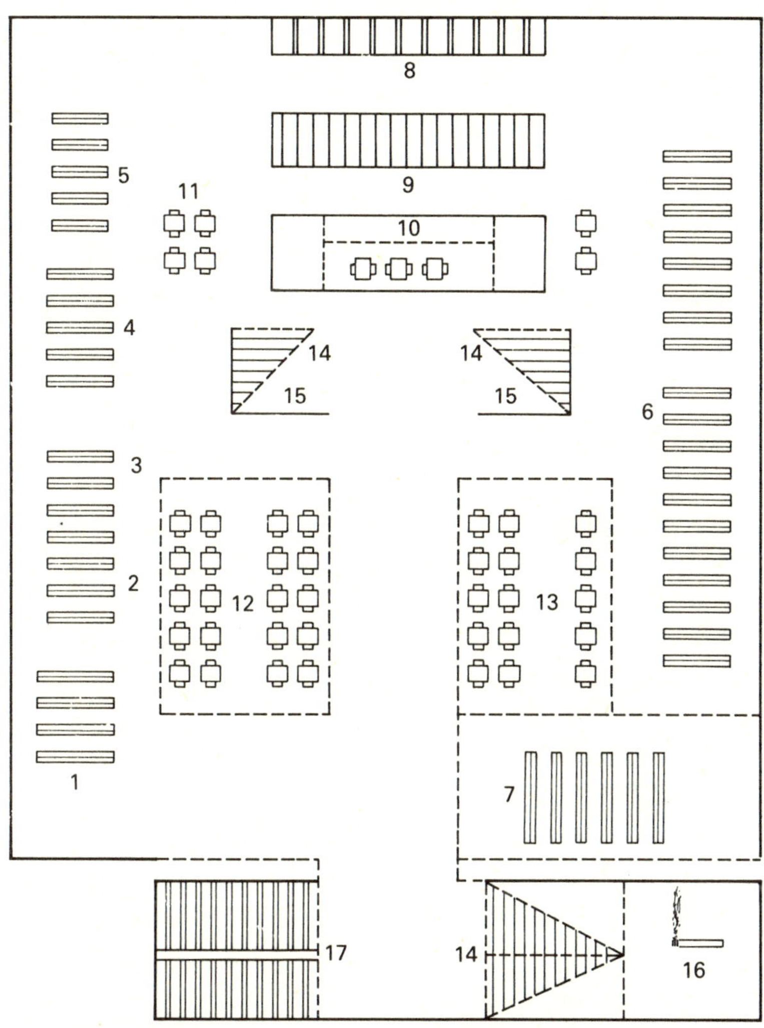

1 General works
2 Philosophy collections
3 History, topology collections
4 Geography, anthropology collections
5 Social sciences
6 Education, languages and literature
7 Oversize books
8 Microfiche storage units
9 Microfilm storage units
10 Microfiche/microfilm reader printers and reading room
11 Reading area
12 Reading area
13 Reading area
14 Stairs
15 Toilets
16 Smoking area
17 Elevators

(c) Third floor, humanities and social sciences

141

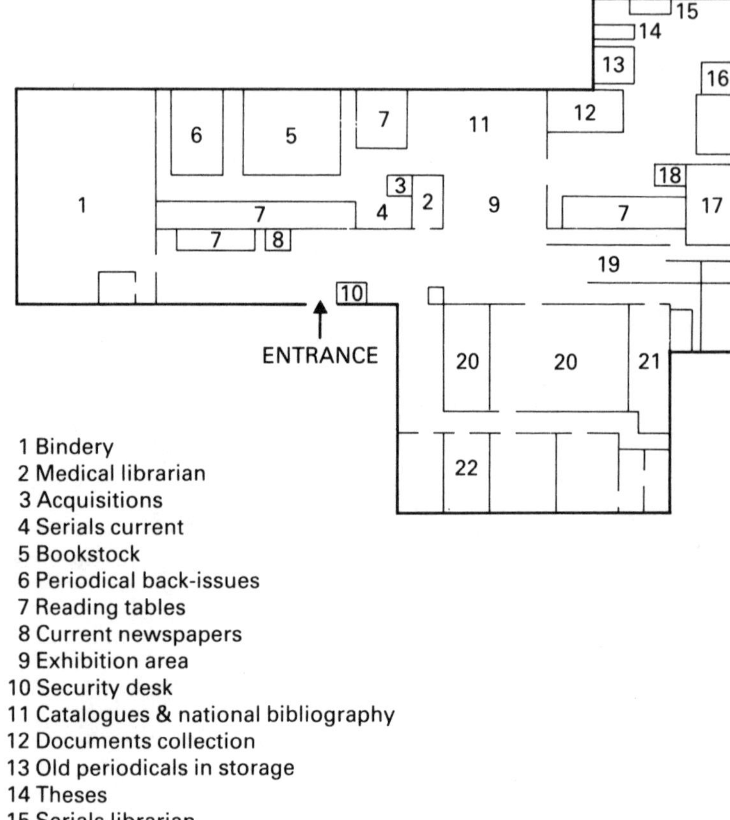

1 Bindery
2 Medical librarian
3 Acquisitions
4 Serials current
5 Bookstock
6 Periodical back-issues
7 Reading tables
8 Current newspapers
9 Exhibition area
10 Security desk
11 Catalogues & national bibliography
12 Documents collection
13 Old periodicals in storage
14 Theses
15 Serials librarian
16 Microform readers
17 Photocopying room
18 Documents librarian
19 Circulation desk & reserved stock
20 Ordering & cataloguing sections
21 Staff rest room
22 University librarian

(a) Township library, Murtala Muhamed Way

Figure 6.2 *Floor plans, University of Jos library, Nigeria*

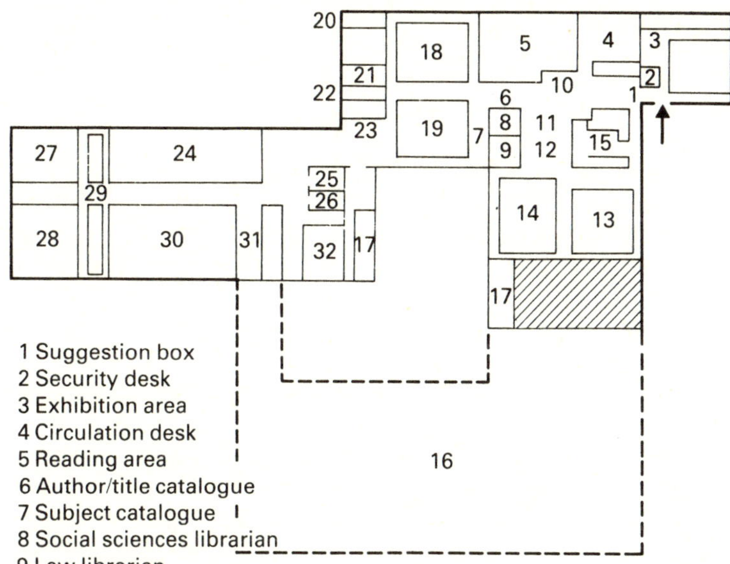

1 Suggestion box
2 Security desk
3 Exhibition area
4 Circulation desk
5 Reading area
6 Author/title catalogue
7 Subject catalogue
8 Social sciences librarian
9 Law librarian
10 Natural science acquisitions
11 Reading area
12 Reading area
13 Law books
14 Social science books
15 Current serials, law, natural and social sciences
16 Extension under construction
17 Toilets
18 Natural sciences serials back sets
19 Natural sciences books
20 Microform reader
21 Natural sciences librarian
22 Photocopying room
23 Deputy university librarian
24 Reading area
25 Education librarian
26 Arts librarian
27 Law and social sciences serials back sets
28 Arts, education and environment science serials back sets
29 Abstracts and indexes
30 Arts, education and environment science books
31 Current serials, arts, education and environment sciences
32 General references

(b) Bauchi Road library

distractions caused by the movement of readers. However, the plan represents the result of the modification of a former warehouse and the building is only for temporary use.

King Abdulaziz University library, Saudi Arabia, occupies a multi-storey building which was wisely planned by Dr Abbas Tashkandy, then dean of library affairs; construction was completed in 1977. Off the entrance hall to the left on the ground floor are the circulation and reference departments, exhibition hall and mosque; lending bookstacks, as well as reference stacks, are on the same floor. At the far end of the ground floor is the technical services area. The long reading areas are divided up by inserting sections of bookstacks. Some libraries would have been inclined to avoid separating the periodicals from the bookstacks related to the same discipline, as proximity encourages the use of periodicals. But here, the first floor contains current and back issues of all periodicals, arranged alphabetically by the title of the journal. In addition, there is a microform room, meeting room, documentation centre, Nassif hall, manuscripts room, dissertation room, discussion room and a separate area containing government publications. The most striking feature of the library is the placing of individual study carrels. There are thirty-six carrel units on the ground floor, each unit consisting of four carrels, making a total of 144; there are also forty-two carrel units on the first floor, i.e. 168 carrels, plus twenty-six single carrels by the windows. Apart from that, the library provides thirty-two cubicles for research students and faculty staff. Each cubicle occupies an area 72" × 94" and is equipped with a chair and a table with a small bookshelf. There are 166 easy chairs ideally located on both floors of the library building. The ever-increasing use of audio-visual materials requires separate areas both for the storage and use of such collections. As is evident from Figure 6.3, the University of Calabar library, Nigeria, has allocated a sizeable space for audio-visual materials as well as for microform collections, although both collections have been separated. In Saudi Arabia almost all the university libraries provide facilities for making use of non-print materials. Figure 6.4 indicates that the King Faisal University Men's Medical library has made available audio-visual study carrels in the library. They are endeavouring to build up a comprehensive range of audio-visual collections.

University library buildings with successful functional designs

144

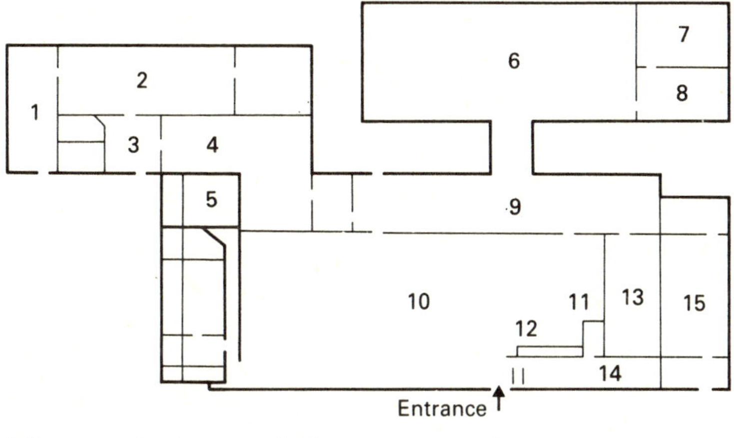

1 Resource development division
2 Technical services bindery division
3 Audio-visual material
4 Reference library
5 WC staff
6 Bound periodicals
7 Govt pub. depository materials
8 Africana collection
9 Current periodicals
10 Lending library
11 Reserve collection
12 Lending desk
13 Microfilm collection
14 Catalogues
15 Office of the university librarian

Figure 6.3 *Floor plan, University of Calabar library, Nigeria*

can be seen in Kuwait, Jordan, Malaysia and Nigeria.

The National University of Malaysia library (see Figure 6.5) is special, as it has ten good-sized seminar rooms. This facility is not available in any other university library, and even those engaged in planning and designing new library buildings do not consider it a necessity. However, thirty-six lockable cubicle rooms provided at the King Abdulaziz University library might be considered an excellent facility for readers.

The University of Karachi library, set up in 1952, was initially housed on the third floor of the department of chemistry building, then for a while in the arts building until 1964[53] when it occupied the present seven-storey building. It comprises reading areas on various floors[54] and provides 980 seats for readers; this is still inadequate for the number of enrolled students. This building was designed by a French architect[55] on a central site, occupying a total area of 296,000 square feet. Before the new building was erected, thirty-two departmental libraries were in existence and their

145

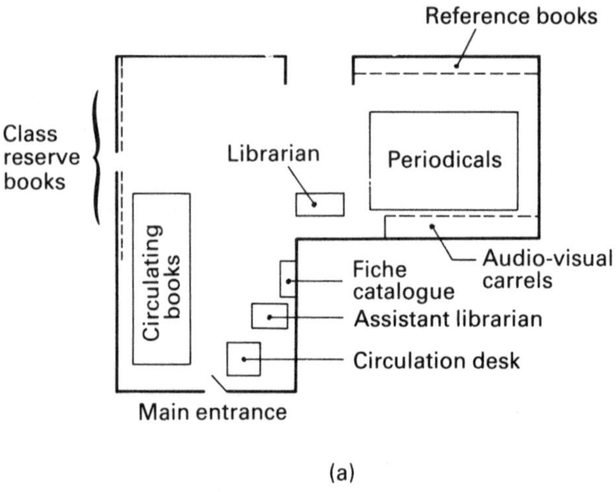

(a)

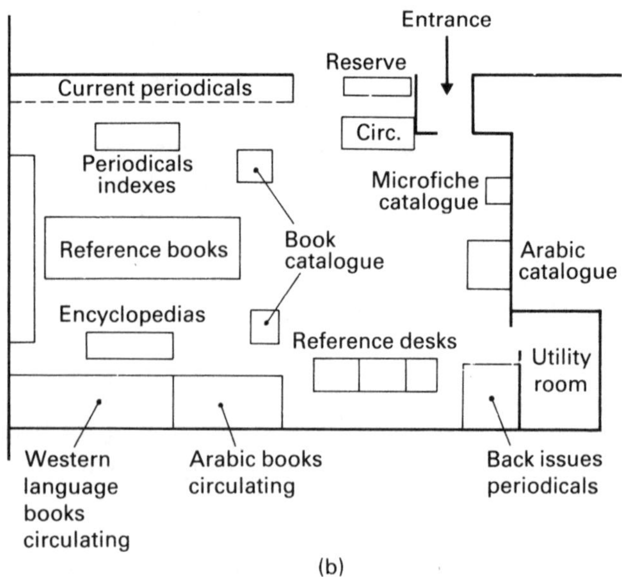

(b)

Figure 6.4 *Floor plans, Men's Medical Library, King Faisal University, Dammam, Saudi Arabia*

Table 6.1 *Reading areas, University of Karachi library, Pakistan*

Type of reading room	Seating capacity
Science	350
Social Science	180
Reference	80
History and oriental	260
Research	25
Documents	30
Periodicals	55
Total seating for readers	980

collections were transferred to the central library upon completion of the new building.

However, there are a vast number of university libraries in Sudan, Pakistan, Saudi Arabia and Nigeria which are housed in cramped quarters and provide a negligible amount of seating for an increasing number of users. At some universities, especially in Saudi Arabia, new campuses, including library buildings, are being planned and are due to be completed during the 1980s, while in some poor Islamic countries the lack of finances is hampering any such proposals for new buildings.

The number of students seated should be a certain proportion of the maximum student population that the university intends to enrol during the next twenty years. 'Norms for seating have become arbitrary figures dictated more by exercises involving finance than by any reliable assessment of actual needs.'[56] The National University of Malaysia, where the library moved to its newly built premises in 1982, accommodates 3,500 readers in its 220,000 square feet of floor space. It comprises four floors, and one of the floors is occupied by the audio-visual division, with viewing theatres, a master control room and a microfilm laboratory. A shortage of seating accommodation prevails in the University of Jordan library (750 seats), University of Al-Gezira library, Sudan (286 seats), King Faisal University library, Dammam (60 seats), Islamic University, Bahawalpur (126 seats) and the Islamic University, Islamabad (50 seats). In fact, in Pakistan, 'most of the university libraries do not have their own buildings and those which have, are not constructed keeping in view the

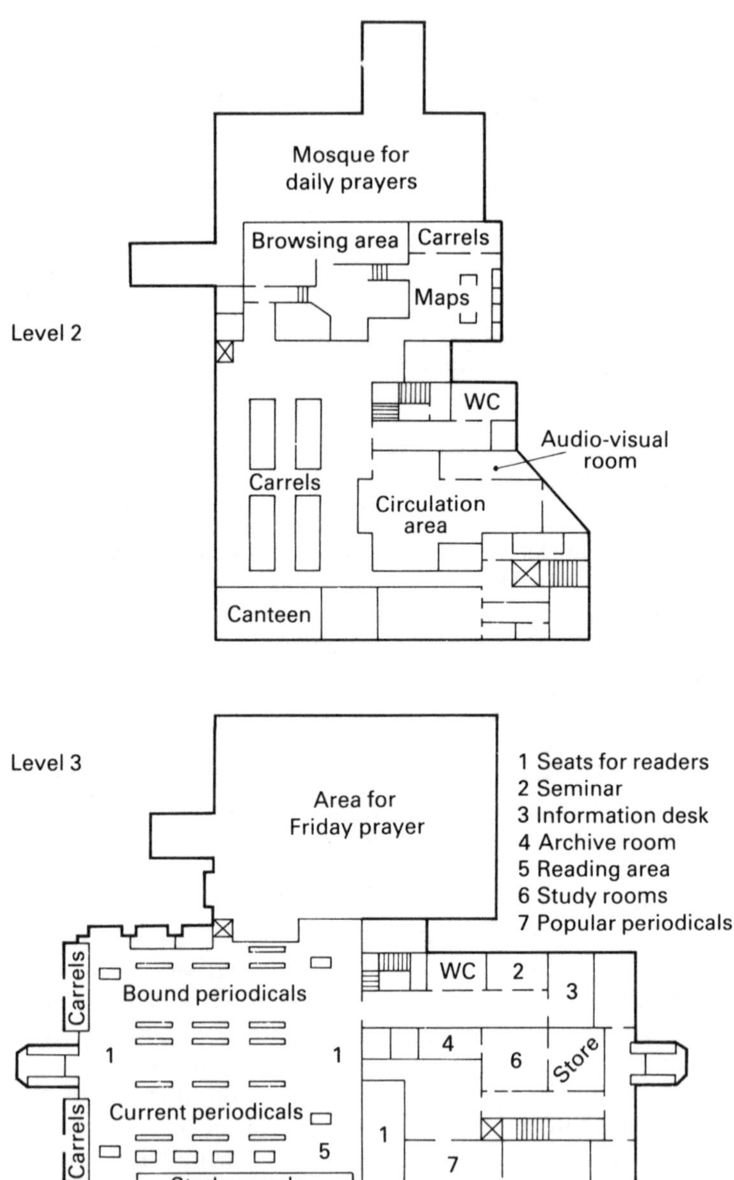

(a) Levels 2 and 3

Figure 6.5 *Floor plan, National University of Malaysia library*

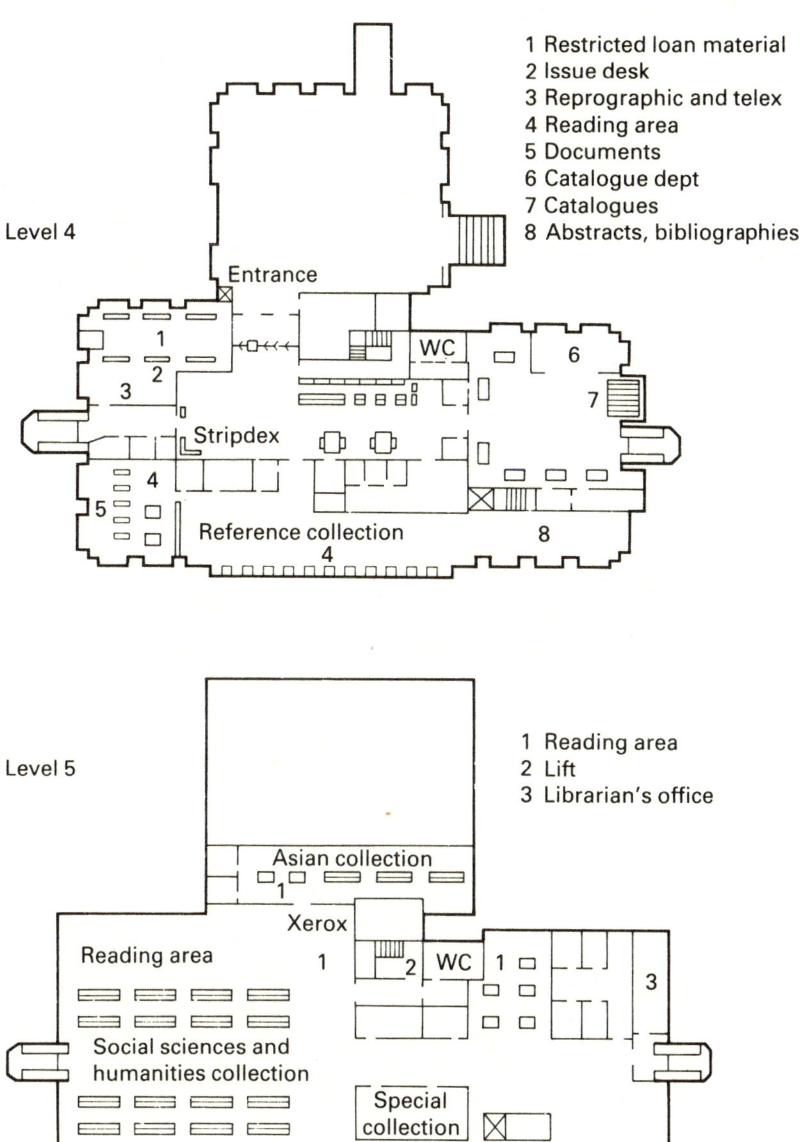

(b) Levels 4 and 5

Table 6.2 *Seating capacity in university libraries*

Country	Library	Reader seats	Carrels	Cubicles	Year erected
Kuwait	University of Kuwait	2,702	675	–	1966
Jordan	Yarmouk University	1,000	200	–	1979
Nigeria	Ahmadu Bello University	2,000	24	–	1976
	University of Jos	2,000	–	–	under construction
Malaysia	Technological University of Malaysia	1,000	41	–	1982
	University of Agriculture	1,900	56	–	1974
	National University of Malaysia	1,500	–	36	1975
	Universiti Sains Malaysia	1,300	30	–	1979

requirements of a modern library . . . the buildings are not functional at all.'[57] It is understood that all university libraries fail to make an adequate provision of places for readers. P. Haward William, while commenting on university library standards, states that 'The number of places will depend on practices in the country concerned. A generally acceptable standard is one reader place for every four students in English speaking countries.'[58] Mason suggests '20 per cent of the maximum student body at one time for resident campuses; 10 per cent for commuting institutions'.[59] The University Grants Commission in the United Kingdom believes that there should be one seat for every five science undergraduates, one seat for every three arts undergraduates, one seat for every three postgraduate science students and one seat for each postgraduate arts student.[60]

In view of the financial limitations with which most developing countries are confronted, and cultural, religious, sociological and environmental factors, it is logical to suggest a minimum seating capacity for university libraries, irrespective of type of readers. Although, it would be ideal to provide over 30 per cent of students and staff with reader places, the minimum standard is seating for one-quarter of the total undergraduate and postgraduate student population. Individual study carrels and cubicles for research students and teaching staff should also be given top priority. Reading space at the ratio of one place for every ten academic and administrative staff should also be provided. This ratio does not imply that faculty members will use the library less than students, but rather that they will to a great extent want to use library materials in their offices.

As we examine the number of reader places and students in the universities of Pakistan, we observe that the University of Agriculture, having a new building, caters more adequately for the needs of users and provides more seats for readers than all other universities in the country. It has made available one seat for every 2.4 students. The University of Engineering and Technology, Lahore, has seating capacity for 250 readers, or one seat for every ten students. Both the University of the Punjab, Lahore, and Quaid-e-Azam University libraries have a very low seating capacity, which is largely due to the fact that they have decentralized library systems and their departmental libraries are also used by students. During the last twenty years, the number of students has increased rapidly, but the number of reading places in most university libraries has remained unchanged. Unlike university libraries in Kuwait and Malaysia, it is not the common practice to provide separate study rooms, like cubicles at the King Abdulaziz University, Jeddah, for faculty members or research scholars.

Different standards for seating accommodation have been put forward by professional librarians. Metcalf has categorized reader space thus:

25 sq. ft. per undergraduate student
30 sq. ft. per graudate student
35 sq. ft. per visiting scholar
70 sq. ft. per faculty member[61]

Jean Bleton recommends that '3 square metres of floor space per reader for seating accommodation may perhaps suffice for reading rooms used by students who need to keep only a few volumes or reference books on their desks'.[62] For special material users, such as maps, a minimum of 10 square feet space should be provided per map user.[63]

To avoid complications in working out space for users, the space for each reader should be calculated on the basis of 30 to 40 square feet, although a higher standard is preferable. Similarly, one in every three postgraduate students should be provided with study carrels where they can leave their research materials on their individual tables, with an adjacent chair and bookcases. If the library is to be used by architectural students, who have to use a large table to spread plans, graphs, and drawings, it is necessary to allow 50 square feet of space for each carrel. Additionally, cubicles for research students or faculty members engaged in extensive research ought to be provided in the library. The ideal study situation, albeit an expensive one, is an individual room of at least 60 square feet, specially designed with a large desk, chair and bookshelf.

Observations suggest that rectangular tables are ideal for study, whereas circular tables may be placed in the relaxation areas near the entrance. Tables are supplied in various sizes, but the most commonly used tables have accommodation for two, four or six readers. At Yarmouk University library[64] and at the King

Abdulaziz University library, there are four-seater tables. Likewise, the King Faisal University library, Dammam, also provides four-seater tables, although some readers spread out their materials in such a way that a four-seater table can hardly be used by another reader. In a university library which has a large number of postgraduate and research students '90 per cent of the small tables may be carrels'.[65] Carrels are useful and convenient, as they are connected with the stacks and require a minimum of cubic footage.[66] Great care should be taken in choosing chairs, as uncomfortable chairs discourage users. All chairs, with or without arms, must fit under tables. Chairs that swivel and roll, as at the University of Petroleum and Minerals library, are best for using microform readers and computer terminals.[67]

The library personnel unit

This unit includes space requirements for the office of the dean of library affairs or director of the university library, deputy librarian, subject specialist librarians, reference librarian, serials librarian and staff in the technical services department. The chief librarian's office needs 400 square feet of space, whereas, for a deputy librarian's office, 200 square feet would suffice, provided provision is made in the library for a meeting room where members of the library staff regularly meet to discuss matters relating to the library activities. The subject specialist librarians' office should be situated adjacent to the reading areas and bookstacks related to their field of specialization. The space required for this purpose should be 150 square feet.

In a staff workroom, where operations such as typing, preparing stencils, photocopying, etc., are carried out, each member of staff should be allocated 100 square feet of space. Likewise, for members carrying out the preparation of books for the shelves, labelling, stamping, minor repairs of books, and pamphlet binding, the same amount of space per person is needed. Metcalf recommends 150 square feet per person for library working quarters, as well as for cataloguers and acquisitions personnel. To wisely and realistically organize and utilize space in the technical operations unit, a big hall, with the required number of partition walls with openings but no doors, would be an ideal solution. As at the University of Petroleum and Minerals library, Dhahran, partition walls, which are not ceiling-high, divide the work areas for individual staff members. These can be put up, removed, re-used or re-set very easily and allow a great deal of flexibility if and when the interior is redesigned. With these movable partitions, nothing is permanently fastened to the floor. Normally made of plaster-board, they are sold in different heights, ranging from 2 feet 6 inches and 3 feet 6 inches to 5 feet 4 inches. The system of workroom partitioning is exceptionally good for university libraries. Optimum utilization of floor space and flexibility in design are the two salient features of the panel system. Libraries having limited funds could make use of this system for erecting study carrels.

Other points which deserve attention in the process of planning are the building's walls, ceilings and floors. Some university libraries are designed and built with a uniform ceiling height for all areas. Others have a ceiling 7 feet 6 inches high in the bookstack areas and a ceiling of varying height, ranging from 9 feet to 15 feet, in the reading areas and the staff workrooms. 'In dual purpose rooms 15 ft. ceilings may be possible.'[68] Although one can make best use of space by 'having lower ceilings in . . . parts of a building',[69] a low ceiling height needs a good forced ventilation system.[70] Without doubt, rooms with high ceilings and large windows add considerably to the operational budget.[71] The ceiling should be demountable, fire-resistant and sound-absorbing. Owing to the operational cost of air-conditioning in the libraries of poor tropical countries, such as Sudan and Pakistan, and less fortunate countries, such as Jordan and Nigeria, it is desirable that the height from floor to ceiling should be at least 8 feet 4 inches or more. Mason suggests a minimum ceiling height of 8 feet 6 inches, but a ceiling height of over 9 feet 6 inches should be avoided, except where a special effect is called for.[72] It is advisable to shade readers from the sun's rays by means of louvres. For interior partitions, metal, glass or plaster-board may be used to give the flexibility so important in library design. It is also vital to provide a structure that is strong enough to withstand heavy floor loads, so that the bookshelves can be placed anywhere. A live load figure for standard bookshelving is 125 lbs per square foot.

Lighting requirements

University libraries are illuminated by both artificial and natural light. In warmer countries, excessive natural light brings with it unbearable heat, thus causing discomfort for readers. It is believed that reading materials, furniture and floor coverings are not damaged by sunlight. Libraries without windows may have little problems with dust, noise, etc., but certainly deprive students of fresh air and daylight which is necessary for students from poor developing countries that cannot afford the installation of air-conditioning systems. Readers prefer to sit facing windows rather than solid brick walls. It is intimidating, even, to have very high windows in the library, thereby denying readers the chance of opening these to enjoy a cool breeze on a hot summer day. To prevent sunlight entering the building in abundance, particularly in summer, Venetian blinds may be used. In a multi-storey building, upper floors can be protected from the sun by a pierced screen attached to the inner wall. This has been done successfully at the Ahmadu Bello University library, Nigeria.

There are different areas in the library which require different levels of lighting. For instance, in bookstack areas, one would need relatively more lighting than in other areas. A variety of lighting systems are in use in various libraries. Some use incandescent light; this is costly and short-lived, but installation is simple. This system is in operation at the Dag Hammarskjold library of the United Nations in New York.

The most commonly used illumination system in university libraries is fluorescent, which has a longer life-span and creates a congenial atmosphere for study. With an incandescent lighting system, it is possible to replace a burnt bulb with the wrong type of bulb, as they all easily fit. But with fluorescent tubes, such mistakes do not occur because of the type of fixture. Diffused and scattered light is preferable in libraries, and fluorescent lights fall in this category. Bad lighting causes readers undue strain and fatigue and becomes a source of irritation.

All lighting experts agree that '5-foot candles are insufficient for ordinary browsing or reading, and 15-foot candles are insufficient for study'.[73] Mason specifies that 'rare book stacks and reading rooms require special lighting'.[74] Long strips of very bright fluorescent lights are not suitable for libraries; diffusers that help to spread the light vertically must be used. However, 60-foot candles are fairly satisfactory for reading areas.

To increase the level of lighting, the colour of furniture, carpet, walls and ceilings plays a significant part. Light-absorbent colours, including green, brown, black, red and pale blue, should be avoided as far as possible. Shining surfaces create glare and disturb readers. Light colours for all the interior furnishings must be chosen so as to eliminate or at least minimize glare. Floodlights surrounding the exterior of the university library building are aesthetically pleasing.

To sum up, the building design should admit considerable natural light. An adequate level of illumination, whether artificial or natural, is most important. According to British Library standards, table top illumination should be 40 lumens per square foot. It should be remembered that in most Western countries cloudy conditions throughout the year necessitate increased artificial lighting in libraries, whereas in most African, Arab and South Asian countries, sunlight is a major source of illumination in daytime, but at night the same standard of lighting will have to be provided. Finally, in addition to a local switch, it should be possible to switch all lights off by a single switch, to avoid the inconvenience of turning off many switches at closing time.

Climatology

To successfully plan a university library building, especially in tropical countries, a knowledge of climatic and atmospheric conditions is imperative. As we examine the climates of Saudi Arabia, Pakistan, Malaysia, Jordan, Sudan, Kuwait, Nigeria and Qatar, it is observed that in certain countries the climate is extremely hot and dry, with temperatures rising to 120°F. In some countries, the climate is humid and relatively warm, while others are quite cold. The architect and the librarian should have complete climatic data available to facilitate the planning process, since temperature, relative humidity and rainfall have a consider-able impact on the design and erection of the library building. Table 6.2 shows climatic information related to the eight countries studied.[75]

In most of these countries, the average maximum daily

156

Table 6.3 *Climatic data*

Location	Average maximum temperature (°F)	Average minimum temperature (°F)	Average humidity %		Latitude	Longitude	Altitude (ft)
			Morning	Afternoon			
Saudi Arabia							
Jeddah	92	73	56	55	21.28 N	39.10 E	20
Riyadh	90	63	54	32	24.39 N	46.42 E	1,938
Kuwait	85	69	64	55	29.21 N	48 E	16
Jordan	74	52	58	38	31.57 N	35.57 E	2,548
Qatar (Doha)	98	62	n.a.	n.a.	25.17 N	51.32 E	n.a.
Sudan							
Khartoum	99	71	38	21	15.37 N	32.33 E	1,279
Pakistan							
Karachi	84	72	80	60	24.48 N	66.59 E	13
Lahore	89	61	62	39	31.35 N	74.20 E	702
Malaysia							
Penang	90	74	77	67			
Kuala Lumpur	90	73	96	63	3.10 N	101.42 E	127
Nigeria (Ibadan)	88	71	96	65	7.26 N	3.54 E	626

temperature is recorded between 84°F and 99°F, although in some places, in certain months of the year, the temperature might be much higher. For instance, Kuwait (104°F in August),[76] Riyadh, Saudi Arabia (107°F in June to August),[77] Lahore, Pakistan (106°F in June),[78] and Khartoum, Sudan (107°F in May)[79] witness extremely hot weather in summer. In Jordan, however, the hottest month is August, with temperatures rising to 90°F.

Rainfall varies because of the tremendous geographical diversity. The total average annual rainfall in Jordan is 10.9 inches and the wettest months are November (1.3 inches), December (1.8 inches), January (2.7 inches), February (2.9 inches) and March (1.2 inches). The driest months include June, July and August. In Karachi, Pakistan, the average rainfall is 7.7 inches. The wettest months are July (3.2 inches) and August (1.6 inches) and the driest months are April, May, October, November and January. In Lahore, another city in Pakistan, the average annual rainfall is 19.8 inches. The wettest months are July (5.5 inches) and August (5.3 inches) and the driest months from October to February. In Sudan, the climate comprises the deserts of the north, where rainfall is minimal, a semi-arid belt in the central plains, and rainfall up to 60 inches in the southern parts of the country.[80]

Saudi Arabia is situated in the arid part of the Middle East and is affected by a Mediterranean climate in the north and a monsoon climate in the south. The average annual rainfall in Jeddah is only 2.5 inches, although in other parts of the country the amount of rainfall varies greatly. On the other hand, in Nigeria, the rainfall in Ibadan averages 44.1 inches and in the wettest months ranges from 4.9 inches (April) to 6.7 inches (September). In Malaysia, annual rainfall in Penang is 107.7 inches, the wettest months being October (16.9 inches), September (15.8 inches), November (11.9 inches) and May (10.7 inches). In Kuala Lumpur the average annual rainfall is 96.1 inches.

Sudan and Nigeria have tropical climates and temperatures do not vary around the year, although the relative humidity in Ibadan is much higher than in Khartoum. Jordan has a distinctly Mediterranean climate with rainfall in winter and dry spells in summer. One has to allow for heating in winter, as it is fairly cold in the winter months. Malaysia is highly tropical and has very wet periods throughout the year. Both Kuala Lumpur (Malaysia) and Ibadan (Nigeria) have relative humidity as high as 96 per cent, followed by Karachi with 80 per cent. At 70 per cent relative humidity or higher, moulds and micro-fungi grow, and damage paper. Also, high humidity develops moisture. It is vital that good air-conditioning in libraries is installed in order to offset the high temperatures and high humidity. Air-conditioning helps in cooling the air and taking off moisture. Saudi Arabia, Qatar and Kuwait have very hot and dry climates, with relative humidity ranging from 32 per cent in Riyadh to 64 per cent in Kuwait. In Sudan, Khartoum is believed to have the lowest and highest relative humidity, i.e. 38 per cent in the morning and 21 per cent in the afternoons. While temperatures reflect the radiation climate, precipitation is the direct consequence of atmospheric motion. In any case, the relative humidity must not be more than 40 per cent throughout the year. It should be borne in mind that 'computer rooms have a very low tolerance of humidity and temperature variations, which warp the data contained on their tapes and interfere with the handling of IBM cards'. Special machines designed for computer rooms, variously sized for different capacity rooms, can be used for rare book stacks and reading rooms. Their ability to closely control variations in humidity and temperature are ideally suited to the requirements of rare book areas.[81]

The maximum temperature for human comfort is believed to be between 70 and 75°F.[82] Dry climates occur in low, as well as higher, latitudes. In the northern hemisphere, the more northern the latitude the weaker the sun and the colder the climate. The more southerly the latitude, the stronger the sun and hotter the climate. Also, the more northern the latitutde, the longer the daylight in summer and the shorter the daylight in winter. Temperature falls with altitude; that is, the higher the altitude, the colder the climate. Every 300 feet above sea level results in a 10°F drop in temperature. Of the countries studied, Jordan has the highest recorded altitude, i.e. over 2,500 feet above sea level, whereas Jeddah, Saudi Arabia (20 feet), Kuwait (16 feet) and Karachi, Pakistan (13 feet), have the lowest altitude amongst the tropical countries.[83] In planning a library, atmospheric conditions are less significant than climatic ones. If the altitude is higher, atmospheric pressure will be lower.

In wet climates, such as in most parts of Malaysia, some parts of Pakistan, Nigeria and mountainous areas in other countries which tend to have heavy rainfall, the library building should be waterproof and well protected from the risk of flooding, especially if the library is in the vicinity of a river or stream. Ground floors of such buildings should be erected a few feet above the ground and a damp course between the foundations and the walls should be properly installed.

In the climatic conditions which prevail in the different countries described above, complete or partial air-conditioning, humidification, de-humidification and ventilation are essential for the library buildings. Air-conditioning which maintains the internal library temperature around 60 to 70°F and humidity around 50 per cent is considered ideal for the optimum comfort of readers. For example, the University of Petroleum and Minerals library, Dhahran, has installed an all-round air-conditioning and humidity control system. The system is a sophisticated one which helps to remove the moisture and to heat the air to a comfortable temperature.[84] The library also has an adequate ventilation system. The University of Malaysia library and the National University of Malaysia library have provided total air-conditioning, the latter having four centrally air-conditioned floors.[85] Likewise, in most universities in rich Arab Islamic countries, such as Qatar, Kuwait and Saudi Arabia, the libraries are fully air-conditioned. But in other countries, as in Nigeria at Ibadan University library, they tend to rely on natural ventilation and use fans for human comfort.[86] Similarly, most of the university libraries in Pakistan and Sudan make use of ceiling fans, since they cannot afford either to purchase air-conditioning systems or to operate them, since running costs are beyond the financial capability of these libraries. In Pakistan, the University of Agriculture library is fully air-conditioned. The University of Engineering and Technology library, Lahore, moved to its new three-storey building in June 1976.[87] It is located in the centre of the university campus.[88] The reading hall is equipped with three air-conditioners which are not in operation, due to shortage of funds. A well-known architect, W. R. Court, planned the library building of Abdullahi Bayero College, Kano, Nigeria with sealed windows; water tanks are placed under the roof of the library, where 'the water will have a cooling effect, and with an air cooling system whereby relatively cool night air may be drawn at roof level and filtered to remove dust'.[89] Some libraries have partial air-conditioning in the libraries.

At the University of Ilorin library in Nigeria, 'although air-conditioners have been installed in the Research Reading Rooms, after persistent demands by library users, it has not been possible to put them to use because of problems created by low voltage and general fluctuations in power supply'.[90] The university library had three split air-conditioners installed in April 1981 for the comfort of readers, but the Nigerian voltage of 180, instead of 220–240, prevented their use.

It is useful to have exhaust fans in the ceiling to remove the heat produced by electric lights and the presence of readers. Also, slow operating centrifugal fans extract hot air from the building, especially in summer, and help to keep the building cool. Library buildings should be designed with overhanging roofs and shaded walkways to encourage cool breezes and protect exterior surfaces.[91] The other significant point in designing the library building in hot climates is to consider the north, south, east and west sides. Sunrays fall on to the south side at an oblique angle and the building gains relatively less heat, whereas sunrays fall horizontally on the west side and it gains excessive heat. 'The unfortunate exposure to afternoon sun'[92] is another reason why the architect might need to change the position of the building. Also, large glass windows produce tremendous heat; these must be avoided, particularly on the west side of the building. The north side will get least sunlight, so one may have windows to let in fresh air, without gaining intense heat. On the east side, small windows may have wooden shutters or Venetian blinds, which can be drawn when excessive heat enters through windows and creates human discomfort. Consequently, proper atmospheric conditions, in terms of temperature, humidity, and removal of dust and other impurities in the air, are essential, both for the protection of the library materials and the comfort and concentration of readers.

Elimination of noise and other amenities

The library building must be protected against fire because the burning of a library building means a loss of knowledge. Also an automatic detector system is more effective when the building is unoccupied, as it is heat- or smoke-activated.[93] An automatic sprinkler system can also help to put out the fire, as long as it is not on a huge scale, in which case the services of a fire-brigade will have to be sought. Moreover, emergency exits should be planned for use as escape routes in case of such incidents.

The areas of the library where conversation has to be carried on, that is, the circulation desk, reference desk, etc., and where noise may be produced by equipment such as photocopying machines and typewriters, should be properly located. Special attention needs to be paid to sound-proofing against external noise, and double glazing is advocated. Interior noise can be reduced by soft furnishing and carpeting which is resilient and esthetically pleasing. In the University of Agriculture library, Faisalabad, interior noise has been reduced by completely carpeting the library. Roger Stoakley states that 'the exterior encourages the public to enter and the interior induces them to stay and explore its resources'.[94]

As many readers can be expected to want to remain in the library for long periods, lavatory and bathroom facilities should be provided, preferably near the entrance. This provision has been made by several university libraries, including the University of Agriculture, Pakistan, and King Abdulaziz University, Saudi Arabia. Readers should be able to obtain drinking water in the library. If the library has to be on more than one floor, the position of stairs should not hinder the movement of readers. One defect in the library building of the University of Agriculture in Pakistan is that there is no lift, which makes the transportation of books extremely difficult.

Since the university library is regarded as an institution of tremendous significance, a site for the building should be chosen with extreme care and wisdom. Keeping in view the fact that it will cater for the accommodation of readers, staff and materials for the next twenty years, provision should be made in terms of square footage for further structural expansion. It is desirable to plan from the outset a modular building which automatically permits both flexibility and expansion.

Chapter 7

Coordination and mobilization

Resource coordination

The coordination of resources is considered to be one avenue of eliminating the wasteful multiplication of printed and non-printed information. It also implies the sharing of available facilities, such as technology, equipment, manpower, skills and services. Mobilization entails maximizing the utility and rapid availability of materials and improving access to the holdings of university libraries participating in a loosely designed, coordinated network. The desire to be self-sufficient has long been abandoned by university libraries in Western countries, largely because of budgetary curtailments, an excessive amount of published literature, readers' diversified information and research needs, storage problems and, above all, the inflationary prices of both documentation and audio-visual resources.

In poor Arab Islamic countries, where university libraries have deficient collections, meagre funds, unsuitable and inadequate premises and a lack of sufficient qualified personnel, the need to cooperate and share is of paramount importance. University libraries in rich Arab Islamic countries do not face some of the problems shared by university libraries in Western, as well as poor Arab Islamic countries. None the less, they lack professionally trained staff, a participative mechanism and the genuine desire to initiate and lead such cooperative ventures at national levels or actively contribute to international schemes of coordination.

In the USA, several cooperative networks have developed because of the desire to achieve economies.[1] These are a means of relieving pressure on the library budget for salaries, materials and other operating expenditures.[2] The expansion of intellectual demands and the rising cost of library operations are the forces responsible for the development of cooperative activities.[3] University libraries cannot operate as isolated entities and ways must be explored for a library to 'cooperate with other libraries without impairing its own efficiency – indeed with a view to extending and improving its own services'.[4] In the United Kingdom, cooperation among libraries is very popular. It traditionally takes two forms, 'the first involving the interloan of materials, the second the peregrination of scholars to where the material is located'.[5] The latter method is totally impracticable and ineffective in Arab Islamic countries, where research students are unlikely to travel far and wide in search of information. The former method, simply involving inter-library lending on a limited basis, is a very familiar practice in many countries. The barriers which hinder or prevent the introduction of networks amongst university libraries include:

1 deficient postal systems
2 unreliable telephone services
3 insufficient and improperly trained manpower
4 lack of bibliographical apparatus, union catalogues, etc.
5 incompatible processing of materials
6 non-availability of telex installations
7 size of library collections
8 lack of financial allocations to bear the cost of coordination
9 negative attitudes to resource sharing
10 lack of a national body to oversee, coordinate and build up networking
11 lack of student enthusiasm for intensive study and research
12 reluctance of large libraries to participate, because of the danger of being over-utilized without compensation

Gelfand has expressly remarked that the 'largest libraries must engage in co-operative activities to augment their resources, for today it is impossible for any library to be absolutely comprehensive in all fields'.[6] The Regional Seminar on Bibliography, Documentation and Exchange of Publications in Latin America, held in Mexico in 1960, also stresed that 'there should be a co-ordination of and broader cooperation among the university libraries'.[7]

University library cooperative practices, with regard to Arab Islamic countries, may be considered under the following heads: interlending activities, telecommunication networks, bibliographical resources and exchange services, and cooperative acquisition systems.

Interlending activities

As early as 1876, Samuel Green proposed that the libraries must remain dependent upon each other in fulfilling the requirements of readers and this could be achieved if books from one library could be issued to the members of other libraries.[8] Alma Jordan recommended an inter-library loan service as an economic and fruitful means for library improvement.[9] James Thompson believes that 'of all the types of cooperative activity, interlibrary lending is the most important'.[10] In Nigeria, libraries have made arrangements whereby each library is prepared to lend to the others and all university libraries open their doors to non-university persons who are regarded as serious readers. University libraries also offer photo-print and microfilm services to help others.[11] An interlending service within the country comprises, in its simplest form, the lending of reading materials to outsiders on an individual basis, the supply of photocopies of parts of documents and articles to other libraries, the supply of microfilm and microfiche of materials to requesting libraries and the lending of documents to other libraries – all for the use of readers. Several university libraries in Nigeria, which include the Universities of Jos, Ibadan, Calabar, Ilorin, Ife and Ahmadu Bello, supply photocopies to requesting libraries. In the academic year 1980–1, for example, the University of Ilorin library sent out requests for books to a number of other universities, most of which were met by the University of Ife library and Ibadan University library, although the latter could not lend works from its reserved Africana collection. Photocopies of articles in periodicals not held in the library are ordered from other libraries both within or outside the country. In one year, the readers of the University of Ilorin were provided with fifty-seven photocopied articles from abroad and thirty-three others, mainly from Ibadan and Ilorin University libraries. Broadly speaking,

> contrary to expectation, we depend more on overseas libraries
> for filling our photocopy requests than on the local libraries for
> various reasons. Firstly, some of the journals from which
> articles were requested are not held by local libraries. Secondly,
> the inability of local libraries to fill requests promptly, even
> where they held the journals.[12]

This was either due to the fact that the journal could not be located
on the shelves, or the non-availability of photocopying paper, or
even the machine itself being out of order. Under such circumstances, it was preferable to contact the British Library Lending
Division at Boston Spa, rather than waiting indefinitely under
unpredictable local conditions.

The situation in some Arab Islamic countries like Saudi Arabia,
Kuwait, Jordan and Qatar is not too dissimilar regarding interlending services. According to Dr Abdullah Isa, 'interlibrary loan
services are provided at three of the seven university libraries in
Saudi Arabia'.[13] King Saud University, Riyadh, not only offers
photostat copies of materials but also supplies microfilms and even
microscopic pictures of the desired documentation, subject to
copyright regulations.[14] At the University of Petroleum and
Minerals library, Dhahran, if the required book is not in stock and
cannot be ordered for some reason, the library endeavours to
acquire it for readers through the interlending procedure within
the kingdom or from abroad. 'Photocopy requests for journal
articles not available in the UPM library can be obtained from
major European Institutions within two weeks.'[15] Within the
Eastern Province of Saudi Arabia, the University of Petroleum
and Minerals library, King Faisal University library and ARAMCO
library have made a reciprocal arrangement whereby readers are
entitled to borrow materials from any of these libraries. The Saudi
Arabian National Centre for Science and Technology, based in the
capital, Riyadh, tremendously helps the universities to supply the
required information.[16] Hundreds of requests for periodical
articles, theses and technical reports are processed at the centre
and a prompt service is rendered to the university libraries in the
country. The outstanding performance of the University of
Petroleum and Minerals library can be judged from the fact that
out of 175 requests for items or photocopies in 1980, 168 were

successfully met and, in 1981, 207 requests were received, whereas 187 items were promptly supplied.[17]

There are just two universities in Jordan; both provide each other not only with photocopies of any document or article, but also lend up to fifty books at a time to the requesting library for a period of one month.[18] In addition, readers from one university are permitted to borrow materials from the other university library, in accordance with the rules and regulations in force. The library at the University of Qatar, the only university in the country, is endeavouring to enter into an interlending network whereby several university libraries in the Gulf States would actively participate in sharing resources and services for the mutual benefit of all concerned. Likewise, the University of Kuwait library is the only university library in the country and, as it has enough bookfunds, is striving to acquire almost anything related to the study and research programmes. It has very close ties, however, with the Kuwait Institute for Scientific Research.

Both in Pakistan and Sudan, inter-library cooperation amongst university libraries is in a rudimentary form and, due to lack of funds, libraries cannot even supply photocopies to other requesting libraries. In many instances, readers of one university library are not entitled to borrow books from other libraries. However, in some parts of Pakistan, such as Faisalabad, Lahore and Karachi, universities, colleges and institutes have reached agreements which allow substantial numbers of readers to enjoy the borrowing privileges of several libraries. In Faisalabad, the University of Agriculture, the Nuclear Institute of Agriculture and Biology, and the Punjab Agricultural Research Institute cooperate in the exchange and provision of information.[19] Similarly, there is the reciprocal arrangement for making available photocopied materials by three libraries in Lahore, namely, the University of Engineering and Technology, the Pakistan Council of Scientific and Industrial Research and the Pakistan Institute of Nuclear Science and Technology. The major problem for most university libraries in poor countries is the non-availability of photocopying machines, and the facility for the production of periodical articles on microfilm or microfiche is almost non-existent.

In Malaysia, inter-library loan services are very well developed and there is appreciable unity among all the five university libraries in the country, along with the National Library which is responsible for coordinating their lending activities and participates vigorously itself in fulfilling the demands of university libraries and acting as a library of last resort. Moreover, university libraries have devoted their energies, resources and efforts to devising a very comprehensive cooperative acquisition and processing programme which will be discussed later in this chapter.

An effective and workable lending network at the national level requires the preparation of an inter-library loan code which must not damage the interests of the university's own reader population. An essential ingredient of such a joint code should be to safeguard and protect each library's right to refuse the lending of materials which they may think are rare, invaluable, fragile and difficult to replace in the event of damage, mutilation or loss.

Numerous national and international conferences held in Arab Islamic countries have paid attention to the issue of inter-library loan coordination without any apparent success. In 1980, the Conference of Saudi Librarians was held from 5–8 April by King Saud University, Riyadh, and amongst the topics under discussion was inter-library cooperation. In the same year, i.e. 15–19 March 1980, the Kuwait Institute for Scientific Research also organized a conference in which cooperation among the Gulf States was considered. Yet again, during 9–10 January 1982, a conference organized by the Arab Bureau of Education for the Gulf States was held in Riyadh; it also paid attention to the issue of inter-library cooperation, but these conferences have not so far produced fruitful results.

Telecommunication networks

Computers, telexes, telephones, postal services, railroad transportation, cargo services, sea routes and airways are all part of national communication networks. The transmission of inter-library loan messages requires good and uninterrupted telephone facilities in all university libraries. To ensure that the message is accurately conveyed and interpreted precisely at the other end, telex installations might be more practical. The urgency of telex communications cannot be misunderstood. To despatch documents destined for another university library located at a considerable distance, very reliable postal services are desirable.

168

In poor countries, university libraries have an ineffective telephone system restricted to local usage, telex services are unheard of, postal systems are extremely deficient and railway transporation is very slow and cannot be depended upon. Under such circumstances, one could not even consider setting up a coordinated network to develop the mobilization and sharing of resources, either locally or nationally. In Pakistan and Sudan, there is an urgent need to improve postal and telephone services. Even in Nigeria, bad roads, an ineffective postal system and telephone network can obstruct the development of cooperative schemes.[20] The communication network amongst university libraries was recently overhauled and substantially improved. At present, the libraries of the University of Lagos and the University of Ibadan have an automated circulation system. In addition, three of the university libraries, namely the University of Ibadan, Ahmadu Bello University and the University of Jos, are linked through telex installations which help convey messages with admirable efficiency. Many other university libraries are either planning or in the process of installing telex systems. Computer centres have also been established in some universities, including the University of Ibadan (IBM 370/135 and IBM 1620), Ahmadu Bello University (CYBER 72 & ICL 1901 A), the University of Lagos (IBM 1620 and IBM 370/145), the University of Ife (IBM/25) and the University of Benin.[21] One of the remarkable developments in the sphere of postal networks is the introduction of a courier service among all the thirteen university libraries in Nigeria. At first, this service was limited to the routes beween Benin, Ibadan and Ile-Ife, but the network has been expanded to cover the entire country and all the university libraries.[22] The routes are:

Lagos – Ibadan – Ilorin – Zaria
Zaria – Kano – Maiduguri – Jos – Sokoto
Ibadan – Ife – Benin – Port Harcourt – Calabar
Enugu – Nsukka

A courier system is an excellent and economical method of communicating messages and documents within the interlending arrangements.

Unlike Nigeria, Saudi Arabia has no courier service and the postal system, as pointed out in the *Third Development Plan*

1981–85, needs a great deal of improvement.[23] However, the Saudi government is bent on a massive and elaborate plan to radically develop both the railway and airmail systems. Even today, Saudi Arabian universities are not far behind in their ambitious targets for the acquisition and utilization of computer technology, as is evident from the fact that all three major universities in the kingdom, King Saud University, King Abdulaziz University and the University of Petroleum and Minerals, have large computer centres. King Abdulaziz University has acquired computers (IBM 3031 and PDP 11/70), but library operations are not so far automated. 'The on-line searching facilities at the UPM through . . . Lockheed's DIALOG and SDC'S ORBIT, both of California, has accelerated the interlending activity.'[24] Once telex and other transmission channels are established in the university libraries of Saudi Arabia, it would be entirely up to the library management to visualize the benefits in designing and implementing networking operations.

More sophisticated telecommunication systems are in existence in one Islamic country on the continent of Asia. The Malaysian peninsula is connected to its eastern states of Sabah and Sarawak by satellite and undersea cables.[25] Malaysian university libraries are staffed with high-calibre personnel who make full use of the available telecommunication facilities in order to promote and strengthen the interlending network within the country. At present all university libraries and the National Library of Malaysia are linked by telex, and this has increased their capability to exchange information. Although there is a van circulating service from the National Library to the University of Agriculture and National University of Malaysia on three days a week, interlibrary lending is rather minimal. Perhaps this is because of the poor response to requests made by the libraries.

Bibliographical resources and exchange services

Inter-library loan networks are universally accepted as a means of augmenting the usefulness of library resources and extending lending privileges to those who do not have physical access to the centres of learning. But no loan network can be successfully envisaged without up-to-date bibliographical information about the holdings of participants. The first and foremost step in each country is the existence of a body designated as a legal depository, responsible for the production of a national bibliography and a national union catalogue of all the university library collections.

In many Arab Islamic countries, like Saudi Arabia, Kuwait, Jordan and Sudan, there are no national libraries in the real sense and no legal depositories; this makes the designing and functioning of interlending networks somewhat complex. Lack of union lists, union catalogues, indexing and abstracting publications, subject bibliographies and national bibliographies also renders the operations of cooperative networks virtually impossible. The First Conference of Saudi Librarians, which was held at the King Saud University, Riyadh, emphasized the resuscitation of the national library and 'stressed the publication of a national bibliography without which bibliographical control over the intellectual output of the nation is inconceivable'.[26] Dr Abdulaziz Al-Nahari, in his Ph.D. thesis, also identified the importance of a national union catalogue, which he believed would 'facilitate cooperation among Saudi libraries in the form of an interlibrary lending system'.[27] Likewise, Dr Saleh Ashoor, dean of library affairs, University of Petroleum and Minerals library, proclaimed the necessity for a national library 'which can maintain a national union catalogue, a national bibliography'.[28] However, the Saudi National Library has been founded in Riyadh, and bibliographical publications are issued by some universities and institutes in the country. The University of Petroleum and Minerals Library, Dhahran, has produced several bibliographical works, which include *Bibliography on Management, 1981*, and the *UPM Library Accessions List*. The latter is a monthly list of new books and periodicals added to the library. Amongst the earliest bibliographies covering works about Saudi Arabia published abroad, was one entitled *Mu'jam al-Matbu'at al-Sat'udiyah*. It was prepared by Shukri al-Anani and published in Riyadh by the Ministry of Education in 1973. In addition, the King Saud University library staff have been very instrumental in issuing and distributing freely, to other libraries in the country, the following bibliographical products:

1 *Union List of Periodicals* (non-Arabic), 3rd edn, 1980
2 *Accessions List* (quarterly) (both Arabic and English)

3 *Catalogue of the Library of Omar Bin Hassan el-Sheikh*
4 *Catalogue of Manuscripts of the University of Riyadh*. No. 4:
   Hadith, Prophet's Traditions and Related Disciplines, 1980

There is a very comprehensive list of King Saud University library publications appended to the *Directory of Libraries in Saudi Arabia*.[29]

Resource-sharing entails convenient bibliographic access to the holdings of participating university libraries. It is, therefore, pertinent to offer regularly produced lists of journals, newsletters, etc., to the other libraries in the scheme. In the Western Province of Saudi Arabia, such practices are prevalent; the University of Petroleum and Minerals library and King Faisal University library exchange computerized lists of periodical holdings.

In the state of Qatar, the National library assumed the responsibility of producing material bibliographies in 1970 and since that time *Kaimat al Intaj al-Fikri al-Qatari* (*Bibliographical Guide to Qatari Literature*) is issued annually with author and title indexes. Owing to the limited amount of literature output, relatively few native authors, an under-developed publishing trade and high printing costs, most of the works included in the national bibliography emanate from ministries and other government departments. In 1972 the National Library also published a *Bibliography of the Arabian Gulf* and issued a second edition in the following year, comprising author and subject indexes. The University of Qatar library issues, fairly infrequently, a list of recent accessions and some subject bibliographies, which are distributed free to those institutions requestion them, particularly in the Arab world.

In the absence of a national library in Jordan, the Jordan Library Association and the University of Jordan library have contributed to the field of bibliographical compilation and publication. The former prepared *Al-Bibliografyia al-Filistiniyah al-Urduniyah 1900–1970* (*The Jordanian–Palestinian Bibliography*). It was published in 1970, in the first issue of an Arabic library journal called *Rissalat al-Maktaba*, and then reissued as a separate publication in 1972.[30] It consisted of 2,740 items, but did not include government publications and books written for schools. The second issue, covering the period up to 1973, was produced in 1974. In 1980, the University of Jordan library turned out a very comprehensive bibliography of all Jordanian publications available in the library. It has a very wide coverage, as it contains all books and theses written about Jordan, pamphlets, statistical reports and official publications, microfilms about Jordan, serials published in the country and literature (drama, poetry, essays, etc.) written by Jordanians. It has author, title and subject indexes. It is anticipated that the University of Jordan library will issue further updates at certain intervals. Again, this is supplied without charge to libraries in other countries.

In Sudan the University of Khartoum leads the field in the bibliographical compilation. It issues the *Sudanese Union Catalogue of Periodicals* and, since 1951, it has been compiling, on behalf of the National Library, a Sudanese bibliography which appears from time to time in *Sudan Notes and Records*.[31] Apart from that, the university library staff have been conscientiously working on the preparation of a catalogue of Sudanese studies in Arabic, and a catalogue of Sudanese collections in the library.

The University of Kuwait library has excelled all records set by numerous university libraries in the Arab world by issuing a series of extremely useful bibliographical publications which include: *Union List of Scientific and Technical Periodicals in Kuwait, 1976, Arab Dissertation Index*,[32] *Source Book on the Arabian Gulf States, Kuwait, Bahrain, Qatar and Oman, 1975*. Other works include:

1 *Selected Bibliography of Kuwait and the Arabian Gulf*, compiled by Soraya M. Kabeel, 1969 (series no. 1)
2 *Selected Bibliography on Kuwait and the Arabian Gulf*, 1970 (series no. 2)
3 *Selected Bibliography on Arab Islamic civilization and its contribution to human progress*, 1970 (series no. 3)
4 *Selected and Annotated Bibliography on Saline Water Conversion*, 1972 (series no. 5)
5 *Selected and Annotated Bibliography on Yemen*, 1973 (bibliography series no. 6)
6 *An Annotated Bibliography on the Industrialization of Proteins from Petroleum and Micro-organisms*, 1977 (series no. 7)
7 a bibliography of the effect of the environmental habitat, structure of cities and their organization, from the engineering point of view, 1978 (series no. 8)

   8 a bibliography on botany, 1978 (series no. 9)
   9 a directory of Arabic periodicals, 1977
  10 a bibliography of Kuwait and the Gulf, 1978

The earliest bibliography since the independence of Pakistan in 1947 was the one entitled *Pakistan, a Select Bibliography*, published in 1951 by the Pakistan Association for the Advancement of Science. The Pakistan Bibliographical Group came into being in 1950 and its products include a *Guide to Works of Reference Published in Pakistan* and a *Guide to Periodical Publications and Newspapers of Pakistan*.[33] Its most laudable achievement was the preparation of a retrospective bibliography, *Pakistan National Bibliography, August 1947 to December 1961*, which was published in 1972. Subsequently, the National Bibliographic Unit of the government's Directorate of Libraries assumed the task of continuing the compilation of the *Pakistan National Bibliography* annually, starting from 1962. The successive issues of this bibliography are being compiled and produced under the leadership of Mr Abdul Hafiz Akhtar, presently project director, National Library of Pakistan. The second biggest source of bibliographical activities is the Pakistan Scientific and Technological Information Centre (PASTIC). Its achievements include the *Directory of Scientific Periodicals of Pakistan, October 1978, List of PASTIC Bibliographies July 1957–June 1978, Index to Theses and Dissertations: Science (Sind Province) 1970–1974*. It also publishes *Pakistan Science Abstracts* quarterly. The University libraries in Pakistan do not make noticeable contributions and only a few of them issue infrequent accession lists or additions to stock and, in view of high postal charges, do not circulate these tools widely.

The bibliographical function in Malaysia was entrusted to the University of Malaysia, which, during 1957–9, published *Ma-lai-ya la-hsueh chung-wen t'u-shu-mu-lu (Catalogue of the Chinese Collection of the University of Malaysia Library)* in three volumes, containing around 130,000 entries. It was not until 1972 that the National Library of Malaysia was founded; five years later it was segregated from the archives unit. It regularly publishes *Bibliografi Negara Malaysia* and the *Malaysian Periodicals Index* and coordinates 'the input of Malaysian agricultural and information materials into AGRIS' (World Agricultural Information Service).[34] However, the university libraries in Malaysia are playing a very

174

active role of great significance in turning out subject bibliographies, accessions lists and periodical directories. Here a few examples of the most recent publications from three of the five universities will suffice.

The Universiti Sains Malaysia has produced:

1 Tang Wan Fong (compiler), *Tesis Danlatihan Ilmiah Di Perpustakaan Universiti Sains Malaysia*, 1981 (theses and academic exercises in the university)
2 *Bibliografi Pendidikan Jerak Jauh* (*Bibliography on Distance Education*), 1981
3 *Bibliografi Alam Sekitar* (*Bibliography of the Environment*), 1980

The Universiti Kebangsaan Malaysia (National University of Malaysia) has produced:

1 *Disertasi Kedoktoran Mengenai Asia Malaysia (1934–1979)*, 1979 (*Doctoral Dissertations on Southeast Asia in the library*), including a list of masters' theses, 1981
2 *Bibliografi Keguruan Perguruan Di Malaysia* (*Bibliography on Teaching and Teacher Training in Malaysia*), 1980

The Perpustakaan Universiti Teknologi Malaysia (Technological University of Malaysia) has produced:

1 *Senarai Bahan – Bahan Tambahan* (*The State, the Family and Education*) by Miriam E. David, 1982

Nigeria, with its substantial Muslim population, is not too different from other Arab Islamic countries in that it also did not have a national library; responsibility for bibliographical control and publications rested with the University of Ibadan library. From 1950 to 1970 Ibadan enjoyed the privilege of being a national depository. It simultaneously commenced publishing a bibliography entitled *Nigerian Publications*. The National Library was set up in Lagos and took over the role of legal depository. The University of Ibadan continued to receive one copy of each book published until it ceased to function as a regional depository because of a new law which made Ahmadu Bello University a depository. Although the National Library was founded in 1962 and officially inaugurated in 1964, it did not assume its full role until 1970. The original title of the bibliography, *Nigerian*

Publications, was changed to *National Bibliography of Nigeria* in 1973. Its bibliographical format was standardized, according to the *British National Bibliography*, in 1976. At first, it was issued weekly with quarterly and annual cumulations, but in 1973 it began monthly publication.[35] Two of the works of the University of Ibadan library deserve a mention. In 1977, it produced a twenty years' cumulation of the national bibliography, *Nigerian Periodicals and Newspapers 1950–1970*.[36] The International Institute of Tropical Agriculture in Nigeria is committed to issuing a *Union List of Scientific and Technical Periodicals in Nigerian Libraries*, a valuable bibliographical tool for resource sharing.[37]

There is an immense need for university libraries in Arab Islamic countries to set up gift and exchange units to maximize the mobilization and transfer of bibliographical and other available resources. Perhaps a formula to compensate university libraries in poor societies might be worked out, so that they may despatch documents irrespective of the cost of postage and packing.

Amongst the eight Arab Islamic countries surveyed the following exchange facilities are readily available for university libraries to strengthen and increase their collections without incurring substantial expense:

Malaysia: National Library of Malaysia, 7th Floor, UMBC
Building, Jalan Sulaiman, Kuala Lumpur
(Head: Encik Saad bin Marzuki)
The National Library, set up in 1971, also acts as a centre for
the exchange of collections and has maintained bilateral
exchange contacts with various universities around the world.
Nigeria: National Library of Nigeria, Serials and Documents
Department, 4 Wesley Street, PMB 12626, Lagos
This department has been functioning since 1970 and arranges
bilateral exchange agreements. They offer government publi-
cations in exchange for periodical publications.
Pakistan:International Book Exchange Centre, c/o Liaquat
Memorial Library, Stadium Road, Karachi-5
(Chief: Abdul Hafeez Akhtar)
This centre operates under the department of libraries and
provides government publications and works on the culture and
history of Pakistan on an exchange basis. It has reached
exchange agreements with a number of countries, including
Australia and the United States.

1 Library building, University of Agriculture, Malaysia

2 Library building, Universiti Sains Malaysia

3 Library building, National University of Malaysia

4 Library building, University of the Punjab, Lahore, Pakistan

5 Library building, University of Karachi, Pakistan

6 Library building, Yarmouk University, Jordan

7 Library building, University of Petroleum and Minerals, Dhahran, Saudi Arabia

8 Library building, Islamic University, Medina, Saudi Arabia

9 Reading area, University of Kuwait library, Kuwait

10 Reading area, King Abdulaziz University library, Jeddah, Saudi Arabia

11 Reading area, Yarmouk University library, Jordan

12 Reading area, King Faisal University library, Dammam, Saudi Arabia

13 Bookstack area, University of Kuwait library, Kuwait

14 Bookstack area, Islamic University, Medina, Saudi Arabia

15 Circulation area, National University of Malaysia library

16 Circulation area, University of Ilorin, Nigeria

17 Reprographic services, University of Jordan library, Jordan

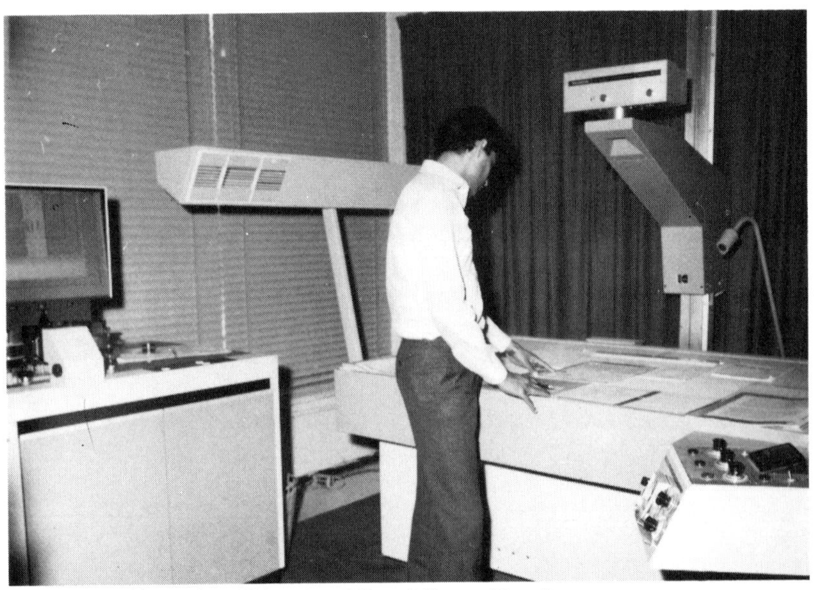

18 Reprographic services, University of Kuwait library, Kuwait

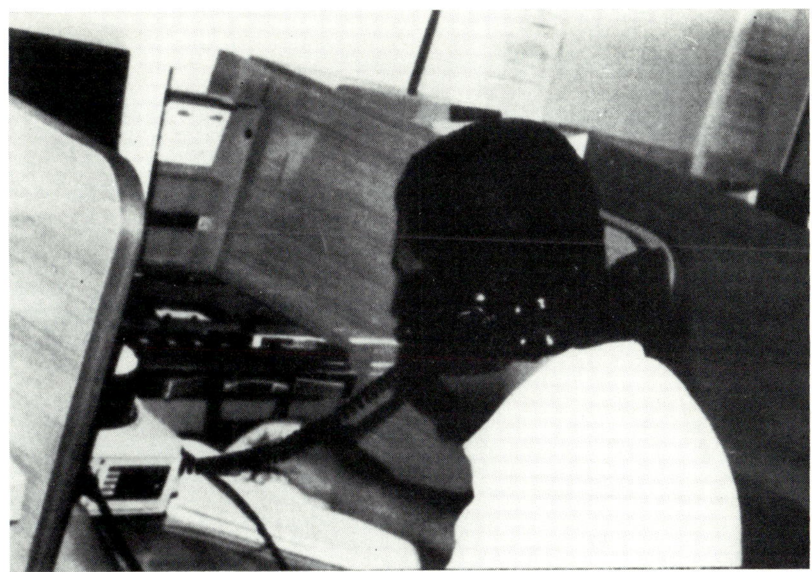

19 Audio-visual carrels, Men's Medical library, King Faisal University, Dammam, Saudi Arabia

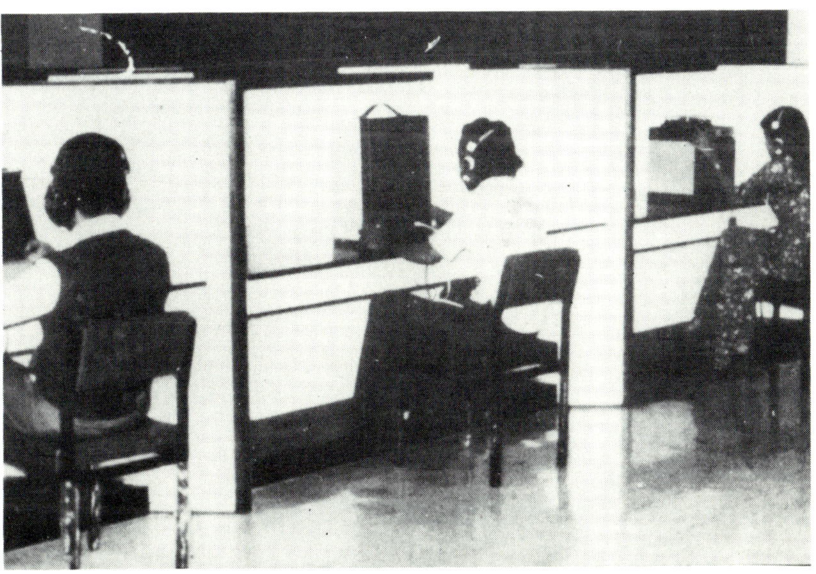

20 Audio-visual department, National University of Malaysia library, Malaysia

21 Equipment for media production, University of Kuwait library

22 Catalogues and exhibition area, King Abdulaziz University library, Jeddah, Saudi Arabia

23 Microfilm reading area, University of Jordan library

24 Periodicals reading room, University of Jordan library

25 Reference room, University of Jordan library

26 Library building, University of Jordan

27 Library building, University of Khartoum

Jordan: The University of Jordan, P.O. Box No. 1682, Jordan
There is no national library or national centre in Jordan to
assume the responsibility for providing exchange facilities so
the university library acquisitions department performs this
function. It reaches agreements with other universities for the
national and international exchange of materials.

In Saudi Arabia, no formal exchange programmes have been
formulated, but university libraries individually operate gift and
exchange schemes, under which bibliographical publications of
libraries, general publications of universities, unwanted periodicals or surplus materials are sent to requesting libraries either as
gifts or on an exchange basis. King Faisal University library,
Dammam, has multiple copies of a computerized book catalogue
listing complete holdings and is updated quarterly. The University
of Petroleum and Minerals library has on-line computer terminals
and cataloguing is completely automated. It can give bibliographical information via computer terminals to other libraries in Saudi
Arabia and neighbouring Arab countries. But the cost of
telephone links might prohibit the use of such a service on a large
scale. Almost all universities have lists of serials, some of them
computer-produced. These are very useful ammunition for exchange purposes.

Cooperative acquisition systems

Without an effective inter-library loan network, unified acquisition
cannot be achieved, and without an efficient telecommunication
and delivery system, the implementation of lending schemes is
inconceivable. There are insurmountable problems inherent in the
formulation of cooperative acquisition policies and their eventual
implementation. However, the need to cooperate emanates from
the need to economize and further the accessibility of resources. It
is vital if 'restrictions have been imposed on purchase funds'.[38]
Obviously Broome is right in quoting Enright, to the effect that
people go to the trouble of cooperating in order to achieve things
which they want and which they do not see themselves capable of
achieving on their own.[39] Cooperative acquisition certainly makes
it possible to achieve both 'comprehensiveness and depth in the
acquisition of materials in certain areas'.[40]

Although there are some very successful schemes, such as in UK (unifying the university libraries of Sheffield, Surrey, Sussex, Reading and Liverpool),[41] British cooperative programmes are not as ambitious as America's Farmington Plan in which around seventy libraries cooperate in obtaining foreign literature on a national basis.[42] In Scandinavia, the Scandia Plan involves Finland, Norway, Sweden and Denmark.[43] No special allocations are made for this purpose and the libraries are assigned subject responsibilities related to the strength of their existing collections. In Germany, the Prussian State Library and the ten university libraries in Prussia are closely cooperating in acquiring materials in their designated areas of specialization.[44] 'Cooperative programmes succeed only as long as each participant perceives them as beneficial to the institution.'[45] Large university libraries are unwilling to participate in cooperative schemes because they fear being excessively used and expect little benefits.

Except in Malaysia and Nigeria, there is hardly any cooperative acquisition network in any of the Arab Islamic countries. In Malaysia, cooperative acquisition has not been very successful; each participant wishes to acquire necessary materials, but due to the interdisciplinary nature of subjects taught in more than one institute, this results in eventual duplication. Syed Salim Agha, chief librarian of the Universiti Pertanian (University of Agriculture), rightly commented that

> The need for a cooperative acquisition policy will only arise if it is clear that the present unnecessary duplication is large. In any case, is it not worthwhile for some form of duplication to exist in a few libraries in the country so that access to them is not limited, particularly so in a developing situation as in Malaysia. However, cooperative acquisition policies aimed at eradicating duplication might be a waste of money, the amount of unnecessary duplication that would be saved in relation to the cost, delays and problems of operating a cooperative acquisition system.[46]

He correctly believes that no restriction on duplication should be imposed so that each library may obtain what it needs. Secondly, the library which is given the responsibility of acquiring almost everything in a specific field should purchase materials for the benefit of all participants. P. Soltani, from the Tehran Book

Processing Centre, has expressed the view that one should be more concerned with the self-sufficiency of libraries, rather than sharing limited resources.[47] Not many librarians would whole-heartedly agree with his viewpoint, since cooperation is the more logical path to augmenting resources without using up meagre funds.

In the Conference of National and Academic Libraries in Malaysia and Singapore, held in March 1974 at the Universiti Sains Malaysia, Penang, the structure of cooperation was fully discussed and, as a result, the Persidangan Perpustakaan Universiti Dan Negara PERPUN (Conference of University and National Libraries) was formed. On 28 June 1975, the first meeting of chief university librarians was held at the Universiti Sains Malaysia and various issues, including cooperative networks, came under discussion. In April 1976, Unesco sent Dr Bjorn Tell, director of libraries, University of Lund, Sweden, to Malaysia as a consultant, naming cooperative acquisition as one of the topics to be investigated. He published a report in 1977 on the pilot project for the development of a library network.[48] Involved in the scheme were the National Library and five university libraries. The group of six have been cooperating on two major projects, namely the PERPUNET Project, concerned with the maintenance of a serials data base which relies on the input of information about library holdings and their location and covers nearly 15,000 serial titles listed in the Malaysian Union List of Serials; and the MALMARC (Malaysian MARC, or Machine Readable Cataloguing) Project, based on the MARC data base from the Library of Congress and the *British National Bibliography*, which is operated in the computer centre of the Universiti Sains Malaysia.[49] This scheme implies a 'commitment on the part of participating institutions to a coverage of particular subject areas'.[50] However, today there is still no functional cooperative acquisition programme such as that envisaged by Dr Bjorn Tell.

The situation is altogether different in Nigeria. The earliest conference on cooperation was held in Salisbury (now Harare), in 1964, when university librarians met to look at the problems confronting university libraries in tropical Africa.[51] It was pre-ceded by a seminar in 1953 at Ibadan, in which twenty-nine librarians from various African countries participated. In 1964, the Nigerian Library Association, in their third annual meeting, recommended the establishment of a Standing Committee on Library Resources to make constructive proposals for the coordination, use and cooperative acquisition of library materials.[52] The committee was later given the task of examining the feasibility of a cooperative acquisition scheme, embracing the National Library and the university libraries. Another development was the formation of a Joint Standing Committee on Library Cooperation in Lagos in 1964. Nine years later, in 1973, the Committee of University Librarians was set up. In November 1975, a meeting of university librarians was held in Lagos and the six existing university libraries agreed to share the African continent for the purposes of cooperative acquisition.[53] Two definite cooperative schemes are in operation. The first is an agreement between the Nigerian Institute of International Affairs and the University of Lagos library for obtaining British parliamentary reports. The second concerns the acquisition of African government documents whereby each of the six older university libraries are assigned areas of responsibility for receiving all publications.[54] The distribution of materials and areas is as follows:

1　Ahmadu Bello University: government publications in French from Morocco and Madagascar, government documents in English from Lesotho, Tanzania and Botswana, and from Sudan in English and Arabic
2　University of Benin: government documents in French from Gabon, Cameroon and Niger, in English from Kenya, Liberia, Zambia and Libya (also in Arabic)
3　University of Ibadan: government documents in French from the Central African Republic, Guinea and Rwanda, in English from South Africa, Swaziland, Mali and Egypt (also in Arabic)
4　University of Ife: government documents in French from Chad, Ivory Coast and Senegal, in English from the Gambia and Malawi, in Spanish and Portuguese from Equatorial Guinea, Angola and Mozambique
5　University of Lagos: government documents in French from Congo, Zaire and Togo, in English from Mauritius, Sierra Leone, Uganda, Ethiopia and Tunisia (also in Arabic)
6　University of Nigeria: government documents in French from Benin, Mauritania and Upper Volta, in English from Ghana, Somalia, Algeria and liberation movements (also in Arabic).

The National Library of Nigeria has been successful in its endeavours to promote the design and mobilization of a national cooperative acquisition programme by means of an Advisory Committee on Library Cooperation.[55]

Cooperative acquisition systems in many countries have proved costly and difficult to operate since libraries feel that their users suffer because of the lack of a positive response from all participating libraries. There is an immense need for university libraries in developing countries to conform to international descriptive cataloguing standards and freely exchange their union catalogues and bibliographical resources. Existing delivery systems should be greatly improved and emphasis should be placed on improving the availability of and access to resources. National bibliographic agencies, where they exist, should not only produce national bibliographies in book form but consider the production of cards for free distribution to all the university libraries in the country. Large university libraries should receive some compensation in return for services to the newly established or poorly stocked universities. Cooperative periodical acquisition is simpler to devise than book acquisition. The idea is to create a Nationwide Availability of Materials (NAM) and prepare for closer links with international systems such as Universal Availability of Publications (UAP), Information Referral Systems for Sources of Environmental Information (INFOTERRA) and the World Science Information System (UNISIST). Several university libraries in rich Arab Islamic countries have embraced computer technology and are occupied in the automation of library processes and operations without any coordination with other libraries in the state or region. In contrast, poor countries are unlikely to share the fruits of speedy and efficient on-line systems unless they possess the technology, capability and trained manpower to participate and share the resources and services of rapidly developing university libraries all over the world.

Notes

Chapter 1 – Library systems and organization

1 University of Ilorin library, *Annual Report 1980–81*, Ilorin, Ilorin University Press, 1980, p. i.

2 Same E. Ifidon, 'New developments in the Nigerian library scene', *Journal of Librarianship*, vol. 10, no. 2, July 1978, pp. 201–11.

3 James Thompson, *An Introduction to University Library Administration*, London, Clive Bingley, 1970.

4 University Grants Committee, Committee on Libraries, *Report*, London, HMSO, 1967.

5 Harrison Bryan, *University Libraries in Britain: a New Look*, London, Clive Bingley, 1976, pp. 25–9.

6 Abdullah S. Isa, 'Proposed standards for university libraries in Saudi Arabia' (Ph.D. thesis), Pittsburgh, University of Pittsburgh, 1982, p. 98.

7 King Saud University, *Al-Laihat al-Sasiyat Li-Maktabat Jamiat Riyadh*, King Saud University Press, n.d., pp. 3–5.

8 Wilfred J. Plumbe, 'Ahmadu Bello University libraries; the first three years', *Nigerian Libraries*, vol. 3, no. 2, August 1967, pp. 46–62.

9 University of the Punjab, *Calender 1977–78*, vol. 1, Lahore, Punjab University Press, 1978, p. 318.

10 University of Engineering and Technology, *Calender 1976*, vol. 1, Lahore, University Press, 1976, p.4.

11 Akhlaq Khan and F. R. Wightman, 'Library Committee on the development of the College/university library', *Pakistan Library Bulletin*, vol. 9, nos 3–4, July–October 1978, pp. 9–19.

12 King Saud University, *Mustakhalsat dauriyat Jamiat al-Riyadh*, vol. 2, Riyadh, King Saud University Press, 1977, p. 9.

13 James Thompson, op. cit., p. 30.

14 University of Petroleum and Minerals, *A Handbook of the University Library 1975–76*, Dhahran, UPM Press, 1977, p. 36.

15 Yarmouk University, *Maktabat Jamiyat al-Yarmok*, Yarmouk University Press, 1979.

16 University of Jos, *Know Your Library*, Jos, Jos University Press, 1982.

17 David Kaser et al., *Library Development in Eight Asian Countries*, Metuchen, NJ, Scarecrow Press, 1969, pp. 238–9.

18 Universiti Kebangsaan Malaysia, *The University Library System*, Bangi, National University of Malaysia Press, 1981.

19 Wilfred J. Plumbe, op. cit., p. 46.

20 W. M. Zaki, 'The role of the People's Open University, Islamabad, Pakistan', *Education in Asia, Reviews, Reports and Notes*, no. 10, September 1976, pp. 13–15.

21 J. S. Parker, 'Library development in the Sudan', *Pakistan Library Bulletin*, vol. 7, nos 3–4, March–June 1975, p. 17.

22 Shaban A. Khalifa, 'Libraries and librarianship in Qatar', *Arab Journal for Librarianship and Information Science*, vol. 1, 4th issue, October 1981, pp. 192–3.

23 Z. Khurshid, 'A report on the workshop on the Development of Libraries and Information Systems and Services in Kuwait and the Gulf Area', *Library Scene*, vol. 5, no. 1, March 1980, p. 19.

24 Abbas S. Tashkandy, 'Saudi Arabia, Libraries in', *Encyclopedia of Library and Information Science*, vol. 26, New York, Marcel Dekker, 1979, pp. 314–16.

25 King Saud University (formerly University of Riyadh), *University Bulletin 1980–81*, Riyadh, King Saud University Press, 1980, pp. 9–10.

26 King Abdulaziz University, *Brief History 1980*, Jeddah, Asphani House, 1980, pp. 10–13.

27 University of Petroleum and Minerals, *A Handbook of the University Library*, Dhahran, UPM Press, 1979, pp. 45–6.

28 King Faisal University, *Catalogue 1982*, Al-Hasa, Dammam, KFU Press, 1982, pp. 168–9.

29 King Faisal University, College of Medicine and Medical Sciences, *College Manual*, Dammam, KFU Press, 1982, p. 15.

30 King Faisal University, *King Faisal University Libraries*, Dammam, Al-Hasa, KFU Press, 1980, p.3.

31 Thompson, op. cit., pp 60–3.

32 Imam Muhammad Ibn Saud Islamic University, *Guide to Imam Muhammad Ibn Saud Islamic University*, Riyadh, King Saud University Press, 1979, pp. 78–80.

33 University of Petroleum and Minerals, *The Library*, Dhahran, UPM Press, n.d., p. 2.

34 King Saud University, 'Maktabat al-Jamiat fi Satur' (leaflet), Riyadh, King Saud University Press, 1979.

35 King Abdulaziz University, *Laihat al-Maktabat*, Jeddah, King Abdulaziz University Press, 1975, p. 39.

36 J. D. Pearson, 'University libraries with special reference to Great
   Britain, Libraries and the challenge of change', paper of the
   International Library Conference held in Kingston, Jamaica, 24–9
   April 1972, edited by K. E. Ingram and A. A. Jefferson, London,
   Mansell, 1975, p. 65.
37 University of Jos Library, op. cit., 1982.

Chapter 2 – The management of university libraries

 1 M. A. Gelfand, *University Libraries for Developing Countries*, Paris,
   Unesco, 1968, p. 50.
 2 L. Wilson and M. Tauber, *The University Library: the Organization,
   Administration and Functions of Academic Libraries* (2nd edn), New
   York, Columbia University Press, 1956, p. 253.
 3 J. D. Mullins, 'The standard of library service', *Library Journal*, vol.
   3, no. 2, April 1878, pp. 52–3.
 4 Alvin Toffler, *Future Shock*, New York, Random House, 1970.
 5 M. A. Gelfand, op. cit., p. 50.
 6 Charles C. Waddington, 'Some principles of administration in libraries', *Journal of Education for Librarianship*, vol. 10, no. 2,
   Autumn 1969, pp. 138–43.
 7 Hasan Ali Al-Zayer, 'The image of change in library administration in
   Saudi Arabia', *Library Scene*, vol. 6, no. 1, March 1981, pp. 16–19.
 8 R. C. Benge, 'Obstacles to scientific management in Nigerian
   libraries', *Nigerian Libraries*, vol. 11, nos 1 and 2, April–August 1975,
   pp. 49–53.
 9 M. A. Gelfand, op. cit., p. 52.
10 Peter Durey, *Staff Management in University and College Libraries*,
   Oxford, Pergamon, 1976.
11 James Thompson, op. cit., p. 38. *An Introduction to University
   Library Administration*, London, Clive Bingley, 1970.
12 Shaban A. Khalifa, 'Libraries and librarianship in Qatar', *Arab
   Journal for Librarianship and Information Science*, vol. 1, 4th issue,
   October 1981, pp. 182–204.
13 Abdulaziz Mohammed Al-Nahari, 'The national library; an analysis of
   the critical factors in promoting library and information services in
   developing countries; the case of Saudi Arabia', Los Angeles,
   University of California, 1982 (Ph.D. thesis), p. 153.
14 Abdullah S. Isa, 'Proposed standards for university libraries in Saudi
   Arabia (Ph.D. thesis), Pittsburgh, University of Pittsburgh, 1982,
   p. 96.
15 Ibid.
16 Institute of Personnel Management (Great Britain), 'Statement on

personnel management and personnel policies', *Personnel Management*, March 1963.

17 P. Pigors and C. A. Myers, *Personnel Administration* (7th edn), New York, McGraw-Hill, 1973.
18 E. V. Corbett, *Fundamentals of Library Organization and Administration: a Practical Guide*, London, Library Association, 1978, p. 56.
19 Elizabeth Stone (ed.), *New Directions in Staff Development*, Chicago, American Library Association, 1971, p. 31.
20 K. D. Metcalf, 'Staff participation in library management in a large research library', *College and Research Libraries*, vol. 18, no. 6, November 1957, pp. 473–8.
21 Noragh Jones and Peter Jordan, *Staff Management in Library and Information Work*, Aldershot, Gower, 1982, p. 159.
22 Harrison Bryan, 'Some problems of size', *Australian Library Journal*, vol. 18, September 1969, pp. 265–76.
23 Douglas McGregor, *Leadership and Motivation*, Cambridge, Mass., MIT Press, 1966, p. 67.
24 K. D. Metcalf, op. cit., p. 476.
25 K. A. Lodewycks, 'Library governance in universities', *Australian Academic and Research Libraries*, vol. 8, no. 3, September 1977, pp. 131–8.
26 G. C. Burgis, 'A system concept of organization and control of large university libraries', in Ross Shimmon (ed.), *A Reader in Library Management*, London, Clive Bingley, 1976, p. 107.
27 Beatrice V. Simon, 'The need for administrative know-how in libraries', in Ross Shimmon, op. cit., p. 23.
28 Charles C. Waddington, op. cit., p. 140.
29 Elizabeth Stone, op. cit., p. 31.
30 Beatrice V. Simon, op. cit., p. 29.
31 Peter Drucker, *Management: Tasks, Responsibilities, Practice*, New York, Harper & Row, 1973, p. 195.
32 Noragh Jones and Peter Jordan, op. cit., pp. 34–5.
33 R. C. Benge, op. cit., pp. 49–53.
34 A. K. Ubeku, *Personnel Management in Nigeria*, Benin City, Ethiope, 1975, p. 301.
35 Roger Stoakley, *Presenting the Library Service*, London, Clive Bingley, 1982, p. 19.
36 Willard Austen, 'Efficiency in college and university library work', *Library Journal*, vol. 36, no. 11, November 1911, p. 566.
37 Michael Gorman, 'On doing away with technical services departments', *American Libraries*, vol. 10, no. 7, July–August 1979, pp. 435–7.
38 Frank P. Hill, 'Organization and management of library staff', *Library Journal*, vol. 22, no. 8, August 1897, pp. 381–3.

39 James E. Herring, 'Personnel management', *Assistant Librarian*, vol. 76, no. 2, February 1983, pp. 24–7.
40 Charles C. Waddington, op. cit., p. 141.
41 John F. Anderson, 'Aspects of main library administration and management', *Library Trends*, vol. 20, no. 4, April 1972, pp. 654–62.
42 Peter Drucker, 'What communication means', *Management Today*, March 1970, pp. 91–3.
43 Charles C. Waddington, op. cit., p. 143.
44 Noragh Jones and Peter Jordan, op. cit., p. 100.
45 Peter Durey, op. cit., pp. 60–1.
46 Syed Hussain Alatas, *Intellectuals in Developing Societies*, London, F. Cass, 1977, pp. 35–47.
47 C. J. Lloyd, 'Staff turnover: problems and solutions', *Library Association Record*, vol. 82, no. 5, May 1980, p. 223.
48 James E. Herring, op. cit., p. 25.
49 Hisham A. Abbas, 'A plan for public library system development in Saudi Arabia' (Ph.D. thesis), Pittsburgh, University of Pittsburgh, 1982.
50 Sudqi Dahbour and Fawzi Shubati, *Director of Libraries in Jordan*, Amman, Jordan Library Association, 1976, p. 10.
51 Theodore C. Hines, 'Programmed learning and in-service training in libraries', *ALA Bulletin*, vol. 58, no. 8, September 1964, p. 720.
52 Wilfred J. Plumbe, 'Ahmadu Bello University libraries: the first three years', *Nigerian Libraries*, vol. 3, no. 2, August 1967, pp. 46–62.
53 Clyde B. Matters, 'Management for library personnel', *Nigerian Libraries*, vol. 2, no. 2, September 1966, pp. 75–82.
54 S. Weeraperumer, *In-service Training in Librarianship*, London, Poets' and Painters' Press, 1971, pp. 10–13.
55 Anthony W. Ferguson, 'Taiwan college and university libraries: problems and prospects', *International Library Review*, vol. 10, no. 4, October 1978, pp. 397–405.

Chapter 3 – Reference and information services

1 University of Ilorin Library, *Annual Report 1980–81*, Ilorin, Ilorin University Press, 1980.
2 King Faisal University, *K.F.U. Libraries, Dammam and Al-Hasa Campuses*, Dammam, KFU Press, 1980.
3 University of Jordan, *The Library of the University of Jordan 1981–1982*, Amman National Press, 1981.
4 University of Petroleum and Minerals, *A Handbook of the University Library*, Dhahran, UPM Press, 1983.
5 University of Petroleum and Minerals, *A Handbook of the University Library*, Dhahran, UPM Press, 1980.

6 Yarmouk University, *Maktaba Jamiat al-Yarmouk, al-waqi wal-tatlaat*, Yarmouk University Press, 1979.

7 James Thompson, *An Introduction to University Library Administration*, London, Clive Bingley, 1970, p. 113.

8 Ibid., p. 112.

9 Shaban A. Khalifa, 'Libraries and librarianship in Qatar', *Arab Journal for Librarianship and Information Science*, vol. 1, 4th issue, October 1981, p. 191.

10 J. S. Parker, 'Library development in The Sudan', *Pakistan Library Bulletin*, vol. 7, nos 3–4, March 1975, p. 23.

11 The Flinders University of South Australia, *The Library: Guide to the Medical Library 1982*, Flinders University Press.

12 James Thompson, op. cit., p. 105.

13 University of Jos library, *Know Your Library*, Jos, Jos University Press, 1982.

14 King Faisal University, op. cit., p. 11.

15 University of Petroleum and Minerals, *A Handbook of the University Library*, Dhahran, UPM Press, 1983, p. 10.

16 University of Petroleum and Minerals, *A Handbook of the University Library*, Dhahran, UPM Press, 1979, p. 13.

17 University of Petroleum and Minerals, *A Handbook of the University Library*, Dhahran, UPM Press, 1980.

18 Yarmouk University, *Dalil al-Maktaba*, Yarmouk University Press, 1981, pp. 25–6.

19 University of Engineering and Technology, *Notification*, 28 October 1974, UET Press, Lahore, p. 607.

20 Muhammad Ramzan, *Library Handbook*, Lahore, University of Engineering and Technology, 1978, pp. 20–1.

21 University of Petroleum and Minerals, *A Handbook of the University Library*, Dhahran, UPM Press, 1983, p. 11.

22 King Saud University, *How to Use the University Library*, Riyadh, King Saud University Press, 1979, p. 10 (Arabic text).

23 University of Ilorin library, op. cit., p. 13.

24 University of Jos, op. cit., p. 29.

25 University of Calabar, *Guide to the Library* (2nd edn), Calabar, Calabar University Press, 1979, pp. 26–7.

26 James Thompson, op. cit., p. 106.

27 Muhammad Ismail Ghazi, 'The problem of book losses in Pakistan', *Pakistan Library Review*, vol. 4, nos 1–2, March–June 1962, p. 34.

28 University of the Punjab, *Student Handbook 1972–73*, University of the Punjab Press, Lahore, p. 55.

29 J. G. Harvey and B. Lambat, 'Librarianship in six south-west Asian countries', *International Library Review*, vol. 3, no. 1, January 1971, p. 28.

30 University of Engineering and Technology, Lahore, op. cit.
31 Norman Roberts, 'University libraries', *Library Association Record*, vol. 73, no. 11, November 1971, p. 211.
32 James Thompson, op. cit., p. 106.
33 King Saud University, op. cit.
34 'Library Timings', Editorial, *Pakistan Times* (English daily), 17 October 1980.
35 Universiti Kebangsaan Malaysia, *Buku Panduan Ahli Akademic Perpustakaan, Tun Seri Lanang*, Bangi, University Press, 1982.
36 University of Nottingham, *Guide to the University Library*, University of Nottingham Press, Nottingham, 1976.
37 University of London, School of Oriental and African Studies, *Library Guide*, London, SOAS, n.d.
38 The Flinders University of South Australia, *Guide to the Library*, Flinders University Press, 1982.
39 Cosmas Enu, 'Nigerian library resources in science and technology and possible avenues for library cooperation', *Nigerian Libraries*, vol. 8, no. 3, December 1972, p. 153.
40 H. R. Verry, 'Document reproduction', *Unesco Bulletin for Libraries*, vol. 17, no. 2, March–April 1962, pp. 71–8.
41 James Thompson, op. cit., p. 123.
42 Norman Roberts, 'University Libraries', *Library Association Record*, vol. 75, no. 3, March 1973, p. 48.
43 Muhammad Saleh J. Ashoor, 'A survey of user's attitudes towards the resources and services of the university libraries in Saudi Arabia' (Ph.D. thesis), Pittsburgh, University of Pittsburgh, 1978, pp. 133–4.
44 Abdulaziz Mohamed Al-Nahari, 'The National Library: an analysis of the critical factors in promoting library and information services in developing countries: the case of Saudi Arabia' (Ph.D. thesis), Los Angeles, University of California, 1982, p. 150.
45 'Sixth-form library visits', *Library Association Record*, vol. 77, no. 4, April 1975, pp. 79–81.
46 R. D. E. Young, 'Introducing freshmen in a Nigerian university on how to make the best use of their library', *Education Libraries Bulletin*, vol. 26, Summer 1966, pp. 10–27.
47 Hazel Mews, 'Library instruction concerns people', *Library Association Record*, vol. 72, no. 1, January 1970, pp. 8–10.
48 University of Jos library, op. cit.
49 Abdullah S. Isa, 'Proposed standards for university libraries in Saudi Arabia' (Ph.D. thesis), Pittsburgh, University of Pittsburgh, 1982, p. 91.
50 Nazir Ahmad, 'Publicizing library resources', *Indian Librarian*, vol. 32, no. 3, December 1977, pp. 122–9.

Chapter 4 – The selection and acquisition process

1 M. A. Gelfand, *University Libraries for Developing Countries*, Paris, Unesco, 1968, p. 67.

2 B. G. Robert, 'The dean looks at the library', *Catholic Library World*, vol. 34, January 1963, p. 242.

3 Wolfgang Budach, 'Struktur und Organisation des Bibliothekssystems der Bremer Universität, *DFW*, vol. 25, special issue, May 1977, pp. 33–42.

4 University of Petroleum and Minerals, *A Handbook of the University Library*, Dhahran, UPM Press, 1983, pp. 8–9.

5 Ahmed Muhammad Al-Ghamdi, 'Maktaba Kuliyat al-Adab wal Aloom al-Insanivat', *Okaz* (Arabic daily), 18 April 1982, p. 17.

6 Ahmed Muhammad Al-Ghamdi, 'Maktaba Kuliyat al-Hindsat', *Okaz* (Arabic daily), 28 February 1982, p. 17.

7 University of Jordan, *The Library of the University of Jordan 1981–1982*, Jordan, National Press, 1981, p. 3.

8 Yarmouk University, *Dalil al-Maktaba* (Arabic text), 1981, Yarmouk University Press, p. 21.

9 W. Olufunmilayo Oyelese, 'Acquisition in university libraries: problems in developing countries', *Unesco Bulletin for Libraries*, vol. 31, no. 3, May–June 1977, pp. 81–6.

10 University of Ilorin, *A Guide to the University of Ilorin Library*, Ilorin, Ilorin University Press, n.d., p. 8.

11 N. O. Oderinde, 'Book provision for libraries', *Nigerian Libraries*, vol. 3, no. 1, April 1967, pp. 24–5.

12 Syed Jalaluddin Haider, 'University libraries in Pakistan', *College and Research Libraries*, vol. 36, no. 5.

13 Muhammad Riaz, 'A report produced for the British Council' (unpublished), Lahore, University of Engineering and Technology, 1977.

14 F. K. W. Drury, *Book Selection*, Chicago, ALA, 1930.

15 W. Olufunmilayo Oyelese, op. cit., p. 81.

16 Hassan Hashim Hetimish, 'The policy of acquisition in the central library' (unpublished report), Jeddah, King Abdulaziz University, 1983.

17 Fazal Elahi, 'Book selection in various kinds of libraries', *Quarterly Journal of the Pakistan Library Association*, vol. 2, no. 1, July 1961, p. 25.

18 J. P. Danton, *Book Selection and Collection: a Comparison of German and American University Libraries*, New York, Columbia University Press, 1963, p. 82.

19 Fazel Elahi, op. cit.

20 University of Petroleum and Minerals, *The Library*, Dhahran, UPM

Notes

Press, 1982, p. 3.
21 Yarmouk University, *Maktaba Jamiat al-Yarmouk: al-waki wal-tatlat*, Yarmouk University Press, 1979, p. 12.
22 National University of Malaysia, *The University Library System* (leaflet), n.d.
23 Herman Fussler, 'Acquisition policy', *College and Research Libraries*, a symposium, vol. 15, October 1953, p. 363.
24 Elizabeth Futas, *Library Acquisition Policies and Procedures*, Phoenix, Arizona, Oryx Press, 1977.
25 *Guidelines for the Formulation of Collection Development Policies*, Library Resources and Technical Services Committee, American Library Association, Winter 1977.
26 C. C. Aguolu, 'Information resources in Nigerian higher education: problems of development and growth', *Libri*, vol. 28, no. 1, March 1978, pp. 21–57.
27 W. Olufunmilayo Oyelese, op. cit., p. 82.
28 A. J. Walford (ed.), *Guide to Reference Material* (3rd edn), London, Library Association, 1977.
29 C. M. Winchell, *Guide to Reference Books* (8th edn), Chicago, American Library Association, 1967.
30 B. S. Gujrati, *Librarianship*, New Delhi Lakshmi Bookstore, 1964, p. 11.
31 *Video and Cable Guidelines for Librarians*, Chicago, American Library Association, 1977.
32 D. Polacheck, 'A method of adult book selection for a public library system', *RQ*, Spring 1977, p. 232.
33 Ronald Norman, 'A method of book selection for a small public library', *RQ*, Winter 1977, p. 144.
34 B. D. Grose, *The Antiquarian Booktrade, and International Directory of Subject Specialists*, Metuchen, NJ, Scarecrow Press, 1972.
35 *The Bowker Annual of Library Book Trade Information* (26th edn), New York, R. R. Bowker, 1981, pp. 359–60.
36 Shaban A. Khalifa, 'Libraries and librarianship in Qatar', *Arab Journal for Librarianship and Information Science*, vol. 1, no. 4, October 1981, p. 196.
37 Yarmouk University, *Dalil al-Maktaba*, Yarmouk University Press, 1976, pp. 12–13.
38 Wilfred J. Plumbe, 'Ahmadu Bello University libraries: the first three years', *Nigerian Libraries*, vol. 3, no. 2, August 1967, pp. 46–62.
39 University of Petroleum and Minerals, *A Handbook of the University Library*, op. cit., pp. 8–9.
40 Ibid.
41 Ahmad Y. Nabry, 'The acquisition of books at Khartoum University', *University Library Journal* (Arabic text), vol. 4, no. 2, April 1975.

pp. 28–45.

42 W. Olufunmilayo Oyelese, op. cit., p. 82.

43 S. N. Vetal, 'Cooperation in medical libraries with special reference to India', *Indian Librarian*, vol. 24, 1969, pp. 53–8.

44 Cavan McCarthy, 'Medical libraries in developing countries: an international approach', *International Library Review*, vol. 10, no. 4, October 1978, pp. 435–6.

45 University of Ilorin library, *Annual Report 1980–81*, University of Ilorin Press, 1980.

46 A. Rahim Khan, 'Foreign literature in the libraries of Pakistan', *Unesco Bulletin for Libraries*, vol. 11, nos 5–6, May–June 1957, p. 113.

47 Unesco, *Agreement on the Importation of Educational, Scientific and Cultural Materials: a guide to its operations* (2nd edn), Paris, Unesco, 1958.

48 M. H. Mirza, 'Book problems during the fourth five-year plan (1970–75)', *Pakistan Librarianship 1970–71*, Pakistan Library Association, Karachi, 1972, pp. 189–92.

49 C. C. Aguolu, op. cit., pp. 21–57.

50 University of Petroleum and Minerals, *A Handbook of the University Library*, op. cit., p. 19.

51 Colin Steele, *Major Libraries of the World*, London, R. R. Bowker, 1976, p. 285.

52 C. C. Aguolu, op. cit., p. 37.

53 Wilfred J. Plumbe, op. cit., pp. 50–1.

54 University of Ilorin library, *Annual Report*, op. cit., p. 3.

55 'Silver Jubilee book exhibition', *Library News Bulletin*, vol. 5, nos 1–4, January–April 1978, p. 4.

56 King Saud University, *University Bulletin, 1980–81*, King Saud University Press, 1980, p. 41.

57 King Saud University, *Catalogue of Manuscripts in Riyadh University*, Riyadh, King Saud University Press, 1980, p. 1 (Arabic).

58 Shaban A. Khalifa, op. cit., pp. 182–204.

59 University of Jordan library, *A Bibliography of Jordan*, Amman, University of Jordan Press, 1980.

60 Z. S. Ali, 'Acquisition through legal deposit–national library experience', *Nigerbiblios*, vol. 1, no. 2, April 1976, pp. 11–12.

61 B. O. Toye, 'Legal deposit in a Nigerian university library: its role in the field of Nigerian studies', *Bendel Library Journal*, vol. 2, no. 1, June 1979, pp. 12–18.

62 A. O. Olafioye, 'The case for publications exchange programmes examined', *Nigerbiblios*, vol. 1, no. 1, January 1976, pp. 12–13.

63 Datuk Haji Hassan Bin Ahmad, 'Malaysia', *Regional Seminar of Experts on Book Planning to prepare a medium term in-service training*

Notes

programme, 19–23 February 1979, Bangkok, Thailand. Unesco Regional Office for Culture and Book Development in Asia, Karachi, 1979, p. 52.
64 W. Olufunmilayo Oyelese, op. cit., p. 83.
65 Agha M. Jaffri, 'Pakistan', *Regional Seminar of Experts on Book Planning to prepare a medium term in-service training programme, 19–23 February 1979, Bangkok, Thailand.* Unesco Regional Office for Culture and Book Development in Asia, Karachi, 1979, p. 61.

Chapter 5 – Size of collections and finances

 1 Verner Clapp and Robert T. Jordan, 'Quantitative criteria for adequacy of academic library collections', *College and Research Libraries*, vol. 26, no. 5, September 1965, pp. 371–80.
 2 R. Marvin McInnis, 'The formula approach to library size: an empirical study of its efficiency in evaluating research libraries', *College and Research Libraries*, vol. 33, May 1972, pp. 190–1.
 3 Rotherford Rogers and David Weber, *University Library Administration*, New York, H. W. Wilson, 1971, pp. 290–1.
 4 Alan M. Cartter, *An Assessment of Quality in Graduate Education*, Washington, DC, American Council on Education, 1966, pp. 114–15.
 5 Melvin J. Voigt, 'Acquisition rates in university libraries', *College and Research Libraries*, vol. 36, no. 4, July 1975, pp. 263–71.
 6 F. W. Lancaster, *The Measurement and Evaluation of Library Services*, New York, Academic Press, 1978, pp. 167–72.
 7 Rose M. Magrill and Mona East, 'Collection development in large university libraries', in *Advances in Librarianship*, vol. 8, New York, Academic Press, 1978, p. 39.
 8 Paul Doebler, 'Special interest marketing, a management strongly for bookselling and development', *Publishers' Weekly*, vol. 209, no. 22, 31 May 1976, p. 138.
 9 Virgil F. Massman and Kelly Patterson, 'A minimum budget for current acquisition', *College and Research Libraries*, vol. 31, March 31 May 1976, p. 138.
10 Anthony W. Ferguson, 'Taiwan College and University libraries. Problems and prospects', *International Library Review*, vol. 10, no. 4, October 1978, pp. 397–405.
11 University of Jordan, *The Library of the University of Jordan, 1981–1982*, University of Jordan Press, p. 1.
12 John F. Harvey, 'Kuwait city libraries', *Indian Librarian*, vol. 28, no. 4, March 1974, p. 193.
13 Colin Steel (compiler), *Major Libraries of the World: a Selective Guide*, London, Bowker, 1976, p. 341.

192

14 Ahmed Muhammad Al-Ghamdi, 'Maktaba Kuliyat al-Adab wal-Aloom al-Insaniyah', *Okaz* (Arabic daily), no. 5801, 18 April 1982, p. 17.

15 Ahmed Muhammad Al-Ghamdi, 'Maktaba kuliyat al-tibb', *Okaz* (Arabic daily), no. 5759, 7 March 1982, p. 17.

16 Ahmed Muhammad Al-Ghamdi, 'Maktaba Kuliyat al-Hindasaht', *Okaz* (Arabic daily), no. 5753, 28 February 1982, p. 17.

17 University of Petroleum and Minerals. *The Library*, Dhahran, UPM Press, n.d., p. 1.

18 University of Petroleum and Minerals, *A Handbook of the University Library*, Dhahran, UPM Press, 1983, pp. 23–4.

19 Abdullah S. Isa, 'Proposed standards for university libraries in Saudi Arabia' (Ph.D. thesis), Pittsburgh, University of Pittsburgh, 1982, p. 82.

20 Ibid.

21 Louis Shores, *Audiovisual Librarianship: the Crusade for Media Units 1949–1969*, Littleton, Libraries Unlimited, 1973, p. 94.

22 Abdullah S. Isa, op. cit., p. 130

23 James Thompson, *An Introduction to University Library Administration*, London, Clive Bingley, 1970, p. 75.

24 Ibid., pp. 75, 79.

25 Guy R. Lyle, *The Administration of the College Library* (4th edn), New York, H. W. Wilson, 1974, p. 201.

26 Akhtar Hanif, 'University librarianship in Pakistan: problems and prospects', *Pakistan Library Bulletin*, vol. 12, nos 3–4, September–December 1981, p. 24.

27 James Thompson, op. cit., p. 91.

28 Lois Jennings, 'Budgeting and decision making', *Australian Special Libraries News*, vol. 14, no. 4, December 1981, pp. 96–107.

29 Ibid.

30 University of Ilorin library, *Annual Report 1980–1981*, Ilorin, Ilorin University Press, 1981, pp. 10–11.

31 W. Summers, 'A change in budgetary thinking', in *Budgeting for Accountability in Libraries*, Metuchen, NJ, Scarecrow Press, 1974, pp. 16–20.

32 Diana Higgins, 'Managing special libraries in times of financial and staffing cuts', *Australian Special Libraries News*, vol. 12, no. 3, September 1979, p. 114.

33 Lois Jennings, op. cit., pp. 98–9.

34 George Morgan, 'Libraries face cutbacks on all sides', *The Times Higher Educational Supplement*, 17 January 1975, p. 11.

35 'The Kingdom's budget for 1399–1400AH/1979–80AD', *Indo-Arab Star*, series no. 3, September 1979, pp. 27–31.

36 Sheikh Muhammad Iqbal, 'The Kingdom of Saudi Arabia: the latest

advances in industry, agriculture and education', *Indo-Arab Star*, vol. 11, series nos 6–7, 1980, p. 12.

37 'Riyadh University', *Middle East Education*, vol. 3, no. 3, April 1981, p. 20.

38 Pakistan, Ministry of Finance, Commerce Division, letter no. 3/(1)/78 TR11, dated 5.8.1978.

39 Pakistan, Ministry of Finance, Provincial Coordination/Economic Affairs Division, letter no. VI/93 C.M.V.78.

40 'Silver Jubilee Book Exhibition', *Library News Bulletin*, vol. 5, nos 1–4, January–April 1978, p. 4.

41 Christabel King, 'Starting from scratch in Sudan's deep South', *Library Association Record*, vol. 80, no. 5, May 1978, p. 237.

42 University of Ilorin library, *Annual Report*, op. cit., pp. 3–4.

43 Wilfred J. Plumbe, 'Ahmadu Bello university libraries', *Nigerian Libraries*, vol. 3, no. 2, August 1967, pp. 50–4.

44 'Statement of Policy regarding gifts and bequests', *American Libraries*, vol. 2, July–August 1971, pp. 721–2.

45 'Statement on appraisal of gifts', *College and Research Library News*, no. 3, March 1973, p. 49.

46 G. R. Lyle, op. cit., pp. 243–51.

47 G. R. Lyle, op. cit., p. 230

48 Giuliana Lavendel, 'Special libraries: a crucial service for research', *Australian Special Library News*, vol. 10, no. 3, September 1977, pp. 113–22.

49 Lois Jennings, op. cit., pp. 96–9.

50 University Grants Commission, *Report of the study group on financial needs of universities*, pt 1, Pakistan University Grants Commission, Islamabad, 1978, p. 12.

51 'Meeting of Experts on the National Planning of Library Services in Latin America', *Unesco Bulletin for Libraries*, vol. 22, November–December 1966, p. 285.

52 James Thompson, op. cit., p. 19.

53 J. O. Dipeolu, 'Objectives and standards of practice for university libraries in West Africa', in John Dean (ed.), *Standards of Practice for West African Libraries*, Ibadan, University of Ibadan, 1969, p. 35.

54 John Dean. 'Organization and services of university libraries in West Africa', in M. Jackson (ed.), *Comparative and International Librarianship: Essays on Themes and Problems*, Westport, Greenwood Press, 1970, p. 125.

55 C. C. Aguolu, 'Information resources in Nigerian higher education: problems of development and growth', *Libri*, vol. 28, no. 1, March 1978, p. 52.

56 Abdullah S. Isa, op. cit., p. 146.

57 C. C. Aguolu, op. cit., p. 53.

58 'Standards for College Libraries', *College and Research Libraries News*, vol. 35, no. 6, 1974, p. 305.
59 James Thompson, op. cit., p. 20.
60 E. J. Wainwright and John Dean, *Measures of Adequacy for Library Collections in Australian Colleges of Advanced Education*, Perth, Western Australian Institute of Technology, 1976, p. 184.

Chapter 6 – Planning and designing buildings

1 Ellsworth Mason, 'Back to the cave, or, some buildings I have known', *Library Journal*, vol. 94, no. 21, 1 December 1969, pp. 4,353–7.
2 Jean Bleton, 'The construction of university libraries', *Unesco Bulletin for Libraries*, vol. 17, no. 6, November–December 1963, pp. 307–15.
3 Frank P. Hill, 'Library building – some preliminaries', *Library Journal*, vol. 24, no. 10, October 1899, pp. 563–7.
4 Rajwant Singh, 'Planning the library building: the role of the librarian, architect and consultant', *Indian Library Movement*, vol. 5, no. 2, June 1978, p. 43.
5 J. A. Fab Akhidime, 'The librarian and library buildings in Nigeria', *NLA Newsletter*, nos 63–4, July/August 1977, pp. 3–6.
6 Nazir Ahmad, 'The growth of academic and special libraries in Australia', *Indian Librarian*, March 1979, pp. 178–81.
7 Ahmad Badr and Mohammed Fathi Abdulhady, *Al-maktabat al-jamiat*, Cairo, Maktaba Gareeb, n.d., pp. 282–3.
8 Mohammed Fathi Abdulhady, 'Maktaba Jamia al-imarat al-Arabia', *Journal of Library Information Science*, 15 (4), October 1981, pp. 33–47.
9 Abdullah S. Isa, 'Proposed standards for university libraries in Saudi Arabia' (Ph.D. thesis), Pittsburgh, University of Pittsburgh, 1982, p. 100.
10 Central Planning Organization, *The Third Development Plan 1980–85*, Riyadh, Ministry of Planning, 1980.
11 John Dean, 'Training and management for library personnel', *Nigerian Libraries*, vol. 2, no. 2, September 1966, pp. 67–74.
12 Peter Hoare, 'Consideration of some planning factors and standards relating to university libraries in tropical developing countries', *Toktor Bilong Haus Buk* (25/26), September–December 1978, pp. 16–27.
13 R. E. Ellsworth, *Planning Manual for Academic Library Buildings*, New Jersey, Scarecrow Press, 1973.
14 M. A. Gelfand, *University Libraries for Developing Countries*, Paris, Unesco, 1968, p. 124.
15 King Faisal University, *King Faisal University Libraries*, Dammam, KFU Press, 1980, p. 3.

Notes

16 *The World of Learning 1981–82* (32nd edn), London, Europa
   Publications, 1981, pp. 1,143–4.
17 Ibid., pp. 897–8.
18 Ibid., p. 876.
19 Colin Steele, *Major Libraries of the World*, London, Clive Bingley,
   1976, pp. 341–2.
20 J. A. Martin, 'Planning new medical library buildings', *Bulletin of the
   Medical Library Association*, October 1969, pp. 368–73.
21 Jean Bleton, 'The construction of university libraries. How to plan and
   revise a project', *Unesco Bulletin for Libraries*, vol. 17, no. 6.
   November–December 1963, pp. 307–15.
22 Ellsworth Mason, *Mason on Library Buildings*, Metuchen, NJ,
   Scarecrow Press, 1980, p. 13.
23 M. Van Buren, 'Interior planning of college and university libraries',
   College and Research Libraries, vol. 17, no. 3, May 1956, p. 232.
24 Frank P. Hill, op. cit., p. 566.
25 Abdullahi Mohammed, 'Communication between the architect and
   the librarian', *Pakistan Library Bulletin*, vol. 12, no. 3–4, September–
   December 1981, pp. 17–19.
26 Herbert Ward, 'Buildings, furniture and fittings', Library Association
   Study School and National Conference, Proceedings, Brighton 1978,
   London Library Association, n.d., pp. 84–6.
27 James Draper and James Brooks, *Interior Design for Libraries*,
   Chicago, ALA, 1979, p. 7.
28 Christabel King, 'Starting from scratch in Sudan's deep south', *Library
   Association Record*, vol. 80, no. 5, May 1978, p. 237.
29 University of Jos library, *Know your Library: Readers' Guide to the
   Library*, Jos, University of Jos, 1982, pp. 21–3.
30 University of Ilorin, *A Guide to the University of Ilorin Library*, Ilorin,
   University of Ilorin, n.d., pp. 9–10.
31 University of Calabar, *Guide to the Library* (2nd edn), Calabar,
   University of Calabar Press, 1979, pp. 10–12.
32 National University of Malaysia, *The University Library System*, NUM
   Press, 1981,
33 K. D. Metcalf, *Planning Academic and Research Library Buildings*,
   New York, McGraw-Hill, 1965.
34 R. W. Henderson, 'The cubook, a suggested unit for bookstack
   measurement', *Library Journal*, vol. 59, no. 20, 15 November 1934,
   pp. 865–8.
35 Ellsworth Mason, *Mason on Library Buildings*, op. cit., pp. 8–9.
36 John F. Harvey, 'Pakistan and Afghanistan librarianship', *Pakistan
   Library Bulletin*, vol. 2, nos. 1–2, September–December 1969, p. 9.
37 John F. Harvey, 'Kuwait city libraries', *Indian Librarian*, vol. 28, no.
   4, March 1974, pp. 191–6.

38 John F. Harvey, *Iranian University Library Standards*, Tehran, Ministry of Higher Education, 1971.

39 R. W. Henderson, op. cit., pp. 865–8.

40 Ellsworth Mason, *Mason on Library Buildings*, op. cit.

41 K. D. Metcalf, 'Special problems in university libraries', *Library Trends*, vol. 2, no. 4, April 1954, pp. 554–61.

42 F. J. Hill, 'The compact storage of books: a study of methods and equipment', *Journal of Documentation*, vol. 2, no. 4, December 1955, pp. 202–16.

43 James Draper and James Brooks, op. cit., p. 31.

44 Mary Larsgaard, *Map Librarianship: an Introduction*, Littleton, Colorado, Libraries Unlimited, 1978.

45 University of Petroleum and Minerals, *The Library*, Dhahran, UPM Press, April 1982, p. 1.

46 Communication, dated 22 November 1982, received from Edward Lim Huck Tee, chief librarian, Universiti Sains Malaysia.

47 Communication, dated 6 January 1983, received from Sulaiman Kalander, chief librarian, University of Kuwait.

48 University of Jos library, op. cit., pp. 17–18.

49 University of Ilorin, op. cit., p. 10.

50 University of Calabar, op. cit., p. 12.

51 Aaron Cohen and Elaine Cohen, *Designing and Space Planning for Libraries: a Behavioral Guide*, New York, R. R. Bowker, 1979, p. 81.

52 M. Saleh J. Ashoor, 'Planning for library automation: the experience of the University of Petroleum and Minerals Library', *Proceedings of the Symposium on New Technology in Libraries: Prospects and Problems for Libraries in the Gulf States, 26–28 April 1982*, Dhahran, UPM Press, 1982, pp. 17–27.

53 Colin Steele, op. cit., p. 290. Steele incorrectly mentions the date of erection as 1954, whereas, in fact, the building was constructed in 1964.

54 'Silver Jubilee Book Exhibition', *Library News Bulletin*, vol. 5, no. 1–4, January–April 1978, p. 5.

55 George Chandler, *Libraries in the East: an international and comparative study*, London, Seminar Press, 1971, p. 63.

56 Norman Roberts, 'University libraries', *Library Association Record*, vol. 75, no. 3, March 1973, pp. 48–50.

57 Akhtar Hanif, 'University librarianship in Pakistan. Problems and prospects', *Pakistan Library Bulletin*, vol. 12, no. 3–4, September–December 1981, pp. 20–7.

58 P. Havard-Williams, 'Standards of service for university libraries', in *A Librarian's Handbook*, compiled by L. J. Taylor, London, Library Association, 1976, p. 442.

59 Ellsworth Mason, *Mason on Library Buildings*, op. cit., p. 8.

60 University of Manchester, Institute of Science and Technology, 'New library buildings', Meeting of the library committee, 1 May 1972, pp. 1–4.

61 K. D. Metcalf, *Planning Academic and Research Library Buildings*, op. cit., p. 97.

62 Jean Bleton, op. cit., p. 311.

63 Mary Larsgaard, op. cit., pp. 208–9.

64 Yarmouk University Library, *Maktaba Jamia al-Yarmouk. Al-waqi wa-altatla'at*, Yarmouk University Press, 1979, p. 6.

65 Aaron Cohen and Elaine Cohen, op. cit., p. 24.

66 P. N. Kaula, *Library Buildings*, Delhi, Vikas, 1971, p. 121.

67 Aaron Cohen and Elaine Cohen, op. cit., p. 109.

68 F. J. Hill, 'Storage in university library buildings', *Unesco Bulletin for Libraries*, vol. 17, no. 6, November–December 1963, p. 338.

69 Ibid.

70 W. Piasecki, 'University library interiors, fixed function or modular', *Unesco Bulletin for Libraries*, vol. 17, no. 6, November–December 1963, p. 347.

71 Jean Bleton, op. cit., pp. 307–15.

72 Ellsworth Mason, *Mason on Library Buildings*, p. 8.

73 Robert T. Jordan, 'Lighting in university libraries', *Unesco Bulletin for Libraries*, vol. 17, no. 6, November–December 1963, pp. 328–9.

74 Ellsworth Mason, *Mason on Library Buildings*, op. cit., p. 34.

75 Meteorological Office, *Tables of Temperature, Relative Humidity and Precipitation for the World*, London, HMSO, 1976.

76 Ibid., p. 34.

77 Ibid., p. 35.

78 Ibid., p. 53.

79 Ibid., p. 69.

80 John O. Voll, *Historical Dictionary of the Sudan*, Metuchen, Scarecrow Press, 1978, p. 2.

81 Ellsworth Mason, *Mason on Library Buildings*, pp. 43–4.

82 Wilfred S. Plumbe, 'Climate as a factor in the planning of university library buildings', *Unesco Bulletin for Libraries*, vol. 17, no. 6, November–December 1963, pp. 316–25.

83 Victor Showers, *World Facts and Figures*, New York, John Wiley, 1979, pp. 508–11.

84 University of Petroleum and Minerals, *Library Scene*, vol. 4, no. 1, Dhahran, UPM Press, April 1979, p. 26.

85 National Univesity of Malaysia library, *The University Library System*, National University of Malaysia Press, Bangi, 1981.

86 Wilfred S. Plumbe, op. cit., pp. 316–25.

87 'Islamia Varsity New Campus', *Pakistan Times* (English daily), 30 August 1980, p. 5.

88 Muhammad Ramzan, *Library Handbook*, Lahore, University of Engineering and Technology Press, 1978.

89 Wilfred S. Plumbe, op. cit., p. 320.

90 University of Ilorin library, *Annual Report, 1980–1981*, Ilorin, Ilorin University Press, pp. 1–2.

91 Aaron Cohen and Elaine Cohen, op. cit., p. 173.

92 Andrea Oppenhamer Dean, 'Sculptural shapes that sit solidly on the ground', *AIA Journal*, mid-May 1982, p. 182.

93 W. N. Randall and F. L. W. Goodrich, *Principles of College Library Administration*, Chicago, ALA, 1941.

94 Roger Stoakley, *Presenting the Library Service*, London, Clive Bingley, 1982, pp. 40–9.

Chapter 7 – Coordination and mobilization

1 Ernest C. Colwell, 'Inter-library cooperation', *Library Quarterly*, vol. 22, January 1952, p. 2.

2 Susan K. Martin, *Library Networks, 1976–77*, New York, Knowledge Industry Publications, 1976, p. 6.

3 Shih-Hsion Huang, 'Library cooperative endeavours in the United States', *Journal of Library Information Science*, vol. 6, no. 1, April 1980, pp. 71–89.

4 James Thompson, *An Introduction to University Library Administration* (3rd edn), London, Clive Bingley, 1970, p. 137.

5 Harrison Bryan, *University Libraries in Britain: a New Look*, London, Clive Bingley, 1976, p. 57.

6 M. A. Gelfand, *University Libraries for Developing Countries*, Paris, Unesco, 1968, p. 113.

7 Ibid., pp. 113–14.

8 S. Green, 'The lending of books to one another by librarians', *Library Journal*, vol. 1, 1876, pp. 15–16.

9 Alma T. Jordan, *The Development of Library Services in the West Indies through Interlibrary Cooperation*, Metuchen, Scarecrow Press, 1970, p. 20.

10 James Thompson, op. cit., p. 138.

11 E. B. Bankole, 'Education explosion and university library development in Nigeria', *Nigerian Libraries*, vol. 3, no. 1, April 1967, p. 5.

12 University of Ilorin library, *Annual Report 1980–1981*, Ilorin University Press, 1980, pp. 6–11.

13 Abdullah S. Isa, 'Proposed standards for university libraries in Saudi Arabia' (Ph.D. thesis), Pittsburgh, University of Pittsburgh, 1982, p. 94.

Notes

14 King Saud University, *How to Use the University Library, 1979–80* (Arabic text), p. 15.

15 University of Petroleum and Minerals, *A Handbook of the University Library*, Dhahran, UPM Press, 1983, p. 5.

16 Mohammed Saleh J. Ashoor, 'A comparative study of UPM library use for 1978–79 versus 1979–80', *Library Scene*, vol. 5, December 1980, pp. 4–5.

17 M. S. Nomani, 'Inter-library lending: problems and prospects', *Proceedings of the Symposium on New Technology in Libraries: Prospects and Problems for Libraries in the Gulf States, 26–28 April 1972*, Dhahran, UPM Press, 1982, pp. 235–45.

18 Yarmouk University, *Dalil al-Maktaba*, Amman, Yarmouk University Press, 1981, p. 46.

19 University of Agriculture, library department, *Annual Report 1978–79*, Faisalabad, 1979, p. 2.

20 Cosmas Enu, 'Nigerian library resources in science and technology and possible avenues for library cooperation', *Nigerian Libraries*, vol. 8, no. 3, December 1972, p. 153.

21 Sam E. Ifidon, 'New developments on the Nigerian library scene', *Journal of Librarianship*, vol. 10, no. 3, July 1978, pp. 201–11.

22 Ibid., p. 204.

23 Saudi Arabia Central Planning Organization, *Third Development Plan 1400–1405 AH (1981–85)*, Riyadh, CPO, 1980, p. 432.

24 M. S. Nomani, op. cit., p. 242.

25 Lim Huck Tee, 'The southeast Asian university libraries network (SAULNET): a proposal and a model for resources sharing in ASEAN countries', in H. D. L. Vervliet (ed.), *Resource sharing of libraries in developing countries*, Proceedings of the 1977 IFLA/UNESCO Pre-Session Seminar for Librarians from Developing Countries, Antwerp University, 30 August–4 September 1977, New York, K. G. Saur, 1979, p. 219.

26 Ahmad Ashfaq and Simon Samoeil, 'First Conference of Saudi Librarians', *Library Scene*, vol. 5, no. 2, August 1980, pp. 8–10.

27 Abdulaziz Mohamed Al-Nahari, 'The National Library: an analysis of the critical factors in promoting library and information services in developing countries: the case of Saudi Arabia' (Ph.D. thesis), Los Angeles, University of California, 1982, p. 192.

28 Mohammed Saleh J. Ashoor, 'A survey of users' attitudes toward the resources and services of three university libraries in Saudi Arabia' (Ph.D. thesis), Pittsburgh, University of Pittsburgh, 1978, p. 137.

29 King Saud University, *Directory of Libraries in Saudi Arabia*, Riyadh, King Saud University Press, 1979.

30 Mahmoud al-Akhras, compiler, *Al-Bibliografyia al-Filistiniyah al-Urduniyah 1900–1970*, Amman, Jamiyat al-Maktabat al-Urduniyah,

1972.

31 R. L. Collison, *Bibliographical Services Throughout the World 1950–59*, Paris, Unesco, 1961, p. 127.

32 University of Kuwait library, *Arab Dissertation Index*, Kuwait, Kuwait University Library, 1972.

33 R. L. Collison, op. cit., p. 112.

34 D. E. K. Wijasuriya, 'IFLA's programmes for bibliographic control and developing country priorities', *IFLA Journal*, vol. 3, no. 3, 1977, pp. 251–6.

35 Patricia H. Shoyinka, 'Bibliographic control in Nigeria', *Libri*, vol. 28, no. 4, December 1978, pp. 294–308.

36 R. L. Collison, op. cit., pp. 109–10.

37 Georgiana K. N. Nwagha, 'Barriers to the accessibility of scientific journals in Nigeria', *International Library Review*, vol. 12, no. 2, April 1980, p. 202.

38 W. A. G. Alison, 'No librarian is an island', *Library Association Record*, vol. 81, no. 11, November 1979, p. 536.

39 E. M. Broome, 'Do developing countries need processing centres?' in H. D. L. Vervliet (ed.), *Resource Sharing of Libraries in Developing Countries: Proceedings of the 1977 IFLA/UNESCO pre-session seminar for librarians from developing countries, Antwerp University, August 30–September 4, 1977*, New York, K. G. Saur, 1979, p. 109.

40 S. B. Aje, 'Cooperative acquisition programmes in Nigeria', in H. D. L. Vervliet (ed.), op. cit., New York, K. G. Saur, 1979, p. 27.

41 Harrison Bryan, op. cit., p. 104.

42 James Thompson, op. cit., p. 143.

43 Harold L. Tveteras, 'The Scandia Plan: a plan for cooperative acquisition of materials', *Unesco Bulletin for Libraries*, vol. 14, no. 4, July–August 1960, p. 153.

44 Carl Wehmer, 'The organization and origin of German university libraries', *Library Trends*, vol. 12, 1963, p. 497.

45 A. Rydings, 'Cooperative acquisition for libraries of developing countries: panacea or placebo?', in H. D. L. Vervliet (ed.), op. cit., p. 79.

46 Syed Salim Agha, report on 'Cooperative acquisitions including book selection based on the use of MARC tapes', communication dated 7 January 1983, received from the chief librarian.

47 P. Soltani, 'The role of processing centres in developing countries in relation to resource sharing', in H. D. L. Vervliet (ed.), op. cit., pp. 136–42.

48 D. E. K. Wijasuriya, 'The Malaysian Research Library Network: a report with comments', received by the author in February 1983.

49 D. E. K. Wijasuriya, 'Resource-sharing; existing arrangements and future developments: Malaysia', *International Library Review*, vol. 12,

no. 2, April 1980, p. 139.
50 Ibid., p. 140.
51 Douglas Valery, 'Conference of university librarians in tropical Africa', *Unesco Bulletin for Libraries*, vol. 29, no. 3, March 1965, pp. 73–6.
52 Nigerian Library Association, 'Minutes of the Annual General Meeting held at the Institute of Administration, Ahmadu Bello University on 4–5 April 1965', *Nigerian Libraries*, vol. 1, 1965, p. 188.
53 W. Olufunmilayo Oyelese, 'Acquisition in university libraries: problems in developing countries', *Unesco Bulletin for Libraries*, vol. 31, no. 3, May–June 1977, p. 82.
54 Sam E. Ifidon, op. cit., p. 204.
55 S. B. Aje, op. cit., pp. 24–32.

Index

More About KPI Books

If you would like further information about books available from
KPI please write to
  The Marketing Department
  KPI Limited
  Routledge & Kegan Paul Plc
  14 Leicester Square
  London WC2H 7PH

In the USA write to
  The Marketing Department
  KPI Limited
  Routledge & Kegan Paul
  9 Park Street
  Boston
  Mass. 02108

In Australia write to
  The Marketing Department
  KPI Limited
  Routledge & Kegan Paul
  464 St. Kilda Road
  Melbourne
  Victoria 3004

KPI